MW01506206

DYING IN
FULL DETAIL

DYING IN FULL DETAIL

MORTALITY AND

DIGITAL DOCUMENTARY

Jennifer Malkowski

Duke University Press • Durham and London • 2017

© 2017 DUKE UNIVERSITY PRESS
All rights reserved
Printed in the United States of America on acid-free paper ∞

Text designed by Courtney Leigh Baker
Typeset in Whitman and Futura by Graphic Composition, Inc., Bogart, GA

Library of Congress Cataloging-in-Publication Data
Names: Malkowski, Jennifer, [date]– author.
Title: Dying in full detail : mortality and digital documentary / Jennifer Malkowski.
Description: Durham : Duke University Press, 2017. |
Includes bibliographical references and index.
Identifiers: LCCN 2016034893
ISBN 9780822363002 (hardcover : alk. paper)
ISBN 9780822363156 (pbk. : alk. paper)
ISBN 9780822373414 (ebook)
Subjects: LCSH: Documentary films—Production and direction—Moral and
ethical aspects. | Documentary mass media. | Death in motion pictures.
| Digital cinematography—Technique.
Classification: LCC PN1995.9.D6 M33 2017 | DDC 070.1/8—dc23
LC record available at https://lccn.loc.gov/2016034893

Cover art: AP Photo/Richard Drew

FOR JOY,
MY GRANDMOTHER,
WHO DIED
A GOOD DEATH

CONTENTS

ACKNOWLEDGMENTS

Many people have supported me through my writing of this project, starting in its infancy at Oberlin College, where Geoff Pingree and Pat Day supervised my honors thesis on death in documentary film and gave me the confidence to pursue an academic career. When I returned to the topic as a dissertation at UC Berkeley, each of my committee members was invaluable. Leigh Raiford was a rigorous and supportive reader, and she helped me lay the groundwork by supervising a qualifying exam field on death and image media—agreeing to read my response papers on atrocity photographs in the middle of a beautiful Berkeley summer, no less. Kristen Whissel's eye for detail and for concise, forceful arguments was a blessing, as was her keen professional guidance throughout my years at Berkeley. Tony Kaes was generous with his time and his encouragement, and he has pushed me to think broadly and write as a member of an intellectual community. Coming to Berkeley, I expected that Linda Williams would be an insightful reader and excellent intellectual resource for her students, but I did not necessarily expect the incredible kindness and collegiality I experienced when I became one of them. I am grateful to Linda for in-depth comments on my work that always let me remain in control of it, active mentoring that left nothing to be desired, and a grounded attitude that allowed me to work with her without feeling too starstruck. Also at Berkeley, I am grateful to Maxine Fredericksen, Gary Handman, and many colleagues in and around the Department of Film & Media who gave generous feedback on drafts and presentations from this project.

After finishing my PhD, I was fortunate to receive funding from the Mellon Foundation as the McPherson Postdoctoral Fellow at Smith College. The time and resources this fellowship granted were essential to the completion of this book, as was the welcoming scholarly community of Smith and the Five

Colleges. In particular, this book would not be what it is—and I would not be the academic I am—without Alex Keller's mentorship and friendship (nor, perhaps, without the restorative Lego playtime breaks that her children, Ava and Max, provided). As I continued work on *Dying in Full Detail* at Miami University, Richard Campbell, Ron Becker, and Kerry Hegarty served as ready sources of encouragement and advice, and Miami's PREP fund provided funding.

Outside these institutions, I am also indebted to Caetlin Benson-Allott, who agreed to mentor me for a year through the Society for Cinema and Media Studies (SCMS) Queer Caucus's mentorship program in its inaugural session and has continued that role—generously and skillfully—ever since. The Visible Evidence documentary conference and its inspiring roster of regular participants has helped me immensely in refining this project, particularly through feedback from and conversations with Alexandra Juhasz, Leshu Torchin, and Jonathan Kahana. Without the tough love of my writing group members Laura Horak, Michelle Baron, and TreaAndrea Russworm, this book would still be on hold as I obsessively rephrased the first sentence of my introduction over and over again. And without the insight and patience of my editor, Courtney Berger, this book would not be a book at all.

My parents, Hilary Pople and Rick Malkowski, and my sister, Kim Malkowski, offered welcome breaks from thinking about my research that certainly improved its quality. Lastly, *Dying in Full Detail* has benefited from the tireless support of my wife, Kate Mason, who is balancing out my professional morbidity by writing her own book on birth. Without her irrepressible optimism, warmth, and willingness to bake me cupcakes, the weight of this project's relentless memento mori might have felt too heavy.

INTRODUCTION

The representation of a real death is . . .
an obscenity. . . . We do not die twice.
ANDRÉ BAZIN,
"Death Every Afternoon"

Don't take pictures o' that. Whattsa matter with you?!?
UNIDENTIFIED SPECTATOR OF JUMPERS
FROM THE WORLD TRADE CENTER ON 9/11

The two preceding quotations are separated by many factors: almost half a century of history, mode of address, circumstance, and level of formality.[1] The first appears in print, written by prominent film critic and scholar André Bazin in a 1958 review, and addresses a hypothetical circumstance in a theoretical mode: if one were to film a human death as it happened, that filming would be obscene. The second is spoken by an anonymous, off-camera individual in raw footage taken during the 9/11 attacks on the World Trade Center. The hypothetical has become actual, the theoretical has become practical, and a man watching individuals jump to their deaths from a burning skyscraper chastises a fellow witness who, like many, chooses to record that fearsome sight. In this moment, a tension becomes starkly apparent between the expanding technological capability to record death and continued social prohibitions against doing so. Together, these quotations hint at the strength, breadth, and longevity of concerns about the documentary capture of death—an act that has long mesmerized and repelled those who make, view, and think about documentary images, but an act that has become increasingly practical with advancements in digital technology.

Dying in Full Detail: Mortality and Digital Documentary will consider the consequences of that new practicality, examining documentarians' recent pursuits of death with equipment that promises to capture its "full detail." In *The Notebooks of Malte Laurids Brigge* (1910), Rainer Maria Rilke composes the phrase I have appropriated for my title. In context, its meaning refers to a style of dying rather than a style of displaying death that my title references. Rilke uses the phrase to describe waning death rituals at the turn of the twentieth century: "Who cares anything today for a finely-finished death? No one. Even the rich, who could after all afford this luxury of dying in full detail, are beginning to be careless and indifferent; the wish to have a death of one's own is growing ever rarer."[2] Rilke and historians alike characterize the twentieth century as an era of death's denial in the West, a time when the "full detail" of life's end was little attended to and kept from the public eye—nowhere more so than in the United States. As contact with death diminished in modern life, the idea of its unsimulated, documentary appearance on film screens became highly charged. In his 1974 writing about the enduring taboo of filming actual death, Amos Vogel expresses the frustration of death's cultural banishment and the grim fascination that it creates with watching life end: "For when we witness unstaged, real death in the cinema we are frightened, caught in the sweet and deadly trap of the voyeur; mixed feelings of attraction and repulsion take hold of us as we anxiously watch the actual end of another being and search his face for hints of the mystery or proper rules of conduct."[3]

As the century approached its end, though, documentarians seemed poised to bring many such taboo moments to the public screen—to reveal death's detail more fully and more often than ever before. Technologically, they were enabled by accessible and affordable digital production and distribution. Culturally in the United States, they were empowered by a turn away from hidden and homogeneous hospital dying back toward an individualized "death of one's own"—and by the public's unabated curiosity to see images of violent death, nurtured in fiction film through the century's suppression of natural death.[4]

Written near the height of Western death-denial culture in 1958, Bazin's essay couples a bold condemnation of documentary death with a less novel condemnation of pornography: "Like death, love must be experienced and cannot be represented (it is not called the little death for nothing) without violating its nature. This violation is called obscenity. The representation of a real death is also an obscenity, no longer a moral one, as in love, but metaphysical. We do not die twice."[5] Bazin focuses on death as a "lived" experience that cannot be successfully mediated by a documentary camera, drawing an ethical line in the sand and demanding that some aura for the death moment be preserved. He also connects the sacred quality of death to its temporal singularity within each lifetime, continuing: "Before cinema there was only the profanation of corpses and the desecration of tombs. Thanks to film, nowadays we can desecrate and show at will the only one of our possessions that is temporally inalienable: death without a requiem, the eternal dead-again of the cinema!"[6]

For Bazin, filmic reproduction profanes death, and yet he acknowledges, "Death is one of those rare events that justifies the term . . . *cinematic specificity*."[7] Although much theoretical writing associates it with photography's stillness rather than cinema's motion, death, after all, is the culmination of a particular process of duration and change: dying. It seems perfect, on that level, for capture by the technology that "mummifies change," as Bazin famously wrote elsewhere about film—although I will demonstrate that video and digital video (DV) have proven more adept at that capture.[8] To "mummify" this most drastic and most mysterious of changes is a quest that has attracted many cameras. The curiosity, I believe, is not just about a desire to see death but also a desire to find out whether a camera could really *show us* death. Could moving image technology meaningfully represent a liminal event that is frequently written about as being unknowable and beyond representation? Would this technology's affordances for mediating the visible world grant it access to the often invisible physiological process of a human body expiring? As Richard Dyer writes, "Western society has had a positive mania for trying to see what's inside the human being, body and soul. The photographic media, too, so clearly at the cutting edge in capturing appearances, have also sought to see and show past them."[9]

For Bazin, to re-present the sight of an actual death would be an acute "cinematic perversion," but during the era in which he wrote, the problem was more theoretical than practical.[10] Despite the American public's persistent—though not universal—desire to see such a documentary moment (manifest since the early years of cinema), catching hold of one on *celluloid* was quite difficult due to technological constraints. Many cameras were not especially mobile, they required expertise to operate, their film stock was expensive, and, for a time, they could run for only a few minutes per reel. Further, distribution options in this era were slight. In contrast to our digitally enabled Internet climate, most outlets for documentary footage—such as the theatrical newsreel—were subject to the type of journalistic gatekeeping likely to suppress any views of documentary death that actually made it onto celluloid. Technology thus helped mediate between the "stop" of ethical condemnations and the "go" of many viewers' desires, keeping the archive of documentary death images sparse through the mid-twentieth century. That balance began to shift in the United States during the 1960s as nascent trends in media solidified (detailed in chapter 1): the widespread adoption of home movie cameras brought the public greater access to recording technologies, and television's continuing infiltration of American living rooms provided more possibilities for the distribution and exhibition of moving images.

These trends have expanded astoundingly in the decades since, as digital technologies have filled these roles and created still others; in a new media environment, instances of recorded death are no longer the rare lightning strikes they once were. Beginning in the 1980s, when both consumers and professional documentarians started adopting video widely, and continuing through today's ubiquitous mobile phone cameras, recording devices became substantially more affordable, versatile, and easy to operate. As videotapes and digital storage supplanted reels of film, operators could record far more material at far less cost and with far fewer interruptions for changing reels. The democratizing effect of these technological shifts has meant, in practice, that vastly *more* cameras are blanketing public space in the digital age, more ready to capture death wherever and whenever it may occur. A further effect of advancing digital technologies is the accessibility of broader distribution for professional documentaries on DVD and paid streaming sites and for nonprofessional documentaries or raw footage on free streaming sites (YouTube, Vimeo, or any number of less well-known and less reputable alternatives).

And yet, the evolution of death's documentary representation in the digital age has not been a simple story of its universal proliferation through improved technologies. In some cases, the affordances of different digital tools align poorly or come into conflict with social, cultural, and economic forces in a way that impedes the circulation of documentary death. In terms of temporality, for example, DV has the capacity to record hours of footage inexpensively, enabling it to track long processes of dying from disease or to record pedestrians patiently at the Golden Gate Bridge until one jumps off it (as the chapters ahead will discuss). Yet this capacity exists in tension with the conventions of Internet video, a primary avenue of digital distribution. On YouTube and similar sites, the brief, spectacle-oriented video is king. The celebration of those qualities curtails video-makers' options for displaying death's duration or its frequent resistance to spectacular visibility, and it reinscribes the overexposure of violent (rather than natural) death. The failure of Google Glass—a glasses-style, wearable computer able to record video from its user's optical point of view—to achieve widespread consumer adoption provides another instructive case. Had it become commonplace, Glass would have expanded individuals' capacity to record death in public space beyond the gains mobile phone cameras have already achieved. And in terms of specific affordances, it would have allowed people to begin their videos more quickly in the face of sudden events, to record hands-free when they are in physical danger, and to record surreptitiously when the doing so openly might put them at risk (as it has, for example, for many recording police violence against Black citizens in the United States in the mid-2010s). But social drawbacks overshadowed Glass's technological affordances: the surreptitious recording capability raised major privacy concerns, and consumers were not thrilled about the aesthetics of wearing lensless glasses with a bulky computer unit attached to them. Glass became a brief fad as a general consumer product—a technological innovation that would have advanced efforts to document death on video, quickly (and probably rightly) sunk by social rejection.

Still, the cheap and easy chain of digital production, distribution, and exhibition has allowed an unprecedented amount of documentary death footage to reach the public. This footage ranges from intimate chronicles of long dying processes—often shot in part by the dying people themselves or their loved ones—to low-resolution, silent shots of killings recorded by mounted surveillance cameras. It has captured suicides, fatal confrontations with police, war deaths, and sometimes even surreptitiously recorded executions. Typified by shots of jumpers plummeting from the World Trade Center, of protesters under attack during the Arab Spring, and of Black victims of fatal police violence in the United States, documentary death footage has played a prominent role in twenty-first-century visual culture, wielding significant political influence.

Coverage of the World Trade Center's destruction illustrates the scope and rapidity of technological changes undergirding this influx of footage. As citizens tuned in to CNN that morning in 2001, they saw the initial use of extreme long shots from the network's own distant, ineffectually zooming cameras evolve into greater reliance on eyewitness video shot by bystanders near the towers with personal, portable cameras. Some of the news networks acquired and aired clips that showed individuals jumping to their deaths, but—as Barbie Zelizer describes—did so amid a storm of ethical controversy, retreating to still images within hours and then to no visual records of the jumps at all.[11] Within a few years of the attacks, the rise of streaming video sites around 2005 would effectively bypass this ethical crisis among professionals. Since then, plentiful

9/11 jumper footage has been readily accessible to anyone with Internet access and the will to watch it, as the citizen journalists who originally shot the footage or other nonprofessionals who have acquired copies have been able to circulate it freely via YouTube and other sites. *Wall Street Journal* columnist Richard Woodward broadly articulates the fears accompanying this shift: "We better get used to living without visual boundaries—and with the curiosity and flexible morality of the viewer as the only limit on what we can see—from now on."[12]

That documentary death footage has multiplied dramatically in the digital age and that public access to it has expanded at a remarkable rate are undeniable realities of our time, but realities whose implications are not readily apparent and are perhaps difficult to face. Difficult or not, the fact that a life ending in front of a camera has become a common sight on digital screens calls for a critical reassessment of documentary death. This reassessment must eschew all-purpose labels like "metaphysical obscenity" in favor of a more detailed and generous analysis—one that examines the content of individual clips, considering both ethics and aesthetics, and accounts for the ways in which these clips circulate and the ways they are received.

Dying in Full Detail undertakes this reassessment, analyzing deaths that are *embodied* and *enframed*: physical (not metaphorical) deaths of visible individuals, caught on camera. Through this analysis, I ask what digital image technologies reveal about death and, in turn, what death reveals about the digital. The affordances of digital image technologies aim to fulfill promises made long ago by photography and then by cinema: to make visible what has been invisible, to make public what has been private. These promises unfold at the level of both production and distribution, as the digital pledges to let us *record* more of what has gone previously unrecorded through widespread and continuous taping and to let us *watch* more of what has gone unseen through instant, global distribution that bypasses old media's gatekeepers. Recording actual deaths presents an ideal test case for such promises. Death is one of the most private experiences of contemporary Western culture, its visibility remains elusive (its occurrence often passing too quickly and unpredictably to be seen or recorded), and distribution of its documentary capture has frequently been interrupted by media gatekeepers. Indeed, representing death has always been among the earliest projects of new image technologies—a challenge through which image-makers seek to prove the magic of their new devices. The results generally expose both the potential achievements of these devices and their inevitable disappointments.

The footage that actually emerges from digital technology's promises to make death newly visible and public proves to be no exception to this trend.

I argue that the digital is unable to show death "in full detail," as it remains beyond representation even amid image technologies that can record it more fully than ever. Failures to fully reveal it on the documentary screen affirm that death is enigmatic and internal, with limited external signs that the camera doggedly pursues. It refuses to appear as a transcendent, identifiable instant capable of video capture. Especially resistant to mediated visibility is the "moment of death," a supposed point of transition from living being to corpse that has fixated image-makers and audiences, and that obscures the more frightening reality that dying is a durational process—a long one, for most Americans. In digital technology's undeniably increased capacity to record and distribute the sight of death, though, I contend that what it actually delivers is increased opportunity to politicize individual deaths through the rhetorical power of their documentary representation. The contribution digital death documentary can make to the world is ultimately more sociopolitical than metaphysical—more wrapped up in the everyday labor of improving human lives than in the irresistible, impossible philosophical pursuit of truly understanding their endings.

Further, I hope to frame digital technology in a way that suits its actual application in the documentary form. Scholarship on digital cinema tends to focus on the highly visible realms of special effects and image manipulation in big-budget fiction film. The changes digital technology has enacted in documentary have been less spectacularly visible but arguably more impactful, vastly expanding what professionals can do with their limited budgets and extending documentary authorship to nonprofessionals. The frequent scholarly conflation of digital cinema with digital special effects has left a dearth of new media theory that speaks well to digital documentary. For example, theorizing digital cinema in one of the field's most-cited, foundational works, Lev Manovich emphasizes that "pixels, regardless of their origin, can be easily altered, substituted for one another, and so on. Live-action footage is thus reduced to just another graphic, no different than images created manually. . . . *Digital cinema is a particular case of animation that uses live-action footage as one of its many elements.*"[13] Manovich affixes this provocative claim broadly to digital filmmaking, but it is deeply misleading in relation to most digital documentary work. Putting aside the ethical factors that may stop documentarians from drastically mucking about with "easily altered" pixels (other than in routine and relatively benign processes like color correction), there is still the reality that altering pixels well takes time and money, and it thus remains beyond the *budgets* of this typically underfunded filmmaking form.

Especially troubling for the study of digital documentary is existing new media theory's fixation on the loss of indexicality. That perceived loss of the physical connection between object and representation has branded digital images as "immaterial" or "disembodied," but this drama of referentiality seems surprisingly irrelevant in the reception of digital documentary.[14] With most documentaries, viewers' Bazinian faith in the direct correspondence between objects in the world and their representation on-screen does not seem to be shaken by digital capture—which is to say, viewers remain suspicious of digital documentary in basically the same ways they have always been suspicious of celluloid documentary. They question whether the editor has tinkered with a chronology of events or whether incidents have been staged for the camera, but I have not seen evidence in viewer response to the works I analyze that they are wary of overt *digital* manipulation on any meaningful scale.[15] And in much new media scholarship's narrow association of materiality and embodiment with indexicality, these terms' more immediate connotations are sacrificed. As I demonstrate in this book, seeing recorded death makes us *feel* embodied, regardless of platform or medium. While we are watching a still-living person plummet 245 feet off the Golden Gate Bridge and hit the water with a devastating force, for example, it hardly matters that sequences of ones and zeroes are communicating this event rather than silver halide grains on a strip of celluloid. Knowledge of such differences—for those who have it—does nothing to lessen the impact of seeing a life end, a digital sight that feels decidedly material, and painfully so. Along these lines, I support Tom Gunning's assertion in "Moving Away from the Index" that the familiar, indexicality-based approach "may have reached the limits of its usefulness," especially in the realm of digital media theory.[16] Gunning draws a distinction between classical film theory, which strives to uncover the essence of the medium, and contemporary film theory, which insists on the experience of watching as central to the medium. Theories of digital immateriality and nonindexicality rely on the former model, but *Dying in Full Detail* will support the latter approach.

Death Culture's National and Historical Context

As much as video and digital technologies have enabled documentary death, the drive documentarians do or do not experience to capture death and the willingness or unwillingness of audiences to look at it are products of culture— for my study, primarily U.S. culture from the mid-nineteenth century to the present. *Dying in Full Detail* is grounded in the experience of U.S. audiences, though inclusive of some of the transnational circulation of death footage from elsewhere to which they are exposed. This national context serves the project beyond simply establishing a manageable scope; the United States presents the most extreme case of the opposing social conditions that typified the twentieth-century culture of death denial. While removing dying bodies from public space and repressing the taboo topic of death in public discourse, mid-century U.S. culture nurtured a simultaneous obsession with its fictional media representation. This national culture creates a complex and high-stakes environment for the entry of documentary death footage, as detailed later. I want to acknowledge, though, that while I sometimes refer to "U.S. death culture" ahead, there is no singular death culture in the United States. Attitudes toward death in any given period vary with race, religion, region, national or ethnic origin, and so on. To give just one example, attitudes toward death in gay male communities at the height of the AIDS crisis differed considerably from those of the American mainstream in that period.

Although most of my case studies are U.S.-based, I intend for my argument, methods, and many of my insights to be broadly applicable for scholars and viewers of global media. The tension between death's visibility and invisibility that forms the core of my argument seems to be a near-universal theme, globally, in documentaries about death, even if its iterations can differ significantly across national contexts. To take one subtopic, documentarians all over the world making films about war and atrocity wrestle with the question of whether and how to make death visible and with alternatives to its direct display when documentary images are lost or were never made. The two most striking examples in the past decade come from Israel's Ari Folman and Cambodia's Rithy Panh. Folman's *Waltz with Bashir* (2008) centers on the director's own role, as an Israeli soldier, in the First Lebanon War's Sabra and Shatila refugee massacre. Ending with video documentation of the massacre's gory aftermath, *Waltz* revives the power of documentary corpse footage—long dulled by this sight's awful ubiquity in the twentieth century—by juxtaposing its harsh, live-action details with the majority of his film's sleek and stylized animation. In *The Missing Picture* (2013), Panh builds on his decades of experience representing the Cambodian genocide on film to tell the story of his own painful childhood surviving labor camps and losing loved ones to the Khmer Rouge. Though the phrase carries multiple meanings, "the missing picture" refers partly to actuality footage of the Khmer Rouge's murders—the audiovisual record of their atrocities, never created or since lost, that cannot be shown in Panh's film. In its absence, Panh relies on other kinds of archival footage, Khmer Rouge propaganda, excerpts of his own films, and—most centrally and evocatively—elaborate dioramas of hand-carved clay figurines. As Leshu Torchin writes, "Where no images of an experience exist, Panh uses something available (or imagined) and thus gestures to the gaps produced through traumatic experience and a compromised historiography."[17] While these have long been among Panh's methods as a documentarian, *The Missing Picture* becomes his most evocative exploration of the value of actuality footage of death, of the extent to which filmmakers and viewers invest in its authority, its supremacy over other kinds of representation. For, as *Dying in Full Detail* will assert more generally, the type of "missing picture" Panh lacks would never meet expectations—would never equal the tragic beauty and truth of his clay pageant.

Further, my discussion of the ways in which documentary death serves political causes—despite its overall failure to illuminate death's "full detail"—also has broad global applications, as actuality images of death are pulled into the service of politics in many, many regions. In some cases, the political causes are massive, transnational in nature, and circulate globally through journalistic and social media. This was true for the 2011 wave of interconnected revolutions in the Middle East and North Africa and the multiple instances of documentary death they produced—most prominently, images of Mohamed Bouazizi's self-immolation in Tunisia and the corpse of Khaled Saeed, beaten to death by police in Egypt. These men's deaths elevated them to martyr status and fueled the coming uprisings in their respective nations, where photographs of them—both alive and dead—frequently graced material protest signs and pro-revolution Internet activism.[18] In other cases, recordings of death circulate on a narrower national level where they spark smaller-scale political organizing. In Foshan, China, in 2011, security cameras recorded two-year-old Wang Yue (sometimes written about as "Little Yue Yue") being struck by two vehicles and lying fatally injured in the road while eighteen passersby neglected to help her. The footage, circulating on local television news and then online, prompted national debate about the Chinese public's moral character and was successfully mobilized to support new Good Samaritan legislation.[19] In Ficksburg, South Africa, in the same year, Andries Tatane was filmed being shot and beaten to death by police while protesting a lack of public services. Footage of the incident—again, broadcast locally on television news and circulated online—propelled further protests and gave Tatane a martyr's role in this activist cause.[20] This book's approach to reading photographs and footage of this nature and its broad consideration of ethical and aesthetic factors in recording death can be applied across national boundaries to cases like these, with the proper consideration of each case's historical and cultural context.

To return to the U.S. historical and cultural context and documentary death's place within it: Robert Kastenbaum succinctly summarizes the state of mainstream U.S. death culture around the turn of the twenty-first century, writing, "We have succeeded more than most societies in reducing the presence of the dead. In part this has been accomplished by keeping people alive longer. In part, though, we have cultivated techniques for keeping not only the dead but also the dying from general view. For most people in other times and places, death and the dead were more a part of everyday life."[21] Death was certainly a prominent part of everyday life upon the birth of modern image technologies in the mid-nineteenth century. Infectious disease tore through populations, especially in growing urban centers, ensuring that "nineteenth-century Americans lived and died in a cauldron of uncontrolled endemic and epidemic diseases of contagion."[22] These hardships were aggravated by the widespread threat of sudden death—still fearsome in its refusal of time for the soul's preparation—from diseases like cholera, and for a few overwhelming years from the massive casualties of the American Civil War.[23]

Nineteenth-century Americans coped with their ever-present mortality by building a culture, as Philippe Ariès describes, in which the process of dying was charged with fierce emotion: joy that the dying person would pass into eternity and salvation, but sharply felt and loudly expressed grief for those from whom he would be (temporarily) separated.[24] The soul's fate remained a key concern in this period, but the presence of the living at the deathbed became a fiercely cherished source of support that rivaled the religious elements of a "good death." To attend the bedside of the dying was a privilege granted to many, as death in this era was far more public and visible than it would soon become. Deathbed visitors largely expected to see life end triumphantly and emotionally—an expectation for sensational dying that persists among media viewers today—so deaths that failed to present those qualities often disappointed.[25] This period of American death culture—concurrent with the rise of photography in the history of image media—hardly foreshadows the denial and suppression of death that would follow in the twentieth century. Discourse on mortality was robust and highly public, because death itself was robust and highly public, and because a dominant Christian religious faith enabled Americans to conceive of death as an exalted event that would lead to a glorious reunion in heaven.

Understanding the persistent saturation of death in U.S. culture through the end of the nineteenth century illuminates the severity of the "brutal revolution" in attitudes that would follow, propelling the country (and much of the Western world) into its much-analyzed era of death denial and creating high stakes for documentary representations of life's end.[26] Observing death culture in the West in 1955—around the height of this "brutal revolution"—noted anthropologist Geoffrey Gorer asserted, "The natural processes of corruption and decay have become disgusting, as disgusting as the natural processes of birth and copulation were a century ago; preoccupation about such processes is (or was) morbid and unhealthy, to be discouraged in all and punished in the young."[27] Death had begun to recede from the public eye in the early part of the century as a result of two major medical developments. First, death rates declined, thanks to improvements in medical care and the control of epidemic diseases—as well as better housing, nutrition, and hygiene.[28] As Americans played witness to fewer deaths in this era of longer life, "the final days of dying, once calmly familiar to everyone, [became] existentially disturbing in ways they once were not."[29] Second, the rise of hospitals in the early twentieth century, and their promise of lifesaving medical intervention from doctors and machines, led to death's spatial displacement starting around 1930, from the home to the hospital.[30] Here, the dying were hidden from the public, first in open wards—where they underwent operations and died in full view of other patients—and then in a deeper layer of concealment as the need for income drove hospitals to offer private and semiprivate rooms.[31]

The style of death that was possible in a twentieth-century American hospital was radically different from the style possible in a nineteenth-century American home, necessitating changes in how people defined the good death. A new trend compromised the personal, spiritual preparation for life's end that had been a central component of a good death since the Middle Ages: that of doctors and family members concealing a terminal diagnosis from the dying person, lest knowledge of her or his immanent demise interfere with medical treatment or hospital routines. An unconscious, speedy end proceeding as privately and invisibly as possible thus became the most valued manifestation of death—a sharp reversal from the fear of sudden death and desire for support and witnesses at the deathbed that were dominant in earlier centuries.[32] Friends, family, and even neighbors, who had been fixtures of deathbeds at home, were now discouraged from gathering beside them and permitted only in limited numbers at set visiting hours.[33]

These changes in customs are symptomatic of how the emotional and spiritual needs of the dying and their survivors became subordinated to the demands of medical care. That Americans abided by this shift in values perhaps speaks to the creeping secularization of U.S. culture and a redistribution of faith—away from God and the certainty that loved ones would reunite in heaven, and toward science and the promise that loved ones could delay their earthly parting. In hospital dying for much of the twentieth century, "spiritual rites of passage" were replaced by "metallic ones" as machines became primary and nurses were taught to do their jobs with mechanical efficiency.[34] Personifying this newly medicalized natural death (arguably more frightening than violent death in the twentieth century), Ariès asserts, "The death of the patient in the hospital, covered with tubes, is becoming a popular image, more terrifying than the *transi* or skeleton of macabre rhetoric."[35]

Enduring death in a hospital, covered with tubes, would likely be easier if it arrived within hours, like nineteenth-century cholera. But as the medical establishment became more successful at prolonging life, a protracted period of suffering and dying was the unfortunate side effect. Death's duration lengthened more dramatically than at any other point in U.S. history. The leading three causes of death in the United States in 1950, for example, all typically produced a great deal of hospital time as death approached: heart disease (which kills only a portion of its victims through sudden heart attacks), malignant neoplasms (cancer), and vascular lesions.[36] For most Americans in this era, the "moment of death"—which this book will track as an object of persistent fixation for documentarians and their audiences—was thus a tiny fragment of a very long process of dying, compared with other historical periods. Furthermore, the "moment," if it ever really had been identifiable, was now obscured by a swarm of drugs and medical procedures that seemed to divide dying into innumerable, often invisible pieces—perhaps making its decreasingly attainable capture on camera all the more enticing.[37]

Lacking the firsthand exposure to dying and the dead that their ancestors had, Americans could not help but rely on other sources of information about what death—this essential and shared human experience—looked like. Cinema has been one of those sources. As Jay Ruby surmises, "Long before most Americans ever see the actual body of a dead person, they see photographic and electronic representations of death—a few are actual, most make-believe."[38] Gorer's 1955 essay sharpens that observation by noting that the make-believe majority of such representations avoid natural death, which Gorer sees as truly taboo, and favor violent death. The deathbed documentaries analyzed in chapter 2 position themselves against this trend, striving to bring the physical and emotional realities of actual, natural dying back into the public eye. Throughout *Dying in Full Detail*, the interplay between "actual" and "make-believe" representations of death will recur, as will the porous aesthetic boundaries between these modes of filmmaking. Generally having seen little in life or documentary to challenge mainstream fiction film's visions of death, viewers respond to "actual" death footage—when it finally does start to appear with any regularity—through the lens of these "make-believe" visions.

Ethical (and Unethical) Approaches
to Recording and Viewing Death

Dying in Full Detail is about the documentary camera's pull toward death's most apparently visible forms—toward publicly displaying dying and dead bodies on-screen—and the impact its footage makes on American visual culture. This book focuses on death that is embodied and enframed, but such displays are complemented in documentary history by other important and eloquent works that approach death more obliquely. In addition to the aforementioned film *The Missing Picture*, this set of documentaries includes *Blue* (1993), in which Derek Jarman opts for a screen of flat color rather than images of bodily decay in his audiocentric chronicle of his own death. In *Grizzly Man* (2005), director Werner Herzog encounters a tape on which a young couple is heard being killed by a bear, and he rejects it on camera, telling its owner, "You must never listen to this . . . you should destroy it."[39] Perhaps Bazin's greatest ally in his argument against recording death is Claude Lanzmann, who pointedly made his nine-and-a-half-hour Holocaust opus *Shoah* (1985) without the shots of corpses that fill other classic Holocaust documentaries, such as *Night and Fog* (1955, Alain Resnais). Resisting documentarians' common pull toward making death directly visible, Lanzmann states unequivocally, "If I had stumbled on a real ss film . . . that showed how 3,000 Jewish men, women and children were gassed in Auschwitz's crematorium 2, not only would I not have shown it but I would have destroyed it."[40] Instead of relying on archival images, Lanzmann evokes past death in the present—grasping at it through the spaces and actions that connote it for living witnesses and perpetrators (a method Panh also adopts in his haunting *S21: The Khmer Rouge Killing Machine* [2003]). Death forms the core of all these documentaries, but the filmmakers restrain it from surfacing visually or aurally, refusing to create Bazin's "metaphysical obscenity."

On the other end of documentary death's spectrum of elision and display lies "death porn." Rather than finding creative ways to evoke death without showing it, as the previously mentioned documentaries do, death porn delights in its graphic display. Seemingly untroubled by ethical concerns, these films and videos strive for "maximum visibility" of bodily pain and destruction that parallels the "maximum visibility" of bodily pleasure Linda Williams writes about in pornography.[41] Gorer, in fact, theorized a similar connection in 1955, long before this content circulated on the Internet and in relation to far more innocent fare, such as horror comics. In both traditional pornography and "the pornography of death," he asserts that "the emotions which are typically concomitant of the acts—love or grief—are paid little or no attention, while the sensations are enhanced."[42]

The most well-known example of the cult death porn genre is *Faces of Death* (John Allen Schwartz), a controversial 1978 release that presents itself as a compilation documentary exploring the profound topic of death, "our own destiny" that we refuse to recognize.[43] An on-screen "expert" guides us: Dr. Frances B. Gröss, who has "compiled a library of the many faces of death" for our edification and narrates these clips. *Faces of Death* quickly communicates its more macabre intentions through the type of footage it uses: gory animal deaths, corpses and autopsies, blatantly staged human deaths (an electrocution, an alligator attack, a cult leader cutting open a follower's chest and eating his innards), and very occasional actuality footage of human death. Still more unsettling than this mix is the way that footage is presented, often with jokes from Dr. Gröss or a comical soundtrack. Actuality footage of a suicidal jump from a building ledge, for example, is accompanied by a jaunty jazz score with the musical count, "and a one, two, one two three four," timed to signal the woman's jump.

Death porn films of this ilk are cataloged with encyclopedic detail in David Kerekes and David Slater's *Killing for Culture: An Illustrated History of Death Film from Mondo to Snuff* (1995), but since the book's publication, death porn's quantity and reach have expanded dramatically with the help of digital technology. High-traffic "shock sites"—analyzed further in chapter 4—gather the Internet's goriest images of actual death alongside footage of nonfatal wounds, spectacles of bodily disfigurement and disability, and often sexual pornography, too.

Makers of death porn recognize a pervasive curiosity about death in an era of its reduced visibility, but they break the "real death" taboo for the sake of taboo breaking and its accompanying titillation. To delight in such an act when the subject matter is actual death is ethically quite different than to do so in relation to sex, as pornography does. The pornography industry—at least, its reputable studios—stages taboo acts of unsimulated sex that are performed by consenting participants who know that the footage will be distributed. This basic level of informed consent is not a privilege that can be granted to people dying suddenly and violently in front of cameras, and the ethical stakes of distributing such footage are therefore extremely high. To present it with a mood of frivolity or as a source of pure audiovisual pleasure is to open oneself up to well-justified ethical condemnation.

The works I analyze in *Dying in Full Detail* generally fall between these two extremes of cautious omission and unabashed enjoyment in their approach to actuality footage of death. These documentarians labor in an ethical and aesthetic borderland, though one increasingly populous in the digital age, striving to represent the unrepresentable, directly and ethically. Not all succeed, as some lose their tenuous grasp on an ethical engagement with death. But all share a conviction, as do I, that images of actual death can do a kind of cultural work—can have a value to the living that justifies the fraught circumstances of their creation.

For documentary death footage to perform this cultural work, it must above all find an audience who is willing to witness it—an act of looking whose ethical complexity parallels that of the act of recording. Not very long ago—in fact, as recently as 2007 when I began researching this topic in earnest—evidence suggested a continuing eagerness among the public to see graphic images of actual death.[44] Questions about the ethics or value of displaying such images, when they were raised, came primarily from professionals in journalism, documentary filmmaking, and academia. These tended to focus on whether it was fair to the deceased or to that person's survivors to distribute documentation of the death and on whether the image served a function valuable enough to account for its explicitness. These individuals questioned our *right* to look at graphic images of actual death, and usually a particular image; a refusal to look would stem from ethical objections to that image's creation or display.

Over just a few years, though, a different kind of objection to looking at documentary death (bundled with various other potentially disturbing recorded sights) gained tremendous momentum in public discourse through the popularization of "trigger warnings"—globally in Internet communities and nationally in U.S. university campus culture. A trigger warning is a caution provided (in writing at the top of a blog post or in a professor's remarks before a course film screening, for example) about potentially upsetting content ahead, giving the audience a chance to turn back or psychologically prepare themselves for the experience of consuming it. These warnings have a long history in feminist Internet culture, but they vastly broadened their reach in the mid-2010s to become a subject of fierce controversy.[45] Resistance to trigger warnings in this era stems, in some measure, from the practice's expansion beyond the specific groups it was once imagined to protect. Many of us in the position to provide such warnings (in our college classrooms, in our writing, in our media-making) agree that a rape survivor, for example, may benefit from advanced notice about a graphic rape scene in a film that might "trigger" a volatile traumatic memory.[46] But applications of trigger warnings and the pool of individuals insisting on them have expanded far beyond this type of specific scenario. At their most extreme, trigger warnings may now be demanded by those who have not personally experienced the uncomfortable things they do not wish to see represented: violence, sex, suicide, self-injury, substance abuse, eating disorders, racism, sexism, classism, homophobia, transphobia, ableism, and so on.[47] Now the culture of the trigger warning feels, to many critics, dangerously oversensitized. No longer calibrated for those people who have actually lived through trauma, trigger warnings often function to shield those with relatively privileged lives from being upset by the traumatic experiences others have to endure.

Proponents of the trigger warning have made refusing to look at disturbing images, like the images of recorded death that this book considers, a much more common and more public practice. Further, they have dramatically shifted the terms under which that refusal is made. Such refusals previously tended to project outward from the individual making them, manifesting an interest in the rights and well-being of others; refusals stemming from trigger-warning culture turn inward, proclaiming one's own right to self-protection from perceived psychological harm. Deeply wary of this turn toward a rhetoric of self-protection, I believe that each of us must interrogate our own experiences and privileges when deciding whether to close our eyes to difficult sights. The images and footage of this nature that are described and sometimes depicted in *Dying in Full Detail* represent, as Susan Sontag writes, "a means of making 'real' (or 'more real') matters that the privileged and the merely safe might prefer to ignore."[48] Those of us among "the privileged and the merely safe" must weigh the necessity of our self-protection against our moral obligation to learn and think critically about the terrible things that happen to others, and—crucially—about the *way* these terrible things are mediated and the consequences of that mediation. Additionally, the type of sights we choose to avoid and our reasons for doing so matter. It is one thing to avoid *The Texas Chainsaw Massacre* because one is upset by blood and gore; it is another to avoid *Night and Fog* because one is upset by dead bodies. And it is one thing to avoid Eric Garner's recorded death at the hands of police because one knows the history of and objects to the spectacularized suffering of Black male bodies; it is another to avoid that footage because one finds it disturbing to watch someone die on camera.

The rise of the trigger warning and its attendant culture makes clear that the desire to see a sight like recorded death is by no means universal. As much evidence as there is that this desire has been strong and persistent throughout the history of photography and film, there are many who feel dread, not curiosity, at the prospect of witnessing a recorded death. The cultural shift toward this dread response, toward a rhetoric of self-protection that trigger-warning culture suggests is likely one consequence of the shift in visual culture that this book describes: the vast expansion of disturbing recorded events available for public view, which digital technology has enabled (though not exclusively caused). When a sight like recorded death is taboo and seldom seen, it may pique curiosity; when it is confronting viewers through video links in news articles and on social media every few weeks in a new form, its generally grim reality registers for many, and that curiosity evolves into apprehension. In my field of research, I do not have the option to avoid images of this nature and, in fact, have to actively seek them out. As a brief personal comment, I will note that the evolution from curiosity to apprehension in the face of documentary death footage is one I have undergone myself during my many years of research for this book.

If trigger-warning culture has contributed something valuable to the matter of creating and viewing potentially disturbing content, it is this: no one should take lightly their request for others to look at horrifying things, especially in media as immersive as photography and film, and especially in a form as sobering as documentary. No matter how sheltered and privileged an audience member might be, no matter how strong one's conviction is that that person *should* see the content in question—that they are morally obligated to do so—it is no small thing to ask someone to witness sights like the ones analyzed in this book. For some, that act of witnessing may pass with little impact, but for others it may leave a psychological mark. On an existential level, it may even drive home the relative powerlessness most viewers have in the face of human cruelty or the chaotic violence of life.

While their effect on audiences will vary, sights like these cannot be unseen—even in the form of small, black-and-white stills in an academic book, with their accompanying description and analysis. Thus, I want to note here that I understand the stakes of writing about the recorded deaths of others and of asking this book's readers to absorb those recordings and think about what they mean. Throughout the process of completing *Dying in Full Detail*, I have aimed to preserve for myself and for my readers the human meaning and emotional impact of these deaths while simultaneously analyzing them in a form (the academic book) that demands, in some measure, critical distance. Writing about this topic with care, compassion, and hopefully some grace has been a vital goal for me as I seek to honor my implicit ethical obligations to readers and especially to the individuals whose deaths—exposed to the public and often deeply unjust in nature—undergird my work.

The Influences and Structure of *Dying in Full Detail*

My writing about the intersection between death and documentary is informed by much related scholarship on photography (Roland Barthes, Sontag, John Berger) and a few film-specific studies (Bazin, Vogel, Michael Renov), where writers have more rarely taken up the subject.[49] No author has been more important to this book than Vivian Sobchack, whose 1984 essay (and its revised 2004 version) "Inscribing Ethical Space: Ten Propositions on Death, Representation, and Documentary" provides an early and ambitious exploration of the topic. In a mere eighteen pages of the *Quarterly Review of Film Studies*, Sobchack provides a cultural context for death in documentary, ten theoretical propositions about it, and a taxonomy of six "gazes" through which the camera might look at actual death, evaluated in relation to ethics.

Sobchack's gazes, which I will reference in multiple chapters ahead, require a brief overview.[50] She grants ethical approval to five of these ways of looking, starting with the "accidental gaze," which applies to death footage captured by chance without a cameraperson's intention to record it. The "helpless gaze" indicates that the cameraperson was restrained from intervening in the death recorded, usually by physical distance or the law (for instance, in the case of recorded executions). Whether helpless or not, the cameraperson who records death with an "endangered gaze" is doing so at the risk of her or his own life, and thus paying an appropriate price for the ethical privilege. An extreme extension of the endangered gaze, the "interventional gaze" shows the cameraperson emerging from cover and safety to record death—sometimes dying while doing so. Finally, the "humane gaze" is more of a stare, "marked by its *extended duration*" and often employed to film natural death.[51] Sobchack praises instances of the humane gaze in which documentarians have been invited by the dying—where the opportunity to consent is possible, unlike in most of the cases these gazes describe. Each of the preceding gazes is ethical, according to Sobchack, because death's recording neither indicates the cameraperson's complicity nor interferes with death's possible prevention. In fact, Sobchack encourages viewers to look for signs of an ethical position "inscribed" within the footage itself—a zoom that indicates physical distance from the death or an obscured view that signifies the cameraperson's endangerment and need to take cover. The "professional gaze" (attributed to professional journalists, in this essay), however, does not inscribe acceptable ethics into its content and does not receive automatic ethical approval from Sobchack. Instead, its content is "marked by ethical ambiguity, by technical and *machinelike compe-*

tence in the face of an event that seems to call for further and more humane response."[52]

With this taxonomy of gazes, Sobchack (implicitly) opposes Bazin's sweeping rejection of documentary death, contributing a welcome insistence that not all recorded deaths are recorded equally. *How* death is documented matters, and viewers can evaluate the ethics of each instance by examining the circumstances and attitude of its recording—often implied in the material itself, through cinematography. Using her essay as a vital foundation, this book affirms Sobchack's insistence that the way death is recorded makes a difference, engaging in the type of close reading that she lacked the space, access, and perhaps desire to undertake in "Inscribing Ethical Space."[53] Further, the works I analyze present opportunities to expand Sobchack's list of gazes, as new ways of looking have emerged in the documentary form that are uniquely digital. In chapters 3 and 4, I propose three digital-era additions to that list: the expectant gaze, the automated gaze, and the ubiquitous gaze.

The chapters of *Dying in Full Detail* progress both chronologically and thematically. Chronologically, the chapters cover photography and film's predigital efforts to record death from the 1830s through the 1970s (chapter 1), video's influx into documentary production in the 1980s and 1990s (chapter 2), the influence of digital production tools in the first few years of the 2000s (chapter 3), and the current climate of digital distribution (chapter 4). Thematically, the book's two halves explore two sides of the mutually informing interplay between death and the digital. The first pair of chapters asks what the digital (sometimes through absence) reveals about death: namely, that it frequently resists visibility and proceeds as an amorphous process rather than an identifiable event. The second pair of chapters reverses the question to ask what death reveals about the digital, emphasizing the latter's unique durational powers, capacity for surveillance, and surprising sense of materiality.

Chapter 1, "Capturing the 'Moment': Photography, Film, and Death's Elusive Duration," situates digital efforts to record death within a long history of photographic and filmic attempts from the invention of the daguerreotype in 1839 through the end of the Vietnam War in 1975. The chapter unifies disparate images—Civil War and lynching photographs, early cinema's execution films, images from Nazi concentration camps, home movie footage of President John Kennedy's assassination, and television news coverage of the Vietnam War—through their struggle to capture the "moment of death." I argue that such attempts form a collective and enduring fantasy for documentarians and their audiences, one that cannot be fully realized because cameras cannot make visible a definitive "moment" within an opaque, durational process of dying. The relative paucity of success in capturing death on celluloid also highlights film's specific technological limitations in that task.

Chapter 2, "The Art of Dying, on Video: Deathbed Documentaries," continues with the opposition between the visible "moment of death" and the nebulous process of dying by examining long-term chronicles of natural dying. This documentary practice gained traction through the rise of analog video and then DV. With newly affordable and user-friendly equipment, both professionals and family members began to bring cameras to the bedsides of the dying, who collaborated in recording their own deaths. Their documentaries—including the filmic precursor *Dying* (1978, Michael Roemer), *Silverlake Life: The View from Here* (1993, Peter Friedman and Tom Joslin), and *Sick: The Life and Death of Bob Flanagan, Supermasochist* (1997, Kirby Dick)—challenge the primacy of the visible "moment of death" by systematically excluding it, despite technology's newfound readiness to capture it. They instead use video's affordances to make the long process of dying newly public, detailing the illness that precedes this "moment" and the mourning that follows it. I argue, though, that this exclusion also reveals a new discomfort with the physicality of dying, as the surprisingly routine "moment" of bodily expiration conflicts with the era's revised model of the "good death" as highly individualized.

Chapter 3, "'A Negative Pleasure': Suicide's Digital Sublimity," analyzes *The Bridge*, a 2006 documentary that exploits the durational affordances of the digital in order to record death in a new and ethically volatile way. With two stations of continually staffed DV cameras, director Eric Steel surveilled San Francisco's Golden Gate Bridge for every daylight minute of 2004, watching for the frequent suicides this structure draws. Culled from ten thousand hours of video, the startling suicide footage included in *The Bridge* made newly visible a type of highly public dying that had remained socially and politically invisible for decades. This display of recorded suicide elicited both a barrage of ethical criticisms and a surge in activist efforts to erect a suicide barrier at the Golden Gate. While the film's harshest critics condemned the mere act of recording these suicides—a common response to death documentaries—I argue that its ethics are fully entangled with its aesthetics. *The Bridge* uses Hollywood conventions to frame suicide as sublime, both terrible and magnificent, and to elevate one graceful jumper into a position as the film's star. These aesthetic choices compromise the film ethically, in light of social scientists' findings that suicides can spread when romanticized through their media representation— an effect that would counteract the project's alleged goal of suicide prevention.

Chapter 4, "Streaming Death: The Politics of Dying on YouTube," moves past professional documentaries with theatrical distribution and ten thousand hours of footage to consider amateur videos as short as twelve seconds that circulate online. I analyze the production and distribution of videos of two violent 2009 deaths, each of which was captured by multiple mobile phone cameras and posted on YouTube. The victims were Oscar Grant, a young Black man fatally shot in Oakland by transit police, and Neda Agha-Soltan, a young Iranian woman killed in Tehran during a protest of that year's elections. Put to use by activists, these two sets of videos achieved disparate levels of success in raising awareness about their injustices and securing support for associated political causes. Analyzing the videos' aesthetics and circulation, I argue that YouTube's failure to provide context for its content—which has prompted scholarly criticisms about its usefulness for activism—can sometimes be politically liberating. However, the centrality of spectacle to success in YouTube's "attention economy" means that the deaths streaming on the site generate interest from the way they look and sound more from than the degrees of injustice they depict. Thus, for activist death footage, I find that only graphically visible death is likely to significantly increase a cause's political visibility.

Finally, my conclusion reflects on the motivations of those who make and view documentary death and on the broad cultural and political work these maligned moving images attempt. I end *Dying in Full Detail* with an acknowledgment that even the recorded reminders of human mortality I write about here are themselves mortal. While a spirit of death denial pervades the public's attitude toward digital recordings—thought immortal, never to curl and decay like celluloid film—the files that store death footage face their own deaths through, for example, neglect in the endless process of migration to new formats that is necessary to sustain them.

The spectacle of "dying in full detail" is what mainstream fiction film has claimed to deliver, what pre-video documentary largely failed to deliver, what Western audiences lost firsthand exposure to in the twentieth century, and what many are curious to see now with the help of digital cameras and distribution. But the promise of spectatorial plenitude in the digital age—that new technology can show us not only death but just about *everything* "in full detail"—cannot hold. Just as we expect too much from death as a mystical, transcendent moment, we also expect too much from technology. Digital video does display the end of life more often and in different ways than its indexical predecessors, photography and film. But as the following chapters will demonstrate, "full detail" remains a fantasy in relation to death, not a visible reality that cameras can capture.

1

CAPTURING THE "MOMENT"

PHOTOGRAPHY, FILM, AND
DEATH'S ELUSIVE DURATION

Death is the unique moment par excellence.
ANDRÉ BAZIN, "Death Every Afternoon"

On-screen, a young actress snorts cocaine in a bathroom stall, then vomits and drops to the floor; she convulses violently, flopping around on the dirty tile until her body stills. An elderly man wheeling his recycling bin to the curb stops and grips his chest; a few seconds later he falls on his lawn, motionless. A rollerblading dog walker reaches exhilarating speed down a sloped suburban street but collides with a car at the bottom; after hurtling over the cracked windshield, her body lies frozen on the pavement as the dogs bark. Each sequence ends in a slow washout as the screen gradually brightens to pure white, with black letters that provide a tombstone's report: Rebecca Leah Milford, 1980–2001; Benjamin Srisai, 1935–2002; Pilar Sandoval, 1970–2005. These death scenes open three episodes of Alan Ball's *Six Feet Under* (2001–5), a celebrated HBO drama about a family that runs a Los Angeles funeral home. Each episode begins with a "death of the week": a mininarrative that lasts between thirty seconds and five minutes, ends in a death, and later links up with the main narrative (usually when the deceased becomes a customer at the funeral home). While the tone and the way in which people die vary with each opening segment, an unwavering but compassionate fascination with the *moment* of death—that inscrutable point when a living being becomes a corpse—unites the many opening death scenes of the series. Benjamin Srisai's fifty-second story epitomizes this focus. It contains no dialogue, no other characters, and only one discernible audiovisual or narrative attraction: a sustained close-up on his face as he dies, first expressing simple pain and then a wide-eyed mixture of shock and wonder. *Six Feet Under's* impressive accumulation of scores of these moments over its five-year run seeks to provide viewers with an answer to a powerful question, one that brushes up against the curiosity to know how death will feel: What is it like to watch a life end?

Part of this book's premise is that fiction film and television have long been the main resources for Americans asking the preceding question because individuals' access to unmediated dying declined so dramatically in the twentieth century. Considering the remarkable distortions and exclusions enacted by most representations of death in the entertainment industry—which rare productions like *Six Feet Under* sometimes attempt to correct—the documentary mode seems a better candidate than fiction for providing enlightening, mediated views of the end of life. However, the pre-video/digital history of documentary photography and film contains few images of death itself. Documentarians rarely succeeded at making that sight visible, proving more capable of showing the before and after—the living person and the corpse. The images that did manage to poise themselves between these states often became icons, achieving that status precisely because they seem to make visible the alluring "moment" of death that is so elusive in the history of photography and film.

This chapter's examination of said history reveals that documenting violent death was less a "road not taken" by indexical media, and more a route attempted with equipment unfit to traverse it. Indeed, within this history a sort of multigenerational quest emerged as image-makers sought to freeze the "moment" of (violent) death in a photograph or contain it within a strip of film. What *Six Feet Under* stages with ease over and over again in twenty-first-century fiction is a moment filmmakers and photographers struggled mightily to document in the nineteenth century and most of the twentieth century— struggling not just because the contingencies of reality made this sight more slippery than in fiction but because of technological limitations. Cameras remained cumbersome and complicated for much of this history, and celluloid

1.1. Benjamin Srisai's "moment of death" (*Six Feet Under*, "The Secret," 2002, HBO).

film stock was expensive. This quest to make actual death visible through documentary media was indeed a technological one, progressing alongside developments in production and distribution equipment. It was a series of attempts—usually on a battlefield, where death was most predictably found—to get the right kind of camera into the hands of a skilled operator lucky enough to find himself in death's vicinity, followed by efforts to bring the resulting image before the eyes of a wide public. Alongside its technological component, the quest was also characterized by ongoing battles with government censorship and the propriety of distributors and exhibitors. And it did not yield a fully linear progression toward the most graphic spectacles; lynching photographs from the late nineteenth century, for example, are far more explicit than battle images from World War II. Accounting for these nuances, the history of documentary efforts to capture the "moment" of death remains most revealing in its failure—or, rather, its scant and partial successes. These expose the limitations of indexical media's capacity to record this fully embodied event—despite their reputation in new media theory as technologies of embodiment and materiality, in contrast to the digital.

Photographic and filmic documentary's true "road not taken" in this history is its potential to depict natural death. While its scattered views of violent death were more realistic and often more political than those of fiction film, the documentary form raised no parallel challenge to fiction in relation to natural death. Documentary's initial use in the mid-nineteenth century to help people contemplate and mourn death (through the postmortem images analyzed later in this chapter) almost wholly disappeared from the public eye for most of the twentieth. In chapter 2, I will return to recordings of natural death and their resurgence in the era of video, but I introduce it here because its imagined archive of absent and hidden images must haunt any discussion of these depictions of violent death. For all that documentary displays of lethal violence promised to *reveal* about death, they also helped to *conceal* their newly shameful counterpart of natural death, supporting its broad displacement from public life and discourse in the twentieth century.

The crucial challenge that natural death poses to the very concept of the "moment" of death is another reason to keep it firmly in mind during this journey through violent death's documentation. The *Six Feet Under* scenes hint at this challenge on a stylistic level: whether the death depicted is sudden or gradual, violent or natural, it is always followed by a slow transition to a pure white screen. In its notable protraction, this type of transition underscores death's necessarily durational rather than instantaneous character, even if that duration is difficult to recognize. The perception of life's end as an instantaneous event—one that could be isolated and made visible in a documentary photograph or a frame of film footage—can only be upheld when death arrives via acute violence rather than withering disease. For in the latter case, how can cameras make that one moment evident? Viewing a barely moving person about to die and a motionless corpse, one does not sense much visible or audible contrast. Anxiety about this blurred line between alive and dead manifested in nineteenth-century fears of premature burial and took a new direction in the twentieth century through medical debates about defining death, spurred by the rise of organ donation. Such uncertainties about death's timing cast doubt on the existence of a "moment" of death available for documentation by all these eager image-makers, and they highlight a subtle psychological function of this photographic and filmic quest. Graphic documentation of violent *moments* of death served as a comforting fiction for a viewing public that would—increasingly, as the nineteenth century and the hypermedicalized twentieth century progressed—be vastly more likely to experience long, painful *processes* of dying.[1]

What follows will track the camera's pursuit of these "moments" of death in documentary images that circulated in the United States from the invention of the daguerreotype in 1839 through the end of the Vietnam War in 1975. My aim will be not to cover every recording or partial recording of death from that period but to focus on the images that strongly registered in U.S. visual culture. In framing this pursuit, I borrow Linda Williams's usage of three temporal modes in "Film Bodies: Gender, Genre, and Excess."[2] Williams identifies three "body genres" that ask spectators' bodies to mimic on-screen sensations: melodrama solicits tears from the audience, pornography solicits orgasms, and horror solicits shudders. She ties each genre to a fantasy and a temporal structure drawn from psychoanalytic theory by Jean Laplanche and J. B. Pontalis. Melodrama investigates the fantasy of the self's origins and the quest to return to them— most symbolically, to the mother's body; the genre's pathos stems from these quests being "'too late!' . . . always tinged with the melancholy of loss." Pornography works through the origins of desire and the fantasy of seduction, creating a "utopian fantasy of perfect temporal coincidence: a subject and object (or seducer and seduced) who meet one another 'on time!' and 'now!' in shared moments of mutual pleasure." Horror tackles the origins of sexual difference and the fantasy of castration, featuring a monster that strikes "too early!" when the characters are not prepared, like the knowledge of sexual difference that one is never ready first to confront. Like Williams, I analyze works that target "the spectacle of the body caught in the grip of intense sensation or emotion" and that owe their maligned status partly to that bodily spectacle.[3]

The ways we talk about death align readily with these temporal modes: it generally feels to loved ones like it arrives "too early" (especially violent death), "on time" for a lucky few, or occasionally "too late" for those who most want to spare the dying from pain. In my use of these modes, though, the desired synchronicity is between actual death—with all its contingencies—and the camera that records it. When the shutter snaps or the film rolls "on time," the camera can seem to make visible the exact transition point between alive and dead. I argue that achieving this scenario was a long-standing goal for documentary image-makers and a widespread desire of audiences in the predigital period, but one that usually proved to be a "*fantasy* of perfect temporal coincidence" (my emphasis). In documentary death's history, the image-maker's actions almost always occur "too late," or death asserts its duration and refuses to become visible in the form of an alluring "moment."[4] Only in the 1960s, at the intersection of great technological development and plentiful violence, did the American public begin to see "on time" encounters between documentary cameras and death.

Keeping "Company with Death":
Corpse Photography and the Temporality of "Too Late"

Connecting the "too late" to melodrama, Williams sees in it the inevitably frustrated desire to return to one's origins, to the body of the mother. In melodrama, "Origins are already lost, the encounters always take place too late, on death beds or over coffins."[5] Like melodrama's coffins, corpses in documentary photography suggest the same temporal mode: death and the camera meet too late for the former's display. Underscoring the finality of death, the corpse is an all-too-material reminder of the "too late"—of our failure to stop a violent death, our tardiness with medical help or intervention in the violence that caused it. The corpse lies there, seemingly outside of time in its utter stillness and imperceptibly slow decay, stubbornly remaining a body that has ceased to *embody* an individual being. The corpse photograph, then, makes a kind of accusation to its creator and viewer: too late to stop a death, they are also too late to display or witness that death. "The decisive moment," in photographer Henri Cartier-Bresson's terms, clearly has passed, unaccompanied by the camera shutter's snap. Such a photograph can drive home the moral failure of preventing death and also the questionable desire it prompts for some: to *see more*, to see the lost object of death itself.

Of course, photography and film, in a very broad sense, have a lost object at their core: the past, which they attempt to preserve. Through these attempts, photography in particular develops a special relationship with death, in both its ontology and its history. Roland Barthes slowly draws out the ontological aspect in *Camera Lucida*, through observations that each photograph "produces Death while trying to preserve life" and creates an "anterior future"—a moment in the past when the death that will befall (or has already befallen) the subject casts a pall over the photo's present. Susan Sontag distills these ideas beautifully, writing, "Photographs state the innocence, the vulnerability of lives heading toward their own destruction, and this link between photography and death haunts all photographs." And André Bazin hints at the special relationship with his insight that the photograph "embalms time."[6] People yearn to preserve the present—as, instant by instant, it becomes the past—because it feels so vibrant and alive, but the photograph turns that life into death. It freezes time and deprives it of animating motion. Thus, photographs that make death their direct subject, rather than their subtext, provide some cathartic acknowledgment of this tragic transformation—a factor that may contribute to the popularity of death photography. As Sontag puts it, "Ever since cameras were invented in 1839, photography has kept company with death."[7]

In the nineteenth century it kept company with corpses, as demonstrated by three major sets of images: postmortem photographs used in mourning practices, views of dead soldiers lying unburied on Civil War battlefields, and photographs that celebrate lynchings by displaying mutilated African American corpses. Then, as photo and film cameras coexisted in the twentieth century, the Holocaust brought a concentrated and high-profile resurgence in the practice of documenting corpses. Whether captured through photography or film, corpse images tend to frustrate viewers' attempts to identify with the victims portrayed, creating emotional distance. As Vivian Sobchack writes, "Our sympathy for the subject who once was is undermined by our alienation from the object that is"—a reminder of one reason that corpse images feel "too late" and that seeing life in the act of being extinguished may feel, uncomfortably, more satisfying.[8]

Postmortem Mourning Photographs

As the camera's first sustained look at corpses, postmortem mourning photographs are also the only major cluster of images to document natural death during indexical media's long period of dominance, offering a rare glimpse of death in familial, domestic space. These images feature recently deceased corpses, handsomely dressed and usually posed as if asleep. They rest on beds or—especially with dead infants or children—in the arms of grieving loved ones. Professionally produced in studios or through house calls, these images emerged at the start of the camera's history and remained common late into the nineteenth century.

Their popularity grew from a number of factors—technology prominent among them. The invention of the daguerreotype brought personal portraiture to the American middle class, no longer the product of expensive hours of posing and painting. Considering the technological limitations that constrained early photographers, corpses actually made ideal portrait subjects. While the living could find the total bodily stillness required of them during prolonged exposure times difficult to maintain, the dead would not mar a sharp image with movement. They presented an opposite challenge, as photographers labored to position their stiff bodies in the convention of "the last sleep": a reclining pose with the "lifelike" appearance of gentle slumber rather than death. Thus, photographs that depict the living and dead together shepherd them in divergent directions, each in the service of a pleasing picture: the corpse is arranged as if alive, while the living subject must discipline their body to imitate death's stillness. These sitters underwent a rather literal version of the metaphorical experience Barthes describes as a "micro-version of death": the photographic subject's feeling that he is transformed into an object for the picture, just as a dying subject is transformed into the object of a corpse. Unsurprisingly, the resulting expressions on the faces of these living sitters—even in portraits disconnected from corpses and mourning—tended to be rather grim.[9]

Cultural attitudes toward death also bolstered the rise of postmortem photography. The strikingly different attitudes that prevail today can make it hard to imagine a time when a mother would bring her dead infant into a portrait studio, or when studios advertised postmortem services in the newspaper. But the mid-nineteenth century was, in historian Philippe Ariès's words, the "age of beautiful death," when death was largely seen as a Romantic passing into eternity, where loved ones reunite. Familiarity with death and corpses was widespread, as the household bedsides of the dying were heavily populated by family and community members. The death of a loved one was a tremendously painful event but was endured through the promise of reunion and through very public, emotional, and elaborate mourning practices.[10] The production and exhibition of postmortem photographs became one of those public practices. Indeed, these portraits went beyond just depicting death as occurring in domestic space; because they were often framed and displayed openly, they also infused that domestic space with death's documentary signifiers.

In *Secure the Shadow: Death and Photography in America*, Jay Ruby articulates a crucial tension at the intersection of mourning and photography: "Mourners are always confronted with two seemingly contradictory needs: to keep the memory of the deceased alive and at the same time, accept the reality of death and loss."[11] He argues that nineteenth-century mourners addressed those two needs with two separate types of images: "memorial photographs" of the living person to preserve happy memories, and postmortem photographs to keep the reality of that person's death ever-present. In my view, these two functions actually unite, balancing delicately, in the ubiquitous "last sleep" pose—one that seems, in some respects, in line with death denial. Barthes broadly asserts that the frenzied pursuit of a "lifelike" appearance in photography reveals the medium's attempts to deny death; on a smaller scale, perhaps posing a corpse as if reclining in a "last sleep" does likewise. But if Ruby's claim that postmortem photos confirmed death while memorial photos preserved life was accurate, then why did studios go to such lengths to create "sleeping," lifelike corpses?

I am more convinced that these photographs convey an ambivalent disavowal of death rather than simple denial. If the latter were a customer's goal, a picture of the subject while living would function more smoothly, or the postmortem views would omit signs of death (for example, mourning attire and accessories, such as rosaries, flowers, candles). Serving Ruby's dual function in a single image, postmortem photographs present a convincing sleep through which to remember fondly the person's life *and* serve as a species of memento mori. This species offers a reminder not only of one's own impending death but also of the fact that the dearly departed in the photo really *has* departed. In this role, the photographs seem to ward off disavowal, encouraging continual acknowledgment of death—even if its image is constructed to match the "beautiful death" ideal. At the same time, the photos engage in the purest form of the new medium's preservational function: a promise to let the living retain some piece of the dead.

This promise resonates most poignantly in the subset of postmortem photographs that had to serve both of Ruby's mourning functions simultaneously, by necessity: those in which no other photograph of the deceased had ever been taken, especially common with infants. In them, the "last sleep" gesture is easiest to assimilate, as it simulates the *life* together that the family imagined but barely experienced. Here, death has come too early and the camera, failing to provide a picture of the living person, too late.

Civil War Battlefield Photographs

During the long popularity of the postmortem portrait through the late nineteenth century, photographic tardiness took on an additional form with the American Civil War—a form that would become very familiar in war coverage—when cameramen missed out on shots of death in battle. Hopes of photographing "moments" of death settled into the realities of photographing corpses, which were plentiful. Drew Gilpin Faust explains that the bloodiest battles killed such a massive number of soldiers that the task of burying the dead often overwhelmed survivors. As "the needs of the living increasingly trumped the dignity of the departed," corpses were left exposed on abandoned battlefields, where Alexander Gardner and his colleagues in Mathew Brady's employ could safely photograph them.[12] Here corpses' stillness once again proved useful. A minor convenience to photographers working with domestic, civilian death, it proved essential in the context of war, making corpses one of the few battlefield spectacles that early cameras could document. Roaming those battlefields, photographers were constrained by more than just the usual long exposure times: the wet-plate collodion process of the day necessitated mobile darkrooms for immediate processing, so these were hauled around in horse-drawn carriages. It took twenty stress-filled minutes from the beginning of negative preparations to the end of processing for each individual image.[13] The era's equipment was thus profoundly unsuited for capturing the frenetic motion of combat, nor would it have been advisable for photographers to spend twenty minutes processing their plates in the middle of a battle.

Indeed, the technology needed to document war well seemed to be invented "too late" for each conflict of the nineteenth and early twentieth centuries, always lagging behind the technology for waging war and out of sync, too, with censorship of war images. Gardner, for example, could have done wonders with the equipment that photographer Ernest Brooks or cameraman Donald Thompson brought to war in 1914—lighter cameras, faster shutter speeds, some handheld capabilities, film that did not require immediate processing—but by that time a new style of fighting enabled by new weaponry made good action shots nearly impossible.[14] Battle was by then long-range, with spread-out troops and excruciating trench warfare that favored advances under cover of night or obscured by smoke or weather. As Brigadier General Andrew Hamilton Russel remarked in a 1918 memo: "When conditions are good for fighting they are, of necessity, poor for photography, and vice versa."[15] In terms of censorship, too, equipment to capture battlefield death well was developed after a window of opportunity had already closed. In the Civil War, Brady's men were self-financed, publishing and exhibiting their own work and thus avoiding the codes of propriety from newspaper and newsreel staffs that later photographers of war death would face. They were also spared any censorship by President Abraham Lincoln's administration, which reasoned that photos of anonymous corpses from past battles would pose no threat in enemy hands.[16]

Comparatively, cameramen at the fronts of World War II, whose equipment gave them greater options for documenting death, were cut off from distributing such images by the U.S. government, which had learned since Lincoln's era about the rhetorical power of war corpses. Not until Vietnam would a minimal synchronicity of image technology, war weaponry, and loose censorship produce a significant archive of documentary death from the battlefield.

Civil War images represent some of the first encounters between cameras and violent death, revealing photographers' attempts to integrate this spectacle into dominant traditions of beautiful (and natural) death. To that end, *Gardner's Photographic Sketchbook of the Civil War* borrows heavily from postmortem photographers' strategies—especially "the last sleep" aesthetic.[17] In *A Sharpshooter's Last Sleep*, for example, a Confederate soldier lies dead, on his back, on the ground: his head tilts gently, his body sinks into the soft grass, and familiar personal objects are arranged beside him (his cap, rifle, tin cup, and blanket). These echo the comforting toys placed with dead children in postmortem portraits. Unable to find bodies that naturally looked this peaceful, Gardner rearranged corpses, in a manner that may offend a twenty-first-century sense of documentary ethics (and general squeamishness). This practice seems to have been an open secret—not disclosed, but often apparent in a simple comparison of images. Indeed, *Sleep* features the same soldier's corpse as the photo *Home of the Rebel Sharpshooter*, dragged from the soft grass into a rocky enclosure for a different pose.[18]

Visual connotations of "beautiful death" in Gardner's work are bolstered by his long and evocative descriptions that accompany each photograph. *Field Where General Reynolds Fell* (an image by Timothy O'Sullivan that Gardner reprints in *Sketchbook*) requires an especially effusive caption to redeem the beauty of corpses in an advanced state of decay, with bloating that has distended their midsections and faces. Gardner's propagandistic description frames these (supposed) Union soldiers as noble, lifelike, and slumbering rather than dead: "The faces of all were pale, as though cut in marble, and as the wind swept across the battle-field it waved the hair, and gave the bodies such an appearance of life that a spectator could hardly help thinking they were about to rise to continue the fight." Gardner must have experienced some cognitive dissonance in writing this redemptive text, since he had penned a much harsher one for the "rebel" corpses in the previous plate—the same corpses, photographed from the opposite side.[19]

Also apparent in the description of *Field* are traces of photographers' frustration with being always and inevitably "too late," with their technological inability to capture death itself. From the faces of the dead Gardner works backward in time, vividly imagining the "moments" of death that his camera could never document:

> Some of the dead presented an aspect which showed that they had suffered severely just previous to dissolution, but these were few in number compared with those who wore a calm and resigned expression, as though they had passed away in an act of prayer. Others had a smile on their faces, and looked as if they were in the act of speaking. Some lay stretched on their backs as if friendly hands had prepared them for burial. Some were still resting on one knee, their hands gripping their muskets. In some instances the cartridge remained between the teeth, or the musket was held in one hand, and the other was uplifted as though to ward a blow, or appealing to heaven.[20]

When read with regard to its specific historical context, this passage is quite revealing about Americans' desire to see "moments" of violent death in the Civil War. It was not just that photographers were eager to enframe them; the families of slain soldiers were desperate for detailed information about just these moments. While today we associate the desire to witness real death with morbid curiosity, Faust explains that nineteenth-century Americans believed that the specific circumstances of the passage from life to death were extremely important and could forecast the soul's fate in the afterlife. To have one's son, father, husband, or brother meet death on some distant battlefield and to be cut off from its witnessing was immensely painful for the many who lost loved ones this way. They wanted to aid the dying in passage from this life, to analyze last moments for clues about salvation, and to absorb the lessons the dying could impart only at that time. Being physically present with a dying man provided answers to crucial questions: Was he calm and courageous? Did he acknowledge and accept his fate? Did he demonstrate faith in God and a belief that he was saved? Did he remember his family?[21]

Faust demonstrates the way fellow soldiers, nurses, doctors, or chaplains tried to compensate for kin's absence at a soldier's "moment" of death by detailing it in condolence letters, and I would argue that *Gardner's Photographic Sketchbook* strives to serve a similar function for a broad audience of mourners. Unable to witness the deaths he describes, Gardner relies on a practice common during the war of studying the corpse to retrieve a sense of the last moment of life. Faust explains, "Many observers believed, as one war correspondent put it, that the 'last life-expression of the countenance' was somehow 'stereotyped by the death blow' and preserved for later scrutiny and analysis."[22]

Strikingly, in an age when photographs failed to display the "moment" of death, the belief arose that death itself created an equivalent: it "embalm[ed] time" on the face and rescued that moment for the type of prolonged contemplation a photo provides. As Gardner reads faces "stereotyped by the death blow" in the *Field* passage quoted earlier, we see him answering the previous paragraph's list of questions. He claims that some soldiers "had suffered severely," but more died with brave dedication to the cause ("their hands gripping their muskets," "the cartridge remained between the teeth"), showed evidence of their salvation ("as though they had passed away in an act of prayer," "appealing to heaven"), and had their bodies cared for ("as if friendly hands had prepared them for burial"). Gardner's descriptions thus attempt to soften the blow of looking at these corpses not just by adding peaceful connotations but by assuring viewers that lost "moments" of death *could* be indirectly grasped through the very photographs that failed to display them directly.

Considering how far from beautiful war death really was at this time—thanks to newly mechanized weapons that could shred flesh and to the disfigurement exposed corpses suffered from decomposition and foraging animals—those photographing it had to expend tremendous effort and creativity to evoke the era's notion of "beautiful death." That they did so is a testament to how desperately the country needed this comforting framework at a time when its citizens were dying in unprecedented, unthinkable numbers. That their equipment made them too late to render visible the "moment" of death, and that the postmoment corpses required ample reframing (through staging and textual rhetoric), make Civil War photos the first in a long lineage of disappointments, as documenting violent death continually frustrated indexical image-makers in pursuit of its "full detail."

Lynching Photographs

A generation after Gardner beautified corpses of the war that ended slavery, a very different death documentation practice took root, opposing African American rights and avoiding conventions of "beautiful death": photographing the lynched bodies of Black men and (some) women. These images continue the tradition of displaying death through corpses, but unlike most other examples in this chapter, their production and circulation were—in the majority of cases—wholly disconnected from grief (an extreme realization of Gorer's "pornography of death" concept). Journalistic incentives to disseminate news of tragic violence were not the driving force, either. Even if we might criticize their profit-driven distribution, most journalistic death photos at least *claim* sympathy for the dead—through an accompanying story or caption—and a desire to educate, not titillate. Lynching photographs make no pretense of sympathy. Like other instances of perpetrator media in documentary history, they were made and circulated primarily to celebrate, not mourn, the murders they document. This attitude is apparent even within the pictures themselves, where enframed lynching participants display emotions that actively oppose grief: pride, excitement, and sated rage. It is important to underscore here that visual documentation of death remains—from these images' hateful origins to their still ethically charged consumption today—a secondary feature of lynching photographs, as their primary drive was a frightening demonstration of white supremacy. Nevertheless, as *the* most graphic documentary images of death that significant American audiences consumed in photography's first century, lynching photographs are essential to this chapter's history.

The lynchings depicted in these photographs are mainly white-on-Black, occurring in the American South from about 1882 to 1930—preceding and overlapping with the era of cinema.[23] Their extreme violence was ostensibly punishment for alleged crimes (with the rape of white women, or just its perceived threat, being the classic justification). But lynchings were more deeply motivated by the economic and social threat African Americans seemed to pose as a new social order eroded their self-effacing deference to former "masters." Members of white lynch mobs that hanged, beat, cut, shot, burned, and stabbed African Americans to death were rarely prosecuted, even though they did not conceal their identities.[24] Indeed much photographic documentation of lynching splits the viewer's attention between two subjects: the mutilated body that hangs by its neck and a crowd of perpetrators and spectators proudly posing below it. The photographs' mode of address was both celebratory, spreading evidence of lynching successes to create an "imagined community" of supportive whites, and threatening, attempting to intimidate African American communities.[25] They circulated with little interference from the U.S. government until 1908, when the Post Office prohibited their mailing through a seldom-enforced law that had no impact on extensive underground circulation. While the postal network spread evidence of a lynching after it occurred, technologies of modernity—telephones, telegraphs, newspapers, cars, trains—worked to announce impending lynchings and transport mobs to their sites.[26] The support of these technologies helped lynchings increase in size, length, complexity, and brutality, satisfying the crowd's desire for ever-grander spectacles of death. One young attendee quickly yearned for a new, more graphic experience, telling his mother, "I have seen a man hanged. Now I wish I could see one burned."[27]

Photography was also a key technology to shape lynching practice, serving two major functions. First, it circulated visceral proof of the event to those not in attendance, significantly expanding its unifying (for whites) or threatening (for Blacks) power.[28] Second, it provided a physical trophy or souvenir for those who participated, making an otherwise ephemeral experience material—and commodifiable. As Leigh Raiford elaborates, "Lynchings spawned a cottage industry in which picture makers conspired with mob members and even local officials for the best vantage point, constructed portable darkrooms for quick turnaround, and peddled their product 'through newspapers, in drugstores, on the street . . . door to door.'"[29] Amateurs (after Kodak's introduction of the personal camera in 1888) and professionals photographed lynchings and eventually could have their images commercially printed as postcards, for either sale or private distribution. That such postcards sold well enough to justify their mass production paints a grim picture of white southern morality in this period. As Dora Apel laments, "The statement about community values and civic pride made by such postcards cannot be underestimated: usually postcards picture the best a community has to offer."[30]

In all three phases of the life of an image—production, distribution, reception—lynching photographs prompt upsetting historical questions. Jacqueline Goldsby affirms that at the most basic moral level, what we desperately want to know is "who took them, who looked at them, and why."[31] Regarding Goldsby's first question, a mixed-media art piece by Pat Ward Williams, *Accused/Blowtorch/Padlock* (1986), articulates the ways in which these photographs' unimaginable production contexts trouble their current viewers. Williams's scrawled notes encircle four views from the same photo that was published in *Life* magazine. The photo displays a lynched man who is chained face-first to a tree trunk and whose hands are bound separately, pulled back harshly behind his body. Williams writes, "WHO took this picture? Couldn't he just as easily let the man go? Did he take his camera home and bring back a BLOWTORCH? . . . WHO took this picture? HOW can this photograph EXIST? *Life* answers—Page 141— no credit." In the face of such agonizing documentary records of death—not just death but nauseatingly brutal and racist murders—lacunae in the historical record feel especially unsettling, unlikely as it is that the answers to such questions would provide any solace.

One puzzling detail that recurs across multiple images hints at perpetrators' (and photographers') disturbing sense of themselves as moral individuals. They often covered corpses' genital areas with cloth in a strange gesture toward presenting "appropriate" displays—a gesture additionally charged by the fact that these victims had usually been lynched for alleged sex crimes. But what viewer would be so disturbed by nudity, or even castration wounds they might see, alongside such graphic death and mutilation? The white women whose treasured purity lynch mobs were so eager to safeguard? That purity would already have been deeply sullied by looking at—either in person or in photographs—lynched corpses like Jesse Washington's, with its burned and contorted frame, missing limbs, and curled, fingerless fists. With these genital coverings, lynching participants carefully avoid any trace of sex while creating some of the most explicit death images in documentary history—perhaps evidence of how much more taboo sex was than death in the nineteenth and early twentieth centuries.

Introducing a recent book of lynching photographs, Hilton Als asks, "Who wants to look at these pictures? Who are they all? When they look at these pictures, who do they identify with?"[32] In thinking about the reception of lynching photographs, the question of identification is particularly troubling because most are gruesome postmortems, each depicting a body whose disfigurement distances it greatly from a living person. Considering the malevolence at play in the images' production, that distancing effect may have been desired, may have, in part, motivated the postmortem timing of these exposures. Contrasting lynching images to the gentler postmortem shots made earlier in the nineteenth century, Goldsby argues: "Failing to restore positive bonds between the viewer and the dead, lynching photographs do not as a rule seek to summon the dead back to an imagined life. Rather, a particular kind of 'scopic aggression' rages in lynching photographs, thwarting any such sympathetic identification between the viewer and the black (dead) subject."[33] In these photos, there are no aids to identification: no illusion of peaceful slumber, no reminders of favorite outfits or trinkets to accompany the corpse, no home or homelike setting, and certainly no final glimpse at the pristine facial features of the deceased. Potential mourners are denied these comforts that photographic technology regularly provided in the nineteenth century. Instead, the brutalized corpse hanging above the mob is intended for hostile display, with maximum visibility of wounds and other marks of humiliation.

The postmortem temporality of lynching photographs is an interesting enigma in this history, because lynching images seem best poised for "on time" synchronicity. Lynching deaths were more predictable, more geographically fixed, and safer for photographers to approach than battlefield deaths. Why, then, do these images overwhelmingly favor corpses, rather than pursuing the "moment" of death? The frenzied movement of such violence may have interfered with stable camera positions and shutter speeds—at least in the early years, possibly establishing an enduring convention. Perpetrators' fears of cameras catching them in the act of murder could be a factor, but their impunity in posing for postmortem shots and the rarity of prosecution cast doubt on that interpretation. I suspect that the radically different aims of lynching photography from most death documentary work—as noted earlier—are more the cause, subordinating the "moment" of death to other gruesome attractions, like wounds inflicted both before and after death that offer a more comprehensive record of the violence. Perhaps postmortem views also best supported the photos' primary goal of illustrating white supremacy through a guarantee that the Black man had been fully, finally subdued—transformed from an allegedly threatening subject to the corpse's powerless object. The variety of violent acts inflicted on the body also makes the precise occurrence of death less central and identifiable, tucked away somewhere in a series of blows, lacerations, burns, and so on.

The fact that cameras, wielded by both professionals and amateurs, turned lynching's extreme racial violence into portable, commercial spectacle makes this an exceptionally bleak chapter in the history of death's relationship with image technologies—and highlights an unsettling trend. Among government censors, image distributors, and the public, attitudes toward documentary death partly depend on the social and racial positioning of the deceased. The idea of publishing photos of white U.S. soldiers who had been shot could cause much hand-wringing in 1917 or 1944; would U.S. citizens be able to handle the sight? This concern becomes absurd when one acknowledges that a number of these citizens already had seen far more gruesome photos of lynched African Americans. Indeed, they may even have kept the postcards.

Concentration Camp Photographs

With the dawn of the twentieth century came the era of the moving image, a time when the once-useful stillness of corpses became an aesthetic liability. Even including photographs, few of this period's iconic images of death or war—the ones that most characterize U.S. collective memory—are of corpses. I close this section with one set that proves an exception, a high-profile revival of documenting corpses that caught and sustained worldwide attention: the photographs and film taken in liberated Nazi concentration camps. British and American forces began this documentary work when they entered camps on the Western Front in April 1945, later joined by the civilian press. The images they captured were comparable to lynching photographs in their visible brutality. But unlike the lynching photographs—or any others in documentary death's previous history—they were quickly released in large quantities, in a concentrated period of time, and through many mainstream sources (newspapers, magazines, and newsreels). Again, as with lynching photographs, I emphasize that interests in the metaphysics of death or the nature of its documentary mediation were not primary in these images' creation or (in most cases) their consumption. But their indelible imagery and unprecedentedly wide circulation make them key texts in the predigital history of documentary cameras' depictions of death.

The U.S. media was suddenly flooded with numerous, if homogeneous, views of corpses: naked bodies stacked "like cordwood" and jumbles of limbs filling mass graves, along with gaunt survivors living among the dead. Several factors prompted such an unchecked display of graphic death from a government that had been suppressing it for decades, in two world wars. First, the Allies had encountered atrocities of confounding immorality and scale that, crucially, could be easily photographed and filmed. The numerous corpses found in Buchenwald or Bergen-Belsen posed none of the typical problems of combat coverage: action that was too sudden or distant, visibility inadequate for film stock, restricted movement, threats to one's life and equipment, and prohibitions about what could be recorded. The greatest challenge image-makers reported overcoming at the camps was revulsion, aided by cameras that allowed them to "close one eye from the horror."[34] *Vogue* photographer Lee Miller, on the scene at Dachau, noted that "by midday, only the press and medics were allowed in the buildings, as so many really tough [soldiers] had become sick it was interfering with duties."[35]

A multitude of eyewitnesses struggled to explain how stunned they were by the cruelty and scale of the Nazis' crimes—and to imagine how such atrocities could be adequately conveyed to a distant public through any form of media. After visiting Ohrdruf, the first camp where the Americans found corpses and prisoners, General Dwight Eisenhower sent word to Washington about "unspeakable conditions. . . . From my own personal observation, I can state unequivocally that all written statements up to now do not paint the full horrors."[36] Eyewitnesses from the military, press, and government felt an overwhelming desire to communicate that horror through documentary images, pushing U.S. officials to "let the world see," in Eisenhower's words.[37] In fact, the Allies developed something of an obsession with letting the world see, and specifically with forcing the German civilians to see the crimes perpetrated by their own government. Mandatory tours of the camps and their dead for locals were common, later supplemented by mandatory screenings in the American and British occupied zones of films documenting the atrocities.[38] Faced with the reality of the camps, many observers seemed gripped by the instinct that the public *had to see* the sights of death that they had, but they were also confronting the difficult truth that a mediated documentary view of these deaths would never feel sufficient.

However, observers' drive to bring these images to the public eye would not have been sufficient without the political usefulness of documenting Nazi atrocities at that point. The U.S. government was not timid in suppressing war images that did not serve its notion of the public good. But just as the prohibition against showing dead Americans lifted when the United States needed to reinvigorate its war-weary citizens, other precedents fell away when it needed to convince the world of Nazi atrocities.[39] Impaired by overly cautious reporting on the camps and a "hangover of skepticism" from World War I propaganda, the public was hesitant to believe written assertions that the Germans has murdered millions of Jews and other innocents in death camps. This skepticism prompted authorities to release visual evidence of the most gruesome varieties: images of decaying corpses, children's corpses, facial close-ups of corpses, and naked corpses (nudity having previously been a sticking point in the display of atrocities).[40]

Struggling to represent a complex system of genocide and murder, the images brought both successes and failures. If the camps had to be seen to be believed, then seeing them through photographs and film did help quantifiably increase American belief in the atrocities—shown by Gallup polls of November 1944 and May 1945.[41] More qualitatively, records of their reception also indicate that these images from the camps made deep impressions on shocked audiences. Hence, the successes of the images as evidence—as much as one hesitates to call explicit views of murdered human beings "successful"—became quickly apparent in 1945, while their failures emerged more slowly. Captions were often missing, inadequate, or inaccurate, and images from one camp would be used to illustrate stories about another, reducing awareness of the plurality of camps and their specific identities. Similarly, information about the individuals pictured (dead or alive) was rarely provided—though news sources, admittedly, may have had little access to it. Haste and sloppiness in 1945 have had unfortunate consequences decades later, as Holocaust deniers fixate on these errors in their efforts to discredit documentation of the camps. In a more general problem that Barbie Zelizer articulates, the seeming interchangeability of the many images conveyed the feeling that the Holocaust was a singular, unified atrocity from which the press could make broad claims about the nature of human evil.[42] It favored these large, symbolic meanings and shed specific contexts, in keeping with the images' main political use: convincing a skeptical public that the Nazis had murdered millions in organized death camps.

Among all the images described in this chapter's section on corpse photography, the photographs from Nazi concentration camps most exude the poignancy of arriving "too late." Unlike the infants who died of disease or the

African Americans whose murders were ignored by their government, the camp deaths both were preventable and had powerful forces working to prevent them. Thus, the vast expanses of bodies in these images underscore the cost of U.S. delay in entering the war, making the American viewer complicit in this tardiness. Further, the encounter between the camera and death again happens "too late" through the Holocaust archive's near-total absence of images showing the actual murders. Such images would have mattered—not only as evidence for courts or skeptics but in the hard lessons each of us experiences in trying to comprehend this event. As some invested in its history have lamented, our understanding of the Holocaust is skewed toward concentration camps that allowed for survivors who could speak of their suffering.[43] At extermination camps like Treblinka, death came quickly to prisoners, and their killers opted not to snap its picture.

While the Holocaust sharply revived the power of corpse photography, it later contributed to a waning in that power over the following decades. Partly, the decline came from familiarity. Photographed bodies of the starved or slain have been used to represent so many famines, genocides, and atrocities that one corpse-strewn patch of ground starts to blur into the next. The Holocaust photographs scarred a young Susan Sontag, who was casually confronted by them in a Santa Monica bookstore in 1945. But they would become a powerful factor in the process of anesthetization she theorized: the process by which repeated exposure to images of suffering and death purportedly drains a viewer's reserves of compassion.[44] The other factor in the declining impact of corpse photography emerged long before the camps were liberated: the motion picture. As its name implies, the medium sought out movement, an attraction that corpses could not provide. This liability is highlighted by the most memorable film footage from the camps, which overcame it: the nightmarish sight of the dead becoming animate, a churning mass of limbs, as bulldozers pushed piles of corpses into mass graves. These shots hint at film's actual target in documenting death, yet to be fully realized: death in motion, exemplified by the "moment" of death.

The Ultimate Change, Mummified:
Film Strives to Encounter Death "On Time"

Slightly more than half a century after daguerreotypes became the first indexical images to document corpses, the invention of film brought a new capacity to register time and movement—crucial to a comprehensive representation of death. Film's ability to render movement seems to align it with vitality and the living, in contrast to photography's aforementioned alignment with stillness and death. There are, however, significant ontological complications with that analogy. First, Barthes's "anterior future" observation applies to film as well as photography: film also makes an imprint of the past that will progress into a fatal future. Second, as Laura Mulvey elucidates in *Death 24x a Second*, the apparent movement of a projected strip of film covers over the underlying stillness of the photographic frames that compose it (with film, typically twenty-four per second). If a photograph signifies death, then by its nature film also does so, "24x a second." Rather than being a pure embodiment of life, film is thus characterized by "the co-presence of movement and stillness, continuity and discontinuity."[45] Bazin evoked the lurking morbidity of film's liveliness in his pithy descriptor "change mummified"—a parallel to his notion of photography as that which "embalms time." If "mummify[ing]" change is the fundamental power of film, then an "on time" encounter with death—where the camera rolls as life expires—should be its most coveted target. For what is death, if not the most profound and enigmatic form of change in human existence?

From film's beginning, its makers pursued death with intensity but found themselves often thwarted by technological and political factors. Photography accompanied film into the twentieth century in this pursuit, with renewed ambition to accomplish what its technological descendent could not: to extract death itself from a stream of time and arrest its motion, freezing this "moment" and making it visible for contemplation. The thrill of being so precisely "on time" in catching death captured the imaginations of photographers and the public, as the instant fame of rare successes demonstrates. In the film-era quest for synchronicity with death, two key periods emerge: cinema's first decade, when reenactments and animal deaths filled in for absent documentary images, and the 1960s, when cameras finally seemed to achieve this controversial aim.

Early Cinema

Early cinema's practitioners recognized the fascination of death's change and frequently put it on-screen in the period before longer narrative films became dominant (around 1907). As Scott Combs notes, "A discernible undercurrent to cinema's early projections is a curiosity to see what death would look like on-screen. From nearly the moment of its invention, cinema got busy staging deaths that looked real."[46] "Looked real" was standard, since footage of death eluded actuality filmmakers for many reasons. Executions offered spectacle and predictability, but by the development of cinema were, for the most part, no longer public events in the United States, nor was their recording permitted.[47] Recording war deaths was a tantalizing prospect for early filmmakers and audiences, but once again was beyond the capabilities of the era's cameras.

As usual, after the late nineteenth century, recording natural death was an overlooked or unwanted option. Perhaps its profile as a tame, domestic form of death was both the quality that made it possible to document and the quality that made it unappealing to filmmakers and audiences who wanted to see this new technology pushed to its limits. The cinema also quickly developed a reputation as a technology not only of change and movement but also of spectacle. Natural death signifies change of the most meaningful order but not a particularly *visible* kind. A soldier slain in the heat of battle offers a stark contrast between energetic motion and deathly stillness, but the apparent contrast between a person dying of tuberculosis and her corpse would be minimal. Sobchack affirms this advantage of violent death as one of her ten propositions about documenting death: "The most effective cinematic signifier of death in our present culture is violent action inscribing signs of mortification on the visibly lived body."[48] Though harder to predict and record, violent death offered not just the spectacle that audiences craved but, seemingly, the brevity that early reel lengths and exhibition practices required. These dictated a fixation on the "moment" of death because little more than *a* moment was ever put on display, with most films lasting less than sixty seconds. Thus, to harness the powerful change death presented, early filmmakers were compelled to frame that change as instantaneous, or nearly so, rather than as a gradual process.

These criteria came together in a string of execution films allowing audiences to glimpse violent "moments" of death that looked real and could be fully contained in short films. In their attempts to stage death realistically, some showcased what the new medium could accomplish by manipulating, rather than just recording, time—as discussed by Combs and by Mary Ann Doane. Films like *The Execution of Mary Queen of Scots* (1895, Thomas Edison) or *Execution by Hanging* (1905, Mutoscope/Biograph) could present believable "moments" of death (by beheading or hanging, here) only by using two shots spliced together to appear continuous—one of a live person and one of a dummy.[49] Though this illusion is playful, its logistics also reinforce the idea of death as a distinct moment. After the splice, the victim became a dummy incapable of independent movement, cinema's primary sign of life. At actual hangings, death did not always arrive so promptly and definitively: if the fall did not break the victim's neck, he could flail wildly on the rope until more gradually asphyxiated.[50]

During this period, electrocution's technological innovation promised to end that prolonged suffering elided by execution films. Combs explains that the method's advocates assured "that its death would be 'instantaneous and painless' and 'devoid of all barbarism'. . . . A switch would now clean up, as it were, visible death, by taking dying out of the spectacle."[51] Two prominent electrocution films, *Execution of Czolgosz with Panorama of Auburn State Prison* (1901, Edwin S. Porter/Edison) and *Electrocuting an Elephant* (1903, Edison), aim to convey the deadly power of electricity to audiences. Though the levels of pain or barbarism they depict are not easily judged, I argue that both films undermine the technology they seem to celebrate by calling electrocution's instantaneity into question. Thus, they undermine the idea of death as a visible, identifiable moment through electricity's promise and failure to deliver it.

No cameras captured President William McKinley's shooting by Leon Czolgosz at the Pan-American Exposition of 1901, nor were any permitted to record the assassin's death by electrocution. To alleviate that absence and add an air of authenticity, Edison's *Czolgosz* reenactment opens with a documentary shot (even advertised in the film's title): a slow pan around the exterior of Auburn Prison, the execution site, taken on the day of the execution.[52] The remaining two minutes show an actor portraying Czolgosz being led out of his cell, a test of the electric chair's current with a row of light bulbs, then the prisoner being strapped in and electrocuted. The actor playing Czolgosz does not writhe after his electrocution like William Kemmler, but to guarantee that his body will permanently still, his executioners send multiple and discontinuous jolts through him. The electrocution itself feels quite prolonged at twenty-five seconds, as its victim cycles through stiffening with the current and relaxing with its cessation thrice before the officials shut off the machine.[53] The performer is recorded from a distance with the chair's straps obscuring his face, and his body stills in the same manner after each convulsion, so the film provides no sign to tell the audience if and when Czolgosz actually dies. If death by electricity strikes instantaneously, then when among those three jolts was the fatal instant? Two officials onscreen quickly labor to resolve this disquieting uncertainty, feeling Czolgosz's pulse and listening for his heartbeat with a stethoscope. Combs uses these characters to demonstrate the film camera's inability to overcome the invisibility of bodily death—even in cases of violent death. Adept at rendering surfaces, the camera cannot access the body's depth, cannot expose the hidden stoppage of organs. Combs argues that it needs a "registrant" who can confirm death by proxy for the audience.[54]

Such a person does not appear in *Electrocuting an Elephant*, and indeed this actuality ends without a clear resolution about whether the elephant is yet dead. Topsy, a performing animal that had killed three men (the last of whom had tried to feed her a lit cigarette butt), was put to death at Coney Island's

Luna Park in front of fifteen hundred spectators.[55] Unlike *Czolgosz*, *Elephant* offers the audience a spectacle of actual death—undoubtedly because animal life was valued far enough below human life that viewing an animal's death in 1903 was not strongly taboo.[56] The film enabled cinema spectators separated from the execution by space and time to watch it along with the fifteen hundred viewers who were physically present. Slightly more than a minute in length, *Elephant* shows Topsy walked to her site of death, then cuts to another shot of her standing in chains. A long, tense stretch of Topsy just standing there is suddenly broken as she goes rigid and smoke billows up from the ground. She falls forward stiffly, but the film continues for another thirty seconds—half of its running time—fixated on the downed animal's body. This lingering gaze contains significant details: the elephant that should be dead is continuously twitching, an obvious splice reveals that she continued moving for longer than the footage's thirty-second duration, and the film's end comes without any apparent motivation, before the body fully stills. Such details prompt questions about just how long it really took electricity to kill. While Topsy's stiffening with the current might seem an instantaneous death blow at first—an "on time" meeting between the film camera and animal death—*Elephant* leaves its viewers without confidence in that interpretation. Combs perceptively extends this uncertainty to the filmmakers themselves, arguing that with the splice at the end it is "as if the camera operator were unsure whether her dying had concluded, or indeed, what might constitute a conclusion."[57] Doane notes that "part of the lure of electricity is the lure of an escape from process, duration, work."[58] *Czolgosz* and *Elephant* expose the false promise of that escape; death by electricity is still a durational process in which the "moment" of transition remains uncertain and invisible. The public's and cinema's attraction to this promise of instant death is an ironic fad to begin the twentieth century, a century that would prolong the length of the dying process dramatically through death's escalating medicalization.

While the extreme popularity of execution films did not endure past cinema's first decade, attempts to display war death began in force early in film history and continued unabated through the ensuing century's many violent conflicts. As discussed earlier, "attempts" is the key word for many decades, as image technologies failed to keep pace with killing technologies. Considering the staggering number of violent deaths modern warfare generated in World War I and World War II, film and photography very seldom recorded them, and images that did emerge were subject to levels of censorship unknown to previous war photographers like Gardner.

Early hopes the moving image brought for documenting war death had to be readjusted quickly during the Spanish-American and Philippine-American wars of the late 1890s, when actuality recordings of faraway battles never arrived. Kristen Whissel describes how the conditions of war and the constraints of technology frustrated those hopes, and how filmmakers turned to reenactments to satisfy spectators' appetites for battle footage. Evincing said appetites, she quotes a *Leslie's Weekly* article from 1900 that anticipated potential American Biograph footage from the Philippine-American and Boer wars: "We are promised some vivid, soul-stirring pictures of actual, grewsome war. . . . Imagine the historical value of a moving picture of the charge at Balaklava, or of the advance upon Gettysburg. There will be other Balaklavas and other Gettysburgs, and the Biograph may get there just in the nick of time."[59] The author leaves little doubt that death—the chief ingredient of "actual, grewsome war"—is among the sights he wants to see in these "vivid, soul-stirring pictures." And his prediction that "the Biograph may get there just in the nick of time" to witness major assaults also hints at the exciting contingency of war death, an event one must have quick reflexes to meet "on time" with a camera.

This writer also references "all the involved processes of photography" that may frustrate the Biograph operators' success in bringing views of war home to American spectators. In practice, these processes—combined with war's realities—did dash the hope of documenting death. Whissel explains that cameras produced crowd-pleasing actualities of troop preparations but were too bulky to traverse the dense, tropical terrain of Cuba or the Philippines in battle. Even if they could have, "the conditions of modern warfare placed limits on both human and machine vision" through, for example, Cuba's thick jungle foliage, the black gunpowder smoke that enveloped American fighters, and the near invisibility of the Spanish (who used smokeless gunpowder that did not give away their positions).[60] Thus, American soldiers severely lacked the visual information needed for their military success, and any documentary cameras that managed to travel the rough campaign trails would find conditions woefully unsuitable for filming.

When the promised films of "actual, grewsome war" failed to materialize, reenactments compensated for their absence but did not reflect the conditions that had prevented their creation. For example, a trio of Edison shorts from 1899—*Advance of Kansas Volunteers at Caloocan*, *Capture of Trenches at Candaba*, and *Filipinos Retreat from Trenches*—instead feature clearly visible enemies firing from orderly lines with only enough gunpowder smoke for dramatic effect as U.S. soldiers defeat them with confidence. These reenactments also feature ideal viewing positions that would have been absurdly dangerous for actuality cameramen: directly in the crossfire in *Caloocan* and in the trench alongside enemy soldiers in *Candaba* and *Retreat*.[61] Though Whissel's analysis focuses on how these reenactments frame American military might, displaying the spectacle of death is an equally central pursuit here. Extending their fiction of uninterrupted vision on the battlefield, death happens right in front of the camera, nearby and fully enframed. Several Filipinos are downed by American bullets early in *Candaba* and *Retreat*, and their bodies lie in the trench through the end of these films. Another short, *Shooting Captured Insurgents* (1898, Edison), combines war and execution reenactments, showing a Spanish firing squad line up and fatally shoot several Cuban prisoners (a propagandistic film likely designed to showcase Spanish brutality). While Filipino and Cuban deaths are fully displayed, only American death is individuated and ennobled, as when a color-bearer gets a spectacular death scene in *Caloocan*: filmed from behind, he stands alongside his fellow U.S. soldiers and waves the flag high, dominating the frame, until he is shot. At that instant, the Stars and Stripes dip as he throws his arms in the air and falls. The flag gives this "moment" of death an air of patriotism and gravitas, while blocking and shot distance afford it full visibility. *Caloocan* provides a vision of what actuality filmmakers hoped they would get: footage in which the contingencies of battle, death, filming conditions, and camera technology would perfectly align and the enigmatic "moment" would be imprinted to celluloid "on time."

Interlude: From Reenactments to Fakes

In *Caloocan*, the actor pretending to be shot does so through war's most familiar "moment" of death pose: he spreads his arms wide and falls backward. This pose responds to the central challenge of representing death in film or photography (one shared by genres and movements as varied as melodrama, pornography, and German expressionism): how to externalize the internal, bringing it into the visible world that cameras can access. The pose appears frequently in nineteenth-century paintings of war—among battling figures in sweeping Civil War landscapes, or as the centerpiece of Frederic Remington's well-known Spanish-American War piece, *Charge of the Rough Riders at San Juan Hill*.[62] This dynamic "moment" of death pose did not surface in war's underwhelming actuality material until 1936, when the French magazine *Vu* published a Spanish Civil War photograph that would be widely reprinted and rise to iconic status. Robert Capa's photograph *The Falling Soldier* shows a Loyalist militiaman on a desolate hillside collapsing backward, presumably hit by enemy fire. Perfectly realizing what Cartier-Bresson would later call "the decisive moment" in photography—now as the "moment" of death—Capa catches the soldier midfall, head thrown back and arms splayed, with his rifle just slipping from his hand.

Gravity's work in progress reinforces the sense of transition the photo exudes, of passage from one state to another: standing up to lying prone, soldier to casualty, alive to dead. Capa announced his "on time" triumph through the image's original title (also loaded with proclamations of its documentary status): *Loyalist Militiaman at the Moment of Death, Cerro Muriano, September 5, 1936*. Here, at last, was the enduring object of desire for generations of image-makers and audiences: death itself, strikingly enframed.

Or so it seemed. Although some doubt remains, the evidence accumulated over decades of *The Falling Soldier*'s study points persuasively to this photograph being staged. Another Capa photo published under it in *Vu* shows a different soldier fallen in exactly the same spot, suggesting multiple takes. There are descriptions of the man identified as the falling soldier being killed in action elsewhere, two days after the picture was taken. Capa claims he took it at Cerro Muriano, but in-depth comparisons of the photographs and Spanish hillsides place the event thirty-five miles away, near Espejo. Espejo was far removed from the battles that day, making Capa's claim that the soldier was killed by machine gun fire implausible. One remarkable aspect of this debunking is the abiding passion among scholars and the public for proving whether the image is documentary or fiction. A Capa biographer calls it "the most debated picture in the history of photojournalism," and major new research on the photograph has been published as recently as 2009, provoking still-heated discussion.[63]

Whether or not the image is staged, it exhibits undeniable artistry in representing war; but the uproar about its origins shows mere artistry to be insufficient for the event purportedly captured. This photograph's reception reveals a historical shift since the late nineteenth century, when staging in Gardner's American Civil War images and reenactment in Edison's battle films did not cause such a stir. The public's willingness to accept (or disinterest in investigating) these works as legitimate views of war—perhaps not precisely "real," but as close as was practical—transformed into greater suspicion as the twentieth century progressed. By World War I, for example, easy-to-record troop mobilization footage was losing its appeal, and demand for hard-to-record battle actualities grew. Filmmakers staged battle scenes to compensate, as entertainment or propaganda. But when staging was detected, these films were increasingly seen as deceptive fakes rather than innocuous reenactments, to the extent that many articles decried them and taught the public to detect their tricks.[64] A harsh 1914 letter in *Moving Picture World* from a representative of the Universal Film Manufacturing Company illustrates this atmosphere: "Anything you see in America of any consequence is a fake. I don't care what it is, if it is relative to the trouble now on the Continent. . . . One of my reasons for writing this letter

1.2. *The Falling Soldier* (1936, © Robert Capa/Magnum Photos).

was the reading of a trade paper advertisement. In my opinion the advertiser is very foolish to try to fool the American people in that manner with some old fake-up junk."[65] Perhaps, based on the tone of these articles, greater efforts were also made to pass staged scenes off as genuine. Capa himself actively courts credulity among viewers, attesting to *The Falling Soldier*'s authenticity in interviews about its creation.[66] Plus, the image does not aesthetically announce itself as staged (as Edison's films did through implausible camera positions). In fact, its blurred quality points to the contrary, implying an aesthetic sacrifice to the unpredictable conditions of battle.

What the Capa controversy reveals, then, is that actual death—not some elegant evocation of heroism or sacrifice in war—is *The Falling Soldier*'s main attraction, and that viewers *care* deeply about death's authentic, documentary recording. Sontag puts it bluntly: "The point of [*The Falling Soldier*] is that it is a real moment, captured fortuitously; it loses all value should the falling soldier turn out to have been performing for Capa's camera."[67] That such an unmasking would compromise the photograph's value so completely gives it a different value to historians. Caroline Brothers argues that in this scenario, "the photograph bears the traces of something broader, of the desired beliefs of a particular historical era. The fame of this photograph is indicative of a collective imagination which wanted and still wants to believe certain things about the nature of death in war . . . that death in war was heroic, and tragic, and that the individual counted and that his death mattered."[68] I would add that this collective imagination also wanted and still wants to believe that dying can begin and end in the same instant, and that this instant can be "embalmed" in time by photography. *The Falling Soldier* and its history tell us that the public embraced a documented "moment" of death, but that such a moment—and one so aesthetically striking—was not likely to stumble into a photographer's viewfinder "on time." In the 1930s, it had to be staged; it would take several more decades for documentarians to close in on the bodily spectacle Capa sought.

The 1960s

Though the 1960s may not have been the "amusement park, full of barely controlled chaos and recklessness," of its reputation, the decade did bring a great volume of violent deaths into U.S. public life via assassinations, political protests, and war in Vietnam.[69] Two that were famously filmed have been seared into collective memory: the assassination of President John Kennedy in 1963 and an impromptu prisoner execution on a Saigon street in 1968. Within the sparse history of documenting death on celluloid that I have outlined, these bits of footage seem like macabre miracles, unlikely products of contingency.

Undoubtedly, they owe much to chance, but developments in technology, politics, and broadcast journalism also had converged to create a somewhat more favorable environment for death and the camera to meet "on time." The footage that emerged in these two cases did not much resemble the straightforward, clean, and noble vision of death playacted on Capa's Spanish hillside, but the 1960s images ignited public interest just as well, demonstrating an appetite for grittier views of real death.

The hold they had and still have over American memory and imagination, I argue, stems largely from the intense type of violent death they document: a gunshot to the head. As a killing method to record, the headshot gives audiences a rare combination of grim attractions. It can display the death blow in gruesome detail, since it is inflicted on a vulnerable and exposed part of the body, *and* it offers an apparent "moment" of death that is far more identifiable than most (among the few types of death whose claims to instantaneity feel plausible). In the decades since, fascination with headshots has only grown, as digital technologies have made their simulation more convincing in movies and their execution a fixture of video games. Indeed, many games that center on combat with ranged weapons incentivize headshots, rewarding players who complete them with experience points or virtual trophies to display on their public profiles.

The headshot that killed President Kennedy on November 22, 1963, was recorded by local Dallas businessman Abraham Zapruder, who brought along his Bell & Howell 8mm home movie camera when he went to watch the president's motorcade. Despite its amateur status, Zapruder's 486-frame film impressively keeps Kennedy on-screen almost continuously from seconds before he was first hit in the neck to seconds after the headshot that killed him. We see the president waving to the crowd as his open-topped vehicle slowly rolls down the street, then his wave transforms into a grasping at his neck. Jackie Kennedy notices that something is wrong with her husband and leans in, at which point the fatal bullet strikes and a small explosion of blood and tissue erupts from his head. A faint, sickening shimmer in that spot remains as his body slumps—the half-recognizable sign of exposed brain matter and torn skin, one assumes. Jackie recoils and crawls out onto the trunk; as a Secret Service agent mounts the moving car's bumper and pushes her back in, an underpass swallows up the vehicle and the film ends. The closest view captured by anyone, Zapruder's film still feels distant in its recording of death. The president and First Lady seem small in the frame, their forms and facial expressions melting into the celluloid's characteristic grain. This lack of proximity is both frustrating and merciful, denying and sparing the viewer a clear look at the president's brains splattering the car or the horror on Jackie's face. In Combs's terms, she would be the film's "registrant," reacting to the death in a way that confirms it has happened for the viewer. In documentary footage of a headshot, though, the registrant becomes a supplemental figure; for once, death can signify itself directly, because it is real and relatively visible.

The images shot by Abraham Zapruder are a fixture of collective memory about this assassination, even connoting the overfamiliar, the too obsessively scrutinized because they are endlessly deployed in the "Who killed Kennedy?" debate.[70] This current sense of iconic visibility obscures the images' absence and even suppression from public view for years after the assassination, with the most stringent censorship centering on frame 313: the "moment" of death headshot. While Zapruder's film offered the most explicit "on time" meeting of a camera and death in history up to that point, its delivery to audiences was decidedly late.

After making his recording, Zapruder went through a nine-hour ordeal to have the film developed, copied, and delivered to the officials gathering evidence—a saga almost unimaginable to today's generation of mobile phone camera operators and YouTube uploaders.[71] As word of the film got around, he was hounded by press representatives wanting to buy the rights; he chose Time Inc.[72] From that point and for the next twelve years, Time Inc. would maintain exclusive legal rights to the film and severely limit how much of it the public could see. The company trickled out its frames through *Life* magazine, initially with four pages of fuzzy black-and-white reproductions in the November 29, 1963 issue. A full week after Kennedy's death, this was the first clear look the American public had at the assassination itself—but only at the parts Time Inc. was willing to share. *Life*'s publisher, C. D. Jackson, reportedly "was so upset by the head-wound sequence" that he decided it should be kept from public view "at least until emotions had calmed."[73] Jackson's decision epitomizes the type of top-down gatekeeping in journalism that helped minimize the number of actuality images of death the U.S. public could access in the predigital era. That first photo spread, ironically titled "Split-Second Sequence as the Bullets Struck," omits frame 313's actual bullet strike, skipping from 270 to 323. *Life* then commenced a teasing routine of getting closer and closer to showing the headshot without doing so. Its October 2, 1964, issue printed a color enlargement of frame 309, then its November 25, 1966, issue did the same for 312, with the caption, "In the next frame, the President received his fatal headshot."[74] Outside the underground circulation of illegally made copies, access to frame 313

1.3. Frame 313 from the Zapruder film (1963, Abraham Zapruder).

seems for years to have been limited to a small, low-quality, black-and-white reproduction in the Warren Report of 1964—the published findings of the official investigating committee.[75]

These details of the headshot's suppression consider only stilled frames, but the sight's greatest impact on the viewer requires the motion its original medium provides. Though the headshot itself can be identified as happening in frame 313, the spray of blood we see exploding outward connotes the individual frame's—the instant's—inability to fully *contain* this spectacle of death. Without the motion of his body's recoil backward and its lifeless sinking into Jackie's lap, Kennedy's filmed death seems decidedly incomplete. Again, an apparently isolated "moment" of death—even the staccato death of the headshot—calls out for its enveloping duration. The public (or the majority, who did not attend the scattered screenings of bootleg copies that began in 1969) could not see that duration until 1975, when Zapruder's moving image was finally screened *in motion* an amazing twelve years after the death he documented. At that point, it aired without Time Inc.'s permission on Geraldo Rivera's nationally broadcast talk show, *Good Night America*.[76] Thus, as much as Zapruder's film represents a leap ahead in the history of documenting death from a production standpoint (technologically enabled by the home movie camera), it also testifies to the impotence of such recording abilities without the more accessible distribution that digital technology would later provide.

In the years since the Zapruder film's halting release from Time Inc.'s captivity, the headshot so long hidden from the public became the focal point of obsessive scrutiny for the film—gazed at over and over as a still frame and as a moving image, at regular speed and in slow motion, from Zapruder's actual distance and blurrily enlarged. The film *JFK* (1992, Oliver Stone) famously re-enacts an instance of this scrutiny, based on real events. Attorney Jim Garrison plays the headshot repeatedly—accompanied by his refrain that borders on incantation, "back and to the left"—for a courtroom full of repulsed spectators. The horror and fascination many feel upon viewing the Kennedy headshot stem not just from its grisliness but from our strange access to the brutal slaughter of such an important public figure. It is one thing to see a skull blasted open, but it is another to see the skull blasted open of a U.S. president whose composure and charm in front of cameras was legendary. Significantly, the lure of bodily spectacle is a quality the film's enthusiasts do not have to admit publicly or even acknowledge to themselves. Investigating Kennedy's murder gives them license to look and look again at its recording. The death's perpetual replay—the "eternal dead-again of the cinema" that Bazin so detested—is thus culturally redeemed by its function as evidence, saving its obsessive viewers from the stigma of morbidity (though usually consigning them to the category of "conspiracy theorists").[77]

In the days following the assassination, Americans lacked images of the death they were struggling to process; they could, however, see footage of a different death that perhaps cathartically channeled their curiosity and filled in for the absent images. The expansion of film technology to a wider public (through home movie cameras) had enabled the recording of Kennedy's death, and days later nascent *video* technology would display his accused assassin's murder on live television. As Lee Harvey Oswald was being transferred from city jail to county jail on November 24, Jack Ruby emerged from a mass of reporters and fatally shot Oswald in the stomach. All major networks had been covering the assassination story continuously, but only NBC was at that moment showing Oswald and caught the murder live. The other networks replayed it from videotape within seconds, using new instant-replay technology developed for televised sports.[78] There seemed to be far less anxiety among exhibitors about showing Oswald's murder than Kennedy's, perhaps because Oswald was seen as an accused assassin less deserving of dignity or because it had been inadvertently shown once already in live broadcast. The fact that this murder was much less graphic than Kennedy's—and that the footage doesn't show Oswald's actual death, which happened later at the hospital—could also have contributed to the decision, underscoring the visual power of a headshot compared with other gunshot deaths. Whatever their rationale, the networks replayed Oswald's murder throughout the day.[79]

Television presents a new distribution medium in this history, but one with many of the same challenges in displaying real death as newspapers and newsreels: like them, TV broadcasts were subject to editorial propriety, government censorship, and commercial interests. However, live television and the emerging video technology that supported it presented a new frontier for death footage, as Oswald's murder shows. This was a wilder, more lawless sphere, where the camera's chance "on time" encounters with death could be recorded and broadcast in the same breath. The element of instantaneity denied journalism's gatekeepers—television producers, in this case—the opportunity to prevent death's transmission. Before the institution of a brief delay in the broadcast of live events that reinstated this gatekeeping power, other live television deaths followed Oswald's. These include the 1974 suicide of Florida newscaster Christine Chubbuck during her own talk show, the 1998 suicide of Daniel V. Jones that ended his standoff with police, the 2012 suicide of Jodon F. Romero (broadcast accidentally on Fox News when operators failed to use their five-second, live feed delay during coverage of a car chase), and the 2015 murder of journalists Alison Parker and Adam Ward during a live local news broadcast.[80]

Although not transmitted live, television's coverage of the Vietnam War kept the spectacle of violent death in the public eye as the 1960s progressed and into the 1970s. Beaming it into American homes in this "living room war," television aired the type of footage camerapersons in previous wars sought but never had the means or permission to actually deliver to audiences. As reporter Leonard Zeindenberg observed, on the eve of the bloody Tet Offensive of 1968, "Certainly the everyday horrors of war have never been so easily available for viewing—crisply edited down to essentials, flashed on the home screen."[81] The accumulated scenes form a veritable cornucopia of war's disturbing visual attractions, including death: troops crawling around and firing their guns in combat, tanks discharging ammunition into buildings, enemies wrestled to the ground and taken prisoner, GIs tossing live grenades into National Liberation Front (NLF) tunnels and then yanking out bloody corpses, huts set alight and engulfed in flames, a Buddhist monk setting *himself* alight and engulfed in flames, bombs cascading out of American planes to pepper the ground below with explosions, children's limp bodies stacked in a village square, burned children running naked down a country road, an impromptu bullet-to-the-temple execution that drops a man to the ground and briefly turns his head into a red fountain of blood. Here were the authentic images of "actual, grewsome war" predicted in cinema's infancy, so many wars ago.

Such images reached American living rooms through a confluence of technological advances and slackened censorship. Chief among the former was television itself, which replaced newsreels as the primary provider of war footage in the United States. Television had become a popular and highly trusted news source, and those with color receivers (sales of which hit their stride in the late 1960s and early 1970s) got added attractions: the jungles were green, the explosions were orange, and the blood was red. The Vietnam footage that fueled the young medium was enabled by developments in recording and transmission equipment. New "lightweight" sound cameras (forty pounds) allowed small crews to traverse difficult terrain alongside GIs. To transmit their footage back to the States, networks could pay $5,000 per five-minute segment for satellite broadcast from Tokyo or fly 16mm reels to New York for airings delayed by about two days.[82]

Despite the sense among government officials that the "horrors of war" now on display were heightening U.S. qualms about this faraway conflict, Presidents Kennedy, Johnson, and Nixon all refrained from official censorship. The challenges were too great: the absence of a declaration of war, the cost of implementation, and concern that South Vietnam would abuse censorship powers.[83] Instead, they gave the press easy credentialing and access to briefings and combat zones, in exchange for adherence to guidelines that mostly protected military strategy—though there was government pressure at points in the war to make coverage optimistic.[84] This rare freedom in documenting and displaying death had disappeared for wartime image-makers since the American Civil War—a freedom that became more useful in the 1960s than the 1860s, as technology allowed for the recording of more than just fields of days-old corpses.

The favorable conditions producing more recorded deaths than in previous wars, however, did not produce as many as one might expect—or as popular understanding of this war implies. While memory may retain the more gruesome images, televised footage of death in Vietnam was actually quite rare; even the category of "heavy fighting" was only shown in 3 percent of news reports.[85] Despite better cameras and little government oversight, image-makers still had the disincentives of going out to combat areas, the dangers they faced upon arrival, the legendary invisibility of the NLF, the contingencies of where and when death would appear, and the whims of TV networks. For all they did show, the networks were nevertheless an obstacle in screening death; still beholden to their advertisers and wary of presenting controversial material, they seemed to volunteer censorship beyond what was sometimes asked of them by the government.[86] Assessing TV coverage of the war, Charles Pach Jr. contends plainly, "Those who remember graphic scenes of death and suffering simply recall a war that television did not show."[87]

The discrepancy between American recollections of the war's images and what the historical record actually bears out seems, to me, less about the faulty memories Pach blames than a mental privileging of quality over quantity. For among the few graphic scenes television *did* show, there are some truly indelible images. Those that became most iconic show the chief of South Vietnam's National Police, General Nguyễn Ngọc Loan, executing handcuffed prisoner Nguyễn Văn Lém on a Saigon street. The impromptu execution happened on February 1, 1968, during the chaotic Tet Offensive that brought the war's violence into Saigon. Partly because Saigon was swarming with reporters—most press people having already been based there—the event was captured by multiple cameras, both on film and as a photograph. Vo Suu recorded the execution on film for NBC. His footage qualified for the expensive Tokyo satellite broadcast, making it to the nightly news on February 2, where it was seen by up to twenty million viewers. Photographer Eddie Adams snapped a picture, *Saigon Execution*, that would run in almost every major newspaper and win him a Pulitzer Prize.[88]

1.4. *Saigon Execution* (1968, © Eddie Adams/Corbis).

Finding the next step in documentary death's evolution after the Zapruder film, Suu and Adams's images take us *closer* to a gruesome headshot. *Saigon Execution* does so by focusing on Lém's facial expression, getting the viewer near enough to contemplate its painful details: eyes cringing, mouth contorted, and skin on the bullet's side of his head seeming to buckle under the impact. Squinting to see such visual information in the Zapruder film, one never finds it. Suu's film footage gives the spectator a sense of being part of the crowd, mixed in among the witnesses and participants shifting around the camera as Loan casually shoos them away with his handgun to make room for the killing he is about to do. One of the dispersing soldiers even walks in front of the camera in a tense moment of *almost* blocking our view of the single shot, delivered point-blank to Lém's temple as he stands maybe ten feet from our position. His body drops heavily, in unison with Loan's gun arm. The general walks away, but Suu's lens lingers on the most disturbing consequence of this new proximity to violent death: Lém's skull is spouting blood as his heart continues to pump, the stream propelled upward a few inches into the air before it sloshes onto the pavement. The blood fights gravity in this fountain-like form for a full three seconds after the body hits the ground, then tapers into a subdued flow. Significantly, NBC had a further seventeen seconds in which Suu zoomed in on the bleeding, but another gatekeeper—*The Huntley-Brinkley Report's* executive producer Robert Northshield—found that "awful rough" and truncated the clip.[89]

Representing only a tiny fraction of documentary images from Vietnam, the shots of death survive best in our collective memory. Adams himself thought little of his photograph's artistry, criticizing its poor lighting and composition, but fixation on its haunting "moment of death" has ensured its longevity and drowned out most aesthetic critiques.[90] Its frozen, "decisive moment" stillness matters here, too. Marita Sturken includes *Saigon Execution* on her list of the war's three most-recalled images but does not include Suu's *moving* images, despite Vietnam's reputation as the television war. Others, including Zelizer and Andrew Hoskins, also claim that war photos endure more than film footage.[91] Photographed and filmed, the execution in Saigon reveals differences between still and moving images of death and why the former endure. Sturken offers several convincing reasons for *Saigon Execution's* primacy in our recollections, compared with the parallel film footage: the photo seems to freeze the moment when the bullet penetrates the man's head and allows us to linger on his facial expression, while the film includes more surrounding footage of the prisoner walking and later the body on the ground spurting blood. It is that frozen facial expression and our ability to *contemplate* it in a corporeal photograph that Sturken prizes over the ephemeral nature of television—at least, television in the decades before VHS and DVR.[92] Sturken adds that the film footage is "extremely difficult to watch," implying that the photograph is less wounding.[93] It seems to me that the *more* wounding medium would be the one seared into memory, but perhaps Sturken's counterintuitive claim reveals a complex interaction between memories of the film and the photo. The latter may serve as a Freudian screen memory for the footage, allowing us to recall the victim's unsettling grimace and forget the more traumatizing blood that surged from his temple a second later.

Sturken also argues that the photo affirms the still camera's ability to capture the "moment" of death—a potential that, as I argue earlier, may make it psychologically appealing to U.S. audiences. Such a photo helps them invest in the notion of death as a moment, keeping faith that it still takes such a temporal form in an age that greatly obscures this "moment" through painful medical treatments that extend both life and the dying process. Where Americans during the Civil War feared an instant death—because they might die without spiritual preparation—Americans during the Vietnam War may have found this type more grimly alluring as it was growing more scarce.[94] Thus, I argue that audiences are drawn to "on time" documentary images in which this "moment" that has largely evaporated in their own lives seems visible, definite—in this case, projected onto the body of an ethnic Other in a distant land. Where is that "moment" in the NBC film footage? If we play the clip without pause or slow motion—operations that viewers could not have performed in 1968—then it disappears, swept away in a durational *process* of dying, however brief that duration is. There is even a sense in which the frightfully powerful fountain of blood in Suu's film subtly undermines the appearance of instant death—that some involuntary force in Lém's body remains vigorous after the "moment" of death that seemed so definitively contained in Adams's photo. The blood's movement thus echoes Topsy's persistent twitching in *Electrocuting an Elephant*. Here, again, is the specter of duration, of dying, haunting even the headshot and its relatively convincing "moment" of death.

While Adams's photograph and Suu's footage give distinct, medium-specific experiences of viewing death, both are more visceral than informative. Northshield, the executive producer who put Suu's film on *The Huntley-Brinkley Report*, himself acknowledged that its news value derived not from its political implications but rather from its striking shots of death.[95] When the scene is reproduced, details of each man's identity and the backstory to the execution usually are ignored. An image of a specific, high-ranking South Vietnamese officer executing a specific NLF prisoner during a specific military offensive becomes a generalized symbol of the war's chaos and injustice. As Sturken notes, Vietnamese kill Vietnamese, and the battle represented is of man against man.[96] In this iconic image, cemented in U.S. memory as epitomizing the Vietnam War, one element is conveniently absent: the United States itself. The slain, wounded, and traumatized U.S. soldiers worrying the American public are nowhere pictured, nor is any sign of the *American* violence and imperialism that was so deeply involved in Lém's death and in all deaths the war produced.

Conclusion: Figurative Wounds

During the thirteen decades surveyed in this chapter, photography and film cameras pursued death (almost always violent death) persistently and caught it rarely. When the "moment" of death did seem to arrive in 1960s headshot images, its impact was sharp—making footage and photos legendary. And yet, the mythical instant—the invisible event seemingly made visible—is never quite as revelatory as we might hope. Stilled in Adams's photo or Zapruder's (long-suppressed) frame 313, it captivates, but it feels incomplete—disconnected from the movement that makes death's fundamental change apparent. When motion is restored in Zapruder's and Suu's films, the "moment" of death a viewer thought she saw slips away—enveloped into the duration of dying. The camera's ability to deliver death, then, is always partial, fragmentary, never in "full detail"—even in the rare cases when it manages to completely enframe that bodily transition. And yet, as I argue throughout this book, these incomplete documentary images of death often fulfill political purposes even when they fail to answer metaphysical questions about the end of life. Some in this chapter, for example, evinced the reality and magnitude of the Holocaust's genocide, helped shift U.S. public opinion against the Vietnam War, and—distressingly—rallied both support for and opposition to brutal lynchings and the white supremacist cause they bolstered.

Documentary images of death were rare in indexical media's era of dominance because the contingencies of where, when, and how death will happen and the minuscule target of the "moment" of death demand more advanced recording technologies. Documentary death crops up with greater regularity in the digital age partly because digital tools make it more practical to record and distribute—as mundane as such a statement sounds in the context of a very powerful subject. Compared with indexical media's history, there are now many more cameras in circulation, able to cover more areas of public space. The cameras are mobile, capable of quick activation, and affordable and user-friendly enough that many people buy and operate them—even incidentally, as one function of a multipurpose mobile phone. These cameras also store their images on capacious and cheap formats, giving operators the freedom to keep recording patiently until death occurs. Film and photography progressed in these directions, too, during their histories; Kodak's introduction of personal cameras in the late nineteenth century yielded more lynching photographs, and the adoption of home movie cameras in the mid-twentieth century provided the best record of the Kennedy assassination. But celluloid never mastered the preceding capabilities as thoroughly as digital has, the evidence of which is in the greater volume of recorded death to be explored in the chapters that follow and the shorter time period they cover.

Digital technologies would help image-makers both in overcoming logistical challenges to recording actual death and in bypassing political obstacles to displaying it. As Abraham Lincoln did not yet understand in the 1860s and as Lyndon Johnson bitterly comprehended in the 1960s, the visual record of a slain human can have tremendous political power. That power is greatest when the body seems caught at the point of transition, the illusory "moment" of death that will make the front page and ensnare the public's attention. The preceding history reveals that in a top-down distribution system, volatile images are routinely suppressed by government censors or news editors. Though hardly a cure-all for such challenges, we shall see significant changes in displaying death come from the Internet's more bottom-up configuration and ability to rapidly transmit photos and videos across any earthly distance.

In contrast to the stalled circulation of the Zapruder film, for example, chapter 4 will trace a very different path from production (via mobile phones) to distribution (on YouTube) for two sets of videos documenting public killings in the twenty-first century. And compared with Edison's reenacted substitute for footage of a high-profile execution in *Czolgosz*, in 2006 the Internet quickly provided videos of the decade's highest-profile execution, of Saddam Hussein, which journalism's gatekeepers at major news outlets had planned to suppress.[97] New (or newly digitized) archives that have arisen with the innovation of streaming video have also begun to unearth the undistributed death footage of the past for broad public access. British Pathé provides a case in point from Europe, having uploaded several actuality death clips to its YouTube channel that were never edited into the company's newsreels and screened— presumably because of their disturbing content, though existing records do not confirm the reason.[98]

Additionally, digital technology now provides greater means for the public to express a *desire* to see documentary death—and, thus, evidence of this long-established desire's vitality in the digital age. For instance, the hunger for documentary images of Osama bin Laden's corpse in the wake of his shooting produced widely circulating Photoshopped fakes, and a computer virus spread through e-mailed links promising photos of the slain leader.[99] As Zelizer notes, a similarly voracious appetite for the perpetrator video of Nick Berg's beheading made terms such as "nick berg video" and "nick berg beheading" the top Google searches after the video's May 11, 2004, release.[100]

Throughout this chapter, I have endeavored to write about not just when and how cameras met death—"too late" in corpse photos or "on time" with the "moment" of death—but why audiences wanted them to and how they experienced these mediated encounters. It is no coincidence that in adapting Williams's temporal modes, my work brushes up against pornography, the genre she associates with "on time" bodily spectacle. Like pornography, the why and how of looking at documentary death has long been subject to moral interrogation, with parallel accusations of prurience and morbidity leveled against their audiences. And like images of actual sex, images of actual death must satisfy a vague standard of "redeeming social importance" to avoid dismissal as "death porn."[101] While not all should be "redeemed" (particularly the lynching photographs), the images discussed in this chapter have all had a social impact and have done more than display the salacious attractions of grisly death. Mourning photographs in the nineteenth century "secured the shadow" of individuals that cameras had often been too late to record in life, helping families grieve for the departed. Civil War battlefield images aided grief on a national scale for a population suffering unprecedented losses and reached back toward the undocumented "moments" of soldiers' deaths to forecast their souls' fates. Lynching photographs aimed to intimidate Blacks and fortify white power, but they also revealed cruelty and cowardice in white southern communities. Concentration camp images evidenced a genocide and struggled to communicate its impact to those across the globe. Zapruder's film documented a murder of world-shaking importance and became a crucial tool in its fraught investigation. And the recording of Lém's execution in Saigon fueled a movement to end the Vietnam War.

And yet, we must not lose sight of the severe limitations of documentary death images, of their inability to fully reveal death or fully connect us with the dying. As Sontag perceptively wrote in 1977, "To suffer is one thing; another thing is living with the photographed images of suffering."[102] Related to this sentiment, there is a point at which my borrowing of Williams's temporalities parts ways with their original use. Williams emphasizes the manner in which bodily sensations connect subjects and spectators. She notes, for example, that weeping melodrama characters can produce tears among the audience, too, physically aligning on-screen bodies with the bodies watching them. Though we may tense and cringe sympathetically with the person dying on camera, similar to Williams's observation that we scream or shudder watching death in horror films, there would be something disingenuous about advancing this parallel—a difference between cringing and bleeding. When a life is actually ending on-screen, there must be a higher threshold for claiming a shared bodily experience.

In considering that threshold, I hold in my mind the gesture of one viewer of documentary death: German filmmaker Harun Farocki. Having seen images of Vietnam's napalm victims, he responds to this experience of spectatorship in his short film *The Inextinguishable Fire* (1969). After reading aloud a news report about the war's violence on camera, Farocki expresses the following concerns: "If we show you pictures of napalm victims, you'll close your eyes. First you'll close your eyes to the pictures. Then you'll close your eyes to the memory. Then you'll close your eyes to the facts. Then you'll close your eyes to the entire context." Searching for a way to communicate the devastating effects of napalm on the human body, Farocki settles on playing the victim himself, picking up a lit cigarette and grinding it into the skin on his forearm in a shocking documentary moment. A narrator intones, "A cigarette burns at 400° Celsius. Napalm burns at 3,000° Celsius." In other words, even this bold action cannot adequately convey the pain at which it grasps.

The Inextinguishable Fire is not a death documentary; it does not fall within this chapter's scope of the U.S. circulation of recorded death in the era of indexical media. I end with it here because Farocki's startling self-injury returns me to broader questions of ethics and understanding that must animate the study of real people dying on camera. His act evokes, for me, the inevitable point at which photographic and filmic images of death and suffering no longer feel adequate. However much these images *can* communicate, whatever impact they *can* have on the directions of politics or the course of wars or the worldview of an individual, they remain deeply limited. I can, as others have done, write about their tactile qualities—how viewers are scarred, jolted, or branded by looking at them. Yet, as Farocki implies: relative to the events these images depict, the sense in which they wound the viewer—the sense in which they burn themselves into memory—is hopelessly figurative.

THE ART OF DYING, ON VIDEO

DEATHBED DOCUMENTARIES

We die with the dying:
See, they depart, and we go with them.
We are born with the dead:
See, they return, and bring us with them.
T. S. ELIOT, "Little Gidding," in *Four Quartets*

When cameras capture violent death, the backgrounds against which they do so are variable: a bustling street, a battlefield, a police station hallway, a train platform, and so on. With natural death, spatial possibilities close down. There is one iconic place where almost all lives end from disease or age on camera, in either fiction or documentary: the deathbed. Douglas Sirk's *Imitation of Life* (1959) offers an archetypal deathbed scene, familiar from so many Hollywood melodramas. In the film's closing moments, wealthy white actress Lora is summoned to the bedside of her beloved African American friend and housekeeper, Annie. A sentimental score plays throughout the scene in Annie's bedroom, where people gather: Lora, close family friend Steve, Annie's minister, her doctor, and another servant. The doctor listens to Annie's heart with a stethoscope and shakes his head gravely to Lora, who becomes distraught.

Annie herself is ashen and fatigued but propped up in bed and alert. Animated by important tasks at hand ("I've got to talk, I've got to!"), she puts her affairs firmly in order: Annie instructs Lora and Steve to find her estranged daughter, Sarah Jane, and deliver her substantial inheritance and Annie's apology for her perceived failings as a mother. Careful not to forget anyone, Annie bequeaths a pearl necklace to Lora's daughter, a mink scarf to the minister's wife, and a "nice, clean fifty-dollar bill" to the milkman at Annie and Lora's old apartment (to whom, Annie reveals, she has been sending money every Christmas, "in both our names"). She directs Steve to a document in which she has fully planned her funeral, then gently ignores Lora's desperate protestations that Annie won't be dying for a long time. Head drooping and eyes closing, Annie says her last words: "I'm just tired, Miss Lora—awfully . . . tired . . ." As she trails off, Lora's panicked reaction confirms what we already know from conventions established by so many fiction films: Annie has just died.

The opening scene of the documentary *Silverlake Life: The View from Here* (1993, Tom Joslin and Peter Friedman) responds directly to this model of on-screen death and the way it has shaped Americans' expectations for their own deaths and those of their loved ones. The film chronicles the physical deterioration and eventual death of its HIV-positive codirector, Tom Joslin. Living with AIDS himself, Tom's partner, Mark, speaks in the first moments of the film, interviewed well after Tom has already died. Describing what he did immediately after Tom's death, Mark explains, "I wanted to close his eye, because it's very strange seeing a dead person staring, and I tried, just like in the movies, to close the eyelid. It doesn't close—it pops back open! As I said to Tom, 'I apologize that life wasn't like the movies.'" Already having seen through Tom's dying process how little death is "like the movies," Mark feels renewed surprise that even this small detail—the ritual of closing the dead's eyes, restoring some sense of peaceful slumber—has been a fiction.

Mark is typical of late twentieth-century Americans in his reliance on fiction film as a guide to what natural death is like. He continues this cultural recourse to fiction in the absence of personal experiences with the dying process (although many gay men of the late 1980s were quickly accumulating those), a recourse that suffuses much of twentieth-century history in the West. As early as 1915, Sigmund Freud remarked on the culture of death denial that he perceived (in Europe): "So we have no option but to find compensations in the world of fiction, in literature, in the theatre for that which we have lost in life."[1] Such a reliance is necessitated by two factors: mainly, the twentieth century's well-documented removal of actual death from the public eye, but also

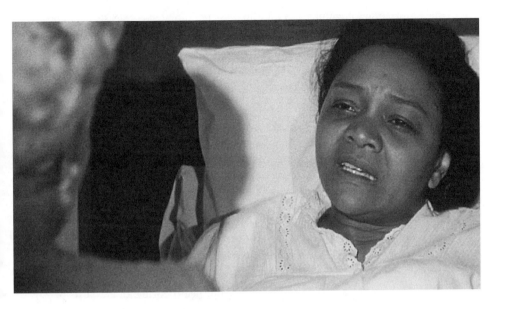

2.1. Annie on her deathbed (*Imitation of Life*, 1959, Douglas Sirk, Universal).

documentary's sluggish response, its failure to rally against that removal and to project recorded dying onto American screens.[2] Chapter 1 detailed the quest to capture, in photographs and on film, violent "moments of death" in a documentary mode—a quest that has proceeded without interruption since the mid-nineteenth-century invention of photography. By contrast, natural death (or its corpses, at least) had documentary exposure in the first few decades of photography through postmortem mourning photographs but virtually disappeared from the public eye during the twentieth century. Writing in 1974, just two years before Michael Roemer's *Dying* would air on PBS, Amos Vogel identifies the extreme paucity of documentary work on natural death: "Although [documentarians] have already documented large areas of human activity and visited all the forbidden places in the world with their light-weight cameras and portable sound, their curiosity, with hardly an exception, has stopped short of death, funeral parlors, morgues or morticians. . . . That this entire area—more universal by far than others covered *ad nauseam*—simply does not exist in contemporary cinema, reveals taboo in its purest form."[3]

Violent deaths in fiction film (and occasionally documentary) may have provided a release for anxiety and curiosity about death during an era of its pervasive denial, but they did so at a remove from the way most American viewers' lives would actually end.[4] In my view, instead of serving a true memento mori function, these highly mediated images of violent death helped to repress awareness of the natural deaths awaiting most Americans (most by a wide margin: only about 7 percent of annual U.S. deaths are by violent means).[5] And fiction film's typical deathbed scenes—especially midcentury Hollywood's—were misleading in preparing Americans to witness or experience these deaths, as Mark's story demonstrates. Such scenes present many points of disjuncture with likely reality, as exemplified by *Imitation*: the nostalgic representation of death at home in an era dominated by hospital death; the appearance of reasonable health in the final hours; the absence of dementia, disorientation, or unconsciousness. Robert Kastenbaum labels this popular convention "healthy dying," free of apparent symptoms.[6] Most of all, fictional deathbed scenes tend to tailor death's duration to narrative (rather than realistic) dimensions, allowing the audience to feel as if the full length of the death has been made visible to them. The process of dying is condensed so that a character like Annie, who had been vaguely ailing for a time from an unidentified malady, seems to become a terminal case just minutes before her clearly identified "moment" of death.

Fiction film's deviations from the attributes of actual dying may reflect the *difficulty* of their representation as much as any desired distance from realism.

As noted in chapter 1, a slow and natural death in bed is an inherently uncin-ematic sight, bereft of the physical motion that defines the medium's "moving image." Vivian Sobchack emphasizes this difficulty in her foundational essay "Inscribing Ethical Space" (1984) through its ten propositions about death in documentary. Propositions two through four draw out the ways in which a violent and abrupt cessation of motion provides "the most effective cinematic signifier of death in our present culture." Sobchack elaborates: "Death can only be represented in a visible and vigorous contrast between two states of the physical body: the body as *lived body*, intentional and animated—and the body as *corpse*, a thing of flesh unintended, inanimate, static."[7] As the deathbed doc-umentaries discussed in this chapter make clear, the "lived body" on its death-bed is rarely "intentional and animated" as the time approaches when it will become a corpse. Between these two states, there is no "visible and vigorous contrast," hence the need for what Scott Combs terms the "registrant": an on-screen witness who will confirm that death, not always visible to the audi-ence, has occurred. Registrants can be human beings—the doctors with their stethoscopes in *Execution of Czolgosz*, Lora with her horrified expression in *Imitation of Life*, the film characters Mark remembers who close the eyes of the corpse—or even, in recent decades, machines. With the advent of EKG and EEG monitors, cinema could rely on machine registrants in hospitals to substitute for the "visible and vigorous contrast" Sobchack describes: though the body remains still before and after death, the lines on the monitor jump around and then flatten.[8]

If the gesticulations of an electronic line on a small monitor seem a poor re-placement for violent death's spectacle of movement, that lack speaks to some-thing almost masochistic about moving image-makers' attempts to document natural death. Ontologically, their medium aspires to embody movement—with film hiding the inherent stillness of its frames in the apparent motion of its projection. The drive to display natural death, then, careens toward ex-posing the medium's own failures in the face of such a powerful metaphysical event. The camera will not be able to show death "in full detail," to show the invisible physicality of it that would not register even if the lens were to pen-etrate the body itself.[9] Buried in this effort to reveal death, is there an impulse to admit to what the moving image *cannot* do? To let it confront a phenomenon "beyond representation" and lay its limitations bare?

Answers to these questions are complicated by a fascinating deviation from film and photography's quest for the violent "moment of death" when docu-mentary once again takes up the challenge of representing natural death, as it had in the mid-nineteenth century through photographs. These deathbed documentaries seek to make natural death newly public and visible in an era when it had become intensely private and invisible. And yet, the "moment" of death that would presumably read as a disappointing failure of moving image technology is simply absent from almost all of them, remaining private. This absence continues even in the deathbed documentaries that seem to directly promise access to that taboo sight, as in Showtime's six-episode documentary series *Time of Death* (2013). Its title references the medical practice of declaring a precise "time of death" for each patient—a bureaucratic protocol that tries to make official the existence of an identifiable "moment" of death. Despite its title and advertising as a series that will take an "unflinching, intimate look" at the deaths of eight people, the series repeatedly flinches at the "time of death."[10] Sometimes there is a gap in footage because the dying party or family members ask to keep that time private or because death happens suddenly without the cameras' presence, leaving the viewer with only a screen of text declaring the time at which this subject died. But in other episodes, the show's crew is present for the death itself but refrains from showing it "in full detail," staying a considerable distance from the bedside or cutting away to loved ones gathered there.

The absence of the "moment" of death redirects attention toward dying as a process—a gradual transformation that carries on past death through the grief of survivors. Instead of grasping for the "moment" of death's nonspectacle of spatial movement, I assert, these documentaries shift their focus to the temporal, seeking to make death's "full detail" visible through *duration* as new image technologies vastly improve the form's temporal capacities. Duration becomes central in these works' attempts to fully represent death because as much as natural death contracts space to the deathbed, it expands time from a "moment" (or the illusion of one) to a prolonged process—a process that gets progressively longer with advancements in medicine. The stretching out of time, then, characterizes two histories of developing technology in the twentieth century that meet in the deathbed documentary: the histories of medicine and of moving images.

At a logistical level, honestly chronicling a long process of dying calls for equipment that can record many hours of material at little cost and can roll for long stretches of time. Offering a cheap and versatile alternative to film stock, video—and later, digital video (DV)—appealed to underfunded documentarians and enabled some people to become documentarians who never could have afforded to with celluloid. After initial (and often unsustainable) forays into documentary video by activist groups and local access TV stations in the 1970s, by the late 1980s documentary filmmakers were adopting video more systematically, and it became an excellent tool for recording natural death.[11] Documentarians of the 1980s and beyond *could* embark on deathbed documentaries because of technological developments, but they *did* largely because of cultural factors: new conceptions of death and dying in the United States, the massive wave of AIDS deaths, as well as trends toward subjectivity, psychological intimacy, and autobiography in documentary.

Among those new conceptions of the end of life was a subtle reshaping of the "good death" to accommodate the altered conditions under which Americans died in the late twentieth century and early twenty-first century. Departing from the step-by-step instructions for dying that the medieval *Ars moriendi* provided and from the universal stages of confronting mortality that Elisabeth Kübler-Ross introduced in 1969, the dominant version of the good death now rejects those one-size-fits-all models. It favors, instead, customized dying rooted in individuality, with each dying person laboring to design and achieve his or her own unique good death. This new good death aligns with broader cultural and social forces: with the emphasis on customization in media and consumer culture in the postindustrial era and with neoliberal mandates for the individual to be self-sustaining and to achieve maximum success in every pursuit.[12] When death is meant to be a final expression of one's unique personhood, the natural "moment of death" becomes a homogeneous obstacle to that expression. Conscious and alert right to the second when her body gives out, *Imitation of Life*'s Annie remains fully herself, personifying her unshakable goodness and distinctive spirit in her last moments. Most actual natural deaths, though, do not allow for such individuality at the end, as body and mind take leave of life asynchronously. When the mind shuts down before the body, the perceived "moment of death" becomes terribly conventional, erasing individuality as unconscious and often emaciated bodies labor to breathe and then stop breathing.

Because it is misleading as a representation of the long process of dying and because it is neither cinematic nor individualized, the "moment of death" so sought after by documentarians capturing violence becomes taboo in documentaries of natural death. By leaving it out, deathbed documentaries bolster a recent fantasy of dying as a fully individualized affair. But, I argue, by leaving it out, they also use the innate strengths of new technologies to expose and reject the temporal fantasy of violent death documentary: that death is a sharp *moment* of transition that cameras can make transparently visible, rather than a prolonged process resistant to cinematic representation. Thus, just as video and digital technologies enable cameras to wait for death, to be finally "on time" in meeting it, documentarians willfully turn those cameras off.

A Death of One's Own: Individualizing the End of Life

The twentieth century's widespread culture of death denial in the West (described in my introduction) arrived alongside the hypermedicalization of death as it moved from the home to the hospital in the early to mid-twentieth century, sharply altering the nineteenth century's dominant vision of "beautiful death" as a romantic and temporary parting. As the nature of the "good death" was evolving, this hypermedicalization also brought new fears of bad deaths. As historian Philippe Ariès articulates: "The death of the patient in the hospital, covered with tubes, is becoming a popular image, more terrifying than the *transi* or skeleton of macabre rhetoric."[13]

This frightening style of high-tech, modern hospital death is hardly the sort that Annie experiences in *Imitation of Life*. In most respects *Imitation* presents a deeply nostalgic version of the good death that predates its 1959 production year.[14] Unlike patients of the period in their sequestered hospital rooms, Annie dies—anachronistically—at home with loved ones gathered around her. She herself, not her doctor, directs how her death will proceed, giving instructions and telling those assembled when to keep quiet and listen. An inconsolable Lora tries to persuade her that she won't die for a long time, but Annie refuses to participate in this twentieth-century denial and maintains focus on her impending demise. In keeping with long-established spiritual expectations of Western dying, she shows concern for her soul's fate, affirming, "I'd like to be standing with the lambs, and not with the goats, on Judgment Day," and demonstrating goodness through her carefully selected bequests and kindness to the old milkman. Annie wraps up her affairs and has planned her own funeral so as not to burden her survivors, for whom she provides. In a moment reminiscent of nineteenth-century beliefs that approaching death would give wisdom to the dying that they could share with those assembled, Annie sagely tells Lora, "Our wedding day and the day we die are the great events of life." And in keeping with the importance of deathbed attendance in the nineteenth century, she registers the tragedy that she cannot say good-bye to her estranged daughter, Sarah Jane, whose absence looms through a large photograph on the nightstand. Lastly, Annie achieves death's optimal duration, concluding earthly business and then promptly dying. She will make no trips to the hospital, will not be covered with tubes or punctured by needles, lingering for months; she simply closes her eyes and is gone. Between her nostalgic death scene and actual deaths at that time—between even the nineteenth and twentieth centuries—there is, as Ariès remarks, a reversal as complete as that of a photographic negative.[15]

In the late 1960s, the previous decades' "brutal revolution" of modern hospital dying that is pointedly *not* pictured in *Imitation* began to generate significant backlash in the United States—a backlash that would later include deathbed documentaries. Doctors came under criticism in "a diffuse rebellion against the medical dictatorship . . . partly spiritual and partly secular."[16] The spiritual and secular elements of this rebellion shared a common goal: to redirect attention from the body of the dying to her personhood (whether through psychology or the soul). Leading the charge was Dr. Elisabeth Kübler-Ross, a Swiss-born psychiatrist who sought to rehumanize end-of-life care with her book *On Death and Dying* (1969), best known for its five stages of psychological reactions to the news that one is dying. According to Kübler-Ross, patients will first experience denial and isolation, followed by anger at their diagnosis, then will attempt to bargain (with God or doctors) for more time, slip into a state of depression, and finally accept the fact that they are going to die.

Though revolutionary in its time, Kübler-Ross's *On Death and Dying* also marks a return to the idea of an instruction manual for death—an idea at least as old in the West as the medieval *Ars moriendi* (*The Art of Dying*), a tract of monolithic, Christian guidelines for the dying that focused on the soul's fate and shaped that era's notion of the good death.[17] Both impose a structure onto the dying process (Kübler-Ross's five stages, the *Ars moriendi*'s five temptations) that has nothing to do with medicine and the body, describing a fierce battle in the mind of the dying that promises a psychological or spiritual reward: ending life at peace or ascending to heaven. Like the *Ars moriendi*, *On Death and Dying* embraces the spirit of the memento mori, affirming, "We should make it a habit to think about death and dying occasionally, I hope before we encounter it in our own life."[18] Both of these pieces of writing and the later deathbed documentaries serve as aids to death's contemplation and as potential guides to achieving the good death—sometimes explicitly announcing this latter function, as in the pointedly titled *The Art of Dying*.

Interestingly, at the time when Kübler-Ross was recentering death into the *mind* of the dying on a psychological level, doctors were doing the same on a physical level. The innovation of heart transplants in 1967 had heightened simmering moral and medical debates about when a patient becomes "dead." Patients who were biologically alive but unlikely to regain meaningful consciousness became important sources of well-oxygenated organs, but doctors removing their still-beating hearts needed a revised definition of death as protection from murder charges.[19] Designating the "moment of death" with legal precision, though, was a fraught task. As an article published in the *Journal of the American Medical Association* in 1968 lamented, "It seems ironic that the end point of existence, which ought to be as clear and sharp as in a chemical titration, should so defy the power of words to describe it and the power of men to say with certainty, 'here it is.'"[20] I have already asserted the difficulty of pinpointing that "moment" with cameras, but here were medical experts, with full access to internal biology, also unable to declare, "here it is."

With transplants on the rise, legal and medical forces together pushed the brain to usurp the heart's role as the single-organ linchpin of human life. Under the new status quo, "In order to be dead enough to bury but alive enough to be a donor, you must be irreversibly brain dead."[21] Coincidentally, this move from heart to brain dovetails with Kübler-Ross and others' focus on the individual in death, with the brain conceived of as the organ that contains unique personhood. Doubts lingered, though, about the besieged theory of life and death as "unequivocal, dualistic categories" governed by a single organ and divided by a distinct moment.[22] These doubts surface periodically through high-profile patients in hotly disputed "brain-dead" states, such as Karen Ann Quinlan, Nancy Cruzan, and Terri Schiavo. As Margaret Lock concludes, "Clearly, death is not a self-evident phenomenon. The margins between life and death are socially and culturally constructed, mobile, multiple, and open to dispute and reformulation."[23] Between death's aggressive medicalization in the twentieth century and the redefinition of its boundary with life, we see the "moment of death" that seemed so clear to chapter 1's image-makers further destabilized by a prolonged process of dying whose end point is not completely evident.

One can understand Kübler-Ross's impulse to provide temporal structure to this sprawling and ill-defined process through her five stages. Her work was both warmly embraced and fiercely criticized in the United States, exposing a passionate concern about the country's deficient death culture but divided opinions on how to improve it. The ensuing decade saw a flurry of discourse on the end of life: books and articles, college classes, support groups, and the emergence of hospice and palliative care as alternatives to Kübler-Ross's chilling vision of typical hospital dying.[24] These seeds of change planted in the 1970s grew into a modest movement that continues into the twenty-first century. Its proponents are united by a core belief: that dying *people* get lost amid the hospital's network of tubes, lines, and machines, the barrage of treatments intended to save their lives, doctors and nurses attuned to bodies but not to emotions, and family and friends unprepared to discuss approaching ends. Thus, the writers, teachers, and caregivers involved in what Tony Walter calls "the revival of death" work to *individualize* dying, transforming it from a cold medical routine into a process undertaken differently by each unique human being. As Larry Churchill put it in 1979, "nobody dies by the book"—an implicit rebuke of *On Death and Dying*, which had been *the* book for the past decade.[25] Now an ambivalent figure for the movement, Kübler-Ross had redirected attention to the personhood of the dying but had also collapsed end-of-life experiences into a rigid, step-by-step formula meant to apply to everyone.

The new movement criticized the reigning model of death in the United States but also sought once again to reshape the good death, working toward what Kastenbaum terms a *nova ars moriendi*. Begun in the United States in the early 1970s, the modern hospice movement has been the greatest force in this endeavor, providing an alternative to hypermedicalized death and inspiring palliative care programs within the medical establishment. Prioritizing meaningful and low-pain dying over painfully prolonged living, hospice offers death at home and also greater attention to the patient's psychological needs. Kastenbaum, who was personally involved in its early years, describes the organization with its own characteristic rhetoric, revealing its alignment with the nova ars moriendi's neoliberal emphasis on individuality: "The terminally ill person's own preferences and lifestyle must be taken into account in all decision making. . . . Hospice patients and their families were not placed on a conveyer belt for the assembling of a standard-issue death."[26] The variety of deaths hospice actually provides may not be as wide as its rhetoric of unique death implies, but the promise of a customized experience—matching the American focus on choice in consumerism—has helped the movement grow. Approximately 45 percent of U.S. deaths (from all causes) now happen under hospice care.[27] Hospice is part of the significant (but not culturally dominant) push to acknowledge dying as a process too long to disregard and long enough to potentially experience meaningfully. Finally abandoning the idea of death as a problem that can-do American determination will overcome—a tantalizing hope in the heady years of the early twentieth century's rapid medical advancements—the culture has turned toward other national values, making death a locus for individual expression and consumer choice.[28]

In this way, the new good death still follows a key principle by which it has been revised throughout history: the good death embodies a given society's highest values.[29] In recent decades, it has come to embody a number of disquieting neoliberal values. These underlie the apparently progressive nova ars moriendi in its focus on the individual and her personal responsibility to craft her own good death through active choices. As Wendy Brown writes, neoliberalism "figures individuals as rational, calculating creatures whose moral autonomy is measured by their capacity for 'self-care'—the ability to provide for their own needs and service their own ambitions. . . . The rationally calculating individual bears full responsibility for the consequences of his or her actions no matter how severe the constraints on this action."[30] Even when that constraint is biological (the impending end of life itself) rather than socio-economic, as Brown envisions, neoliberal subjects are conditioned to succeed, to achieve—to succeed at dying well, to achieve the good death. Doing so compensates for the subject's (eventually inevitable) failure to optimize her own health—what Nikolas Rose describes as her obligation to successfully manage risk by acquiring health knowledge, continually monitoring her own body, and actively making healthy choices.[31] In other words, while the ideal neoliberal subject safeguards her health in order to remain a productive, consumptive being, there are still ways in which her death—once it becomes unpreventable—can align with neoliberal values.

The neoliberal rhetoric of this nova ars moriendi grounded in individualism and productive choice is everywhere apparent in discourse on death. In scholarly work, Walter notes that "in a culture of individualism that values a unique life lived uniquely, the good death is now the death we choose"; Carlo Leget asserts, "We have become very sensitive to the unique wishes of each authentic individual" in death; and Ernest Becker frames the end of life as the last opportunity for individuals to discover and express their true selves.[32] Extensions of this idea in the popular press sometimes take a tongue-in-cheek tone, as in a self-help book called *To Die with Style!* (1974) or the infamous Timothy Leary's *Design for Dying* that posits "Designer Dying" as "the hip, chic thing to do. . . . Even if you've lived your life as a complete slob, you can die with terrific style."[33]

In a culture increasingly framing death as individualized, a call has also sounded to gather and share those unique experiences. Voiced by many writers, this call for "stories over stages" (as Churchill puts it, referencing Kübler-Ross's five stages) implicitly holds hopes for both the dying and the living: that talking about their situation will be liberating to the dying, and that having examples of the nova ars moriendi will help the living plan for their own good deaths.[34] Here we arrive at the function of documentary in this complex culture. Deathbed documentaries oppose the fetishized "moments" of violent death that other documentarians have pursued, the "standard issue" death that has characterized modern hospital dying, and even the equally standardized steps away from that model that Kübler-Ross took. Instead, they tie together many strands of post-1960s U.S. death culture: they tell the personal stories death scholars have called for, challenge the centrality of the "moment of death" by excluding it in favor of the long dying process, and model the nova ars moriendi with a focus on highly individualized dying. Indeed, this individualization trend complements not just the era's death culture but also its media culture, as the rise of video and then digital production and distribution afforded opportunities for smaller, personal projects and more customized audiences.

These technological affordances of video and DV, and the deathbed documentaries they enable, also engage with the nova ars moriendi's neoliberal elements. Anthony Giddens stresses that the subject in the age of neoliberalism must be ever-focused on self-identity, which "has to be routinely created and sustained in the reflexive activities of the individual."[35] These "reflexive activities" can incorporate a drive toward self-improvement (including in caring for one's own body) and a continual, introspective evaluation and narrativization of one's choices (including one's choices in how to die). By watching a documentary tracking the successful—or instructively unsuccessful—deaths of others, the neoliberal subject potentially gathers resources to prepare a death of her own that will express her unique personhood. By making or participating in a documentary tracking her own death, the neoliberal subject publicly articulates her well-crafted self-identity through her customized good death.

Despite the warmth of its rhetoric and its many appeals compared with midcentury hospital dying, the neoliberal nova ars moriendi's emphasis on individual self-identity—and the highly individualized death documentaries that help shape it—can undercut the power of shared experience and the memento mori. In the Ars moriendi or Kübler-Ross's stages, we are all equally implicated. Similarly, many of the skeletons who shadow the living in traditional memento mori iconography are stripped of identity, mere bones; they could be anyone, which is partly the point. Not so in documentary chronicles of avowedly unique dying. Rather than prompting a hard look ahead to our own future deaths, these films may instead allow a damaging distance between the viewer and the dying—offering an implicit (and likely unintended) assurance that since I am so different from this singular human being on-screen, this documentary is not previewing the death that awaits me. The films may thus become tools of disassociation, allowing a gaze at the death of another without the burden of identification.

There are other troubling elements of this video corpus, too: the death stories told through documentary tend to focus on a narrow range of subjects, demographically speaking. The dying people featured in these documentaries are men more often than women, white more often than of color, and middle or upper class more often than working class (sexualities and gender identities outside U.S. norms, by contrast, are strongly—even disproportionately—represented). These trends match similar problems in scholarship on U.S. death culture, and the sense in which death's naively touted universality usually comes back to the deathbed of this dominant version of the Everyman.

In fact, there are notable divergences based on identity in how individuals are likely to meet their inevitable ends. An African American male in the United States, for example, is about two and a half times less likely to die from natural causes—the type of dying portrayed in deathbed documentaries—than a white female. While the likelihood of violent death for an African American male remains low overall, its threat looms culturally larger for some such individuals (as Oscar Grant's death, analyzed in chapter 4, illustrates) and may discourage them from identifying with "universal" deathbed scenes.[36] I note this example of divergence along racial lines as a reminder that U.S. death culture is not monolithic and that my own assertions about the imbalance between violent and natural death in U.S. media do not carry the same psychological consequences for all audiences.

A New Machine at the Deathbed: The Camera

The first significant deathbed documentary to be made in the United States is less guilty of the offenses mentioned here than most that would follow it. Michael Roemer's *Dying*—made on 16mm film (as discussed later) with support from the National Endowment for the Humanities and airing on PBS in 1976—strives to represent individualized dying through a representative range of U.S. citizens rather than one dying person. The filmmakers include footage of three terminal cancer patients in the Boston area, recorded over a period of five to six months each: Sally, a forty-six-year-old white woman; Bill, a thirty-three-year-old white man, married and with young children; and Reverend Bryant, a fifty-six-year-old African American grandfather.

Sally's segment comes first, showing the woman in her room at a medical institution.[37] Her head has been shaved, and she looks old beyond her years. She speaks directly to the filmmaker, reporting that she has a brain tumor, that there's nothing that can be done for it, and "All you have to do is wait." And wait she does through a death of a languid, slowly unfolding duration. That duration resonates with the present tense of the film's title, *Dying*, which underscores the idea of death as a process, not an event. Sally spends some time at this institution learning how to function in her somewhat debilitated body, joking with nurses and encouraging other patients, staring out the window as she listens to Beethoven. Then she moves home to the care of her elderly mother, where she spends quiet days watching her mother bake and listening to music while her mother knits. As these days of waiting stretch on, Roemer accelerates time with shorter and shorter chunks of Sally's life as death seems to approach. In these scenes she moves from sitting in a wheelchair drying dishes to sitting and being fed by her mother to lying in bed, seemingly unable to speak. The passage of time is signified through Sally's body in two poignantly opposed progressions: her hair grows longer, and her motor functions shut down. Though Roemer's editing seems to propel us in an orderly and measured way toward Sally's death, its "moment" is not shown in the film and does not arrive in the time frame we expect. On-screen text informs us that Sally became comatose late in 1974 and died on June 24, 1975—*two years* after her initial hospitalization and at least six months after the last footage of her that Roemer includes.

The next segment, titled "Harriet and Bill," begins with uncertainty as the title couple is shown in the waiting room of a doctor's office, speaking with each other tensely. Harriet is visibly upset, but the next shot of Bill on an exam table lets the audience know that he is the one dying. The segment follows Bill and Harriet through their family routines: taking their young sons to the lake, having family meals, and going to medical appointments. Because the two are featured as a couple, one might expect this segment to center emotionally on death severing the bonds of romantic love. But that nineteenth-century model of dying is nowhere in evidence. Seemingly an even *older* lens for viewing death is in place, as Harriet reacts to Bill's demise less as an emotional blow than as a disruption of social and economic life. She tells Bill's doctor, "I would rather be left now, and then I would have a chance to maybe get them another father or something," and she confesses, "I prayed that that chemotherapy wouldn't work . . . if he's gotta go, why can't it just be quick and get it over with?"[38] The duration of twentieth-century dying that bothers Harriet features prominently—as it did in Sally's segment—and once again the camera leaves well before death, with only on-screen text telling us its date. The last shot of Bill evokes fiction film's model of "healthy dying": appearing physically well, he reclines on a lawn chair in his yard, staring into the distance and ignoring Harriet.

Dying's final segment observes how Reverend Bryant, an African American grandfather and pastor of a Baptist church, copes with terminal liver cancer. Roemer's crew is with him when his doctor delivers the bad news. They record his momentary despair and his quick psychological recovery. Bolstered by religious faith, a loving family, and a deep sense of satisfaction about the life he has lived, Bryant speaks with Roemer about how he will proceed, knowing that he will die soon: "I don't think that Rockefeller could be as happy as I am. I'm the happiest man in the world. . . . The time I have on the topside of this earth, I'm going to try to live it out the happiest and the best that I know how." He decides to take a trip to the South with his family to see his childhood home and his parents' graves, preaches a sermon on dying, then takes to a deathbed set up at home with family life bustling nearby. The now-expected on-screen text informs the audience that Bryant died on January 23, 1975, but then the film proceeds with a long sequence shot at his funeral. As a choir sings and person after person walks past his open casket, affectionately touching his hands, Roemer ends *Dying* not with the title act but rather with mourning. This shift at the film's end implicitly reflects cultural variations in "the good death," taking up the greater emphasis placed on expressive mourning rituals in defining the "good" African American death—an emphasis often seen in media representations of such deaths, including Annie's elaborate funeral that closes *Imitation of Life*.

Made in the mid-1970s, *Dying* is historically situated not only in a decade of death's fierce "revival" but also in a period of transition for documentarians. In the United States, the style of direct cinema—enabled by smaller, lighter, and more versatile film and sound recording equipment—that felt so fresh in the 1960s was by that time experiencing significant revision and opposition (though many documentaries are still made in this style today). The documentary form was becoming invested in deeper explorations of its subjects' psychologies and biographies than the "fly on the wall" production mode could easily achieve. On one level, then, a turn away from the physical and toward the psychological manifested in both death culture and documentary filmmaking during the 1970s. The most common manifestation in the latter was a willingness to let subjects acknowledge and interact with the camera and crew, especially in the increased use of interviews.[39] Staying true to the basic observational mode that direct cinema exemplified, Roemer nevertheless felt free to defy the movement's dogma. Not restricting himself to natural light, he warmly lit some scenes artificially; rather than playing the "fly on the wall," he interviewed the dying to let them narrate their experiences directly (ideologically essential for a post–Kübler-Ross death culture that prioritizes speaking and listening to the dying). Interviews and warm lighting help Roemer frame most of the film's deaths as good ones, disassociated from the aesthetic sterility and emotional distance—reminiscent of "bad death" in the hospital—that a direct cinema style can evoke.

Though the style may still have felt too detached for some (Ariès critiques *Dying* for "reducing [death] to the state of an ordinary thing"), the film garnered gushing reviews from critics.[40] It provoked highly emotional responses, characterized by the reminiscences of Susan Kubany, an employee at WGBH, where *Dying* was produced: "I refused to allow anyone to watch 'Dying' alone. At last count, I had seen it 97 times, possibly more than any other person. Critics with whom I had had solely a professional relationship, sobbed in my arms at the end, close friends for having shared such an experience."[41] Though it has limited distribution today, *Dying* outlived its initial PBS run and its reels were made available for the era's popular thanatology college courses, accompanied by suggested discussion questions.[42]

Dying represents the entry of a new machine—the camera—at the death-bed, a site smothered by technology in the twentieth century. At that point, death's "revivalists"—especially in hospice and palliative care—were busily thinning the tangle of tubes, lines, and beeping instruments that surrounded the dying. They were reacting in part to a fear Kübler-Ross articulated: "We displace all our knowledge onto machines, since they are less close to us than the suffering face of another human being which would remind us once more of . . . our own mortality."[43] The documentary camera, though, is one machine that promises to reproduce and display the face of the dying rather than obscuring it—to carry its sign of "our own mortality" to wider audiences. But in another way, the camera is merely a stopgap in addressing this aspect of twentieth-century America's virulent death denial, for machines typically allow us to avoid two distinct aspects of the "suffering face" of a dying person: the face as sign, signifying death, but also the face as outlet for interactive communication. As Kübler-Ross emphasizes throughout *On Death and Dying*, there is an awkwardness and fear associated with actually *talking to* the dying—a fear that the camera indulges, letting us gaze as voyeurs at the "suffering face" without having to respond to it.

Regarding the documentary camera's aptitude for contributing to a nova ars moriendi, there are two types of impact this machine can have. First, it can be a tool for the dying to use in assembling their individualized good deaths. Second, it can transmit their death stories to the living in the imperative mode of the memento mori or the instructive mode of the *Ars moriendi*. For the dying, the camera provides listeners through the crew and the documentary audience that its presence implies—outlets serving the philosophy of "expressive death," whereby the patient must talk and be listened to in order to cope with the end of life (a sort of "talking cure" for the mortally incurable).[44] That function is apparent in *Dying* with Sally, who has plenty to say and not many loved ones to say it to; with Bryant, who relishes the chance to take stock of his life verbally; and with the soon-to-be-bereaved Harriet, who uses the camera on multiple occasions to confess her desire for Bill's death. More than just a counselor or confessor, though, the camera also supplies Sally, Bryant, and Bill with an additional layer of temporal structure in the long and amorphous process that so defines modern dying. Overlaying five or six months of a documentary's shooting schedule onto this process gives them appointments with people who are not doctors and a way to mark time other than through physical deterioration.

Reflecting on the production of *Time of Death*, executive producer Miggi Hood notes, "It turns out when you put a camera on someone who is dying, they keep going. It keeps them looking forward, it gives them a distraction from the inevitable."[45]

Further, the camera offers a sense of purpose to those who invite it to their deathbeds—a way to make a rote biological process *mean* something other than just "the end." A sense of lost purpose makes dying a demoralizing experience in a culture that places such value on productivity and individual accomplishment.[46] When Sally says of her brain tumor, "All you have to do is wait," her "have to do" takes on two meanings: waiting is the only task she is assigned, and waiting is all she has—the only opportunity now extended to her. The purpose Roemer's film gives Sally is especially clear, as she seems to want to be remembered as someone who died well. The camera gives Sally a compelling reason to strive for that experience, to discover and embody her own good death. At times, she overtly performs the role of the irrepressibly cheerful and fearless dying woman, hamming it up as she jokes with the nurses or shouts carefully pronounced encouragements to another patient. While direct cinema tried to guard against this potential "acting for the camera," Sally's behavior is framed more accurately by the principles of the related documentary movement, cinema verité. Verité documentarians use the camera not as direct cinema's invisible recorder but rather as a tool of provocation, helping authentic feelings and behavior to emerge that would otherwise remain hidden.[47] Even if Sally's positive attitude looks a bit artificial, Roemer thinks of the film as giving her a reason to nurture it and to find enjoyment in the last portion of her life. *Dying* promises that her actions will travel beyond a small circle of medical staff and family, benefiting others who will one day find themselves in her position.[48] As Combs elegantly writes of films in general, "The cinema wants to solve the basic problem of the loneliness of death, to mediate the event of someone's death so that it communicates to the outside world."[49] As Sally's case demonstrates, this project in documentary takes on a poignancy and an urgency it does not carry in fiction.

And what will the living—those for whom Sally performs—take from deathbed documentaries like *Dying*? How do these films contribute to the nova ars moriendi? At the most basic level, this initial documentary look at natural death seeks simply to make public what has been kept private in decades of cultural denial. In the memento mori mode, it offers an impetus to "think about death and dying occasionally . . . before we encounter it in our own life," as Kübler-Ross advises. The film also presents two potential examples of the good death through Sally and Bryant, reflecting on some of its common features in

1976: both appear to die at home rather than in a hospital (aligning with the fledgling hospice movement), both acknowledge that their lives are ending and strive to make their remaining time enjoyable and meaningful, and both rely on family members for support.

Though *Dying* may seem instructive through its models of the good death, the film—and all deathbed documentaries—must contend with a tension inherent in the post-1960s nova ars moriendi. If the good death is now the individualized death, then the very notion of an ars moriendi becomes obsolete; the dying can neither rely on shared rituals and norms nor pattern their own deaths directly on others they have seen unfold (either in life or through documentary film). As A. H. Hawkins articulates, "Perhaps one reason why dying seems so difficult today is that individuals are expected not only to confront their own death—in itself a task arduous enough—but also to *create* a death" in a process I have aligned with neoliberal ideology.[50] In this light, the good death we cannot replicate (Sally's, Bryant's) becomes perhaps less instructive than the bad death we can strive to avoid, included in *Dying*—I argue—through Harriet and Bill's segment. Bill dies a "bad death" by multiple twentieth-century standards. Unlike *Imitation's* Annie, he cannot master the timing of his exit. Harriet waits for him to die, anxious for it to proceed quickly, and the audience waits, as well, expecting to see his body start deteriorating. But Bill lingers in his illness and remains mostly healthy in appearance, resisting the "right" duration of dying for either his loved ones' desires or the conventions of death in cinema. And by the new "bad death" standards of his own era, Bill fails to achieve the kind of individualized death that affirms his unique spirit. In *Dying*, he reads as a nonperson—a blank surface on which both disease and the desires and anxieties of others (Harriet) inscribe themselves.

Roemer himself, who wrote about *Dying* as being designed to help the living get past their fear of death, does not regard it as instructional in the next step, in *how* to die well. His remarks echo the spirit of individualized dying that was strengthening in 1976: "You can't learn to die as though it were a skill. People die in the way they have lived. Death becomes the expression of everything you are, and you can bring to it only what you have brought to your life."[51] This quotation from Roemer, with its assertion that dying is "an expression of everything you are," mirrors the emphasis *Dying* places on different facets of its title experience: specifically, that dying is more fundamentally about psychology and selfhood than physiology. In line with the 1970s death culture that reacted against previous decades' tendency to focus on *only* the dying body, Roemer's film favors the mind, striving to represent "dying in full detail" on a psychological but not physical level. Without hiding the body, Roemer nevertheless de-emphasizes it, largely through timing. He excludes the "moment of death," the climax of bodily dying, and even footage shot *near* the "moment." Scenes that show the subjects in a state of heightened physical debilitation are few and markedly shorter than others—as if the story of dying is more or less told once the body's deterioration usurps psychological and spiritual reflection. Only at rare moments in the film is the dying body displayed *as* a dying body in any graphic way. The most notable comes a few minutes into Sally's segment when she happens to turn her shaved head to the side and exposes to the camera a sprawling, craterous indentation on her skull—presumably the site of a previous surgery on her tumor.

Instead of showcasing the dying body, Roemer prevents it from overshadowing the dying person—a challenging task in his chosen medium, which is so well suited to displaying the material world. Roemer's desired emphasis is most apparent in a gorgeous close-up he creates of Bryant in an interview, as he passionately distills the value of his life and how he will savor what remains of it. The tight shot's larger-than-life composition and warm lighting cinematically disconnect Bryant's broad smile and still-vibrant eyes from the rest of his withering body. Disorienting us from where we are in the timeline of Bryant's long process of dying, the shot grasps at time*less*ness. It enforces a focus on Bryant's words—his feelings about his wife, his assertion of happiness—which transcend the blunt statement his unseen body, with its marks of illness, would make.

While critical reception of *Dying* was overwhelmingly positive, Stefan Fleischer's harsh 1978 critique in *Film Quarterly* offers an important objection to the film's mind/body priorities. Noting the psychological orientation of Roemer's film, Fleischer protests, "But dying is not first of all a mental problem. The most brutal and the most inescapable fact about dying . . . consequently the fact most systematically repressed, is the nature of the physical process itself—pain, incapacity, and the withering away of flesh."[52] Fleischer supports his argument by selecting and disregarding parts of the film carefully, but the essay nevertheless exposes an interesting level of unrest in the fledgling death revival culture. Though the cultural context of *Dying* seems to align it smoothly with the rebellion against the body-obsessed, hypermedicalized death culture of the mid-twentieth century, Fleischer's critique reveals an emerging backlash. He expresses a feeling that the pendulum had swung too far in the other direction, from obsession with the body to obsession with the mind. Moving into the 1980s and 1990s, with the dual influence of the AIDS crisis and the wide adoption of video and DV, deathbed documentaries would return to the body of the dying.

"Death 24x a Second," Death 30x a Second:
How Film and Video Record Death Differently

Before examining subsequent deathbed documentaries on video, it is helpful to consider the fact that *Dying* was shot on film and to ask how these media each enable certain kinds of documentary work on death.[53] Though it changed production conditions more in degree than in kind, video has made a new relationship possible between death and the moving image. In the case of natural death, there are four main areas in which shooting death on video or DV instead of celluloid matters: cost, durational capacities, crew requirements, and aesthetics.

With a videotape (and its later DV variations) costing a small fraction of the equivalent reels of film stock, the former's adoption by documentarians brought the price of projects down considerably. In this mode of filmmaking that has rarely attracted big budgets and box office returns, that change made a dramatic impact on the types of topics and approaches documentarians could pursue. The consequences of this price difference between film and video are plainly articulated by Ross McElwee, another documentarian experimenting with new forms and subjects during a period of technological transition. Of his meandering, autobiographical documentary *Sherman's March* (1986), he writes: "I shot perhaps twenty-five hours of film [over five months]. I did not have a very big budget and had to marshal my film stock carefully. I sometimes wonder how much more footage I would have shot if I had been shooting video."[54]

The cost of film stock or videotape is an issue of particular importance for deathbed documentaries because of the length of the dying process. Illustrating this temporal challenge, for one episode *Time of Death* uses an automated DV camera mounted on a tripod to record its dying subject, Cheyenne, deteriorate at a glacial pace over the course of a whole night. Temporal markers flash on the screen during this sequence as Cheyenne's girlfriend comes in and out of the room—10:18 P.M., 1:05 A.M., 3:32 A.M., 6:34 A.M.—and its time-lapse editing conveys just how long it can take for this last phase of the dying process to conclude. With Cheyenne's "time of death" announced on-screen as 6:36 A.M., this sequence alone required more than eight hours of continuous recording. To chronicle death thoroughly, then—and to do so for multiple dying individuals, as *Time of Death*, *Dying*, and others do—requires a significant commitment of time and footage.

Further, this topic remains a hard sell, even among documentary enthusiasts. Writing favorably about *Dying*, Michael Kearl laments, "Such shows, however, are rare. The emotions and fears they evoke are too great, their exhibition too 'real' for the comfort of their escapist viewers, to garner the viewer ratings required to subsidize their production."[55] In his attack on *Dying*, even Fleischer acknowledges that if Roemer had tried to make "an ugly film" conveying the ugliness of death as a physical process, it may never have aired on PBS or been funded at all.[56] *Dying* carried a sizable $330,000 price tag (about $1.3 million in 2013, adjusting for inflation) but was made under the auspices of WGBH and the National Endowment for the Humanities. The very few deathbed documentaries shot exclusively on celluloid share this type of pedigreed patronage—most notably, well-established documentarian Frederick Wiseman's *Near Death* (1989).[57]

It is economically unsurprising, then, that a concentration of deathbed documentary production in the United States did not appear until advances in video and DV technology in the 1980s and 1990s combined with the cultural forces discussed earlier. At that point, microbudget projects became possible—usually arising out of the wish to document one specific person's death rather than beginning as an idea for a documentary that then found dying patients to record (as *Dying* and *Near Death* began). Examples include *Sick: The Life and Death of Bob Flanagan, Supermasochist* (1997, Kirby Dick) and *Southern Comfort* (2001, Kate Davis), in which filmmakers were drawn to the stories of two fascinating individuals who were dying. *The Andre Show* (1998, Beverly Peterson) and *Death: A Love Story* (1999, Michelle LeBrun) were prompted by deaths within filmmakers' own families: of an adopted HIV-positive son and a husband, respectively. And *Silverlake Life* features a filmmaker turning his camera on his own slow dying. Davis emphasizes how crucial affordable video equipment and tapes have been to this kind of documentary work: "*Southern Comfort* is an example of finding a story and just going and taking a small camera and doing it. I had no support when I started, no funders were interested. . . . But with a DV camera, one can shoot a film for virtually nothing."[58]

Though video's capacity to shoot for long periods at a stretch is more essential to chapter 3's central documentary, *The Bridge*, it also plays a role in deathbed documentaries. The expanding duration of dying as a process recommends a recording device that can be patient—able to sit and wait with the dying, unsure of when important moments in this process will occur and how they will signal themselves. An anecdote mentioned by David Kerekes and David Slater in their study of cult films, *Killing for Culture*, helps illustrate this point. Describing a documentary called *On the Bridge* (1992, Frank Perry) about the director's battle with cancer, they explain, "Perry talks of how he toyed with the idea of filming his own death, pressing the trigger of the film camera when he felt himself slipping away. This because the film magazine would only be 10 minutes duration."[59]

In addition to (and in aid of) reducing costs, video reduces the necessity of having a crew of trained operators to create a death documentary. In each of his visits to Sally, Bill, and Bryant, Michael Roemer had to bring a three-person crew to handle the camera, sound, and lighting equipment.[60] Video shooting allows for less intrusive, more intimate encounters at the deathbed in later productions. Peterson and LeBrun are able to be alone with just their dying loved ones and a camera, and easy-to-use DV cameras make that possible for nonprofessionals, too, in Kirby Dick's *The End* (2004) and *Time of Death*. Dick follows the final months of five hospice patients partly through professionally shot footage and partly through footage the dying and their families record on cameras he lends them; *Time of Death* similarly lends out cameras to participants and mounts them on car dashboards, unstaffed, for capturing private conversations while subjects drive together. Also taking advantage of user-friendly cameras, *Silverlake Life* and *The Andre Show* include video diary segments shot by the dying themselves, alone with just the camera. Even a debilitated AIDS patient and a young child, in these films, have the minimal strength and knowledge, respectively, required to videotape themselves. Video cameras thus allow for the kinds of stories (over stages) Larry Churchill calls for: stories told directly by the dying.[61]

With all the practical advantages video and DV provide for death documentarians, there is one outcome of this technological transition that is more ambiguous: the changed aesthetic qualities of a video image, compared with a celluloid image. This contrast is starkly apparent in Wim Wenders and Nicholas Ray's death documentary, *Lightning over Water* (1980), which was shot on both 35mm film and Betacam videotape. As the image switches back and forth from film to video (a fairly early, low-definition type), the audience must readjust over and over to the soft, undersaturated video with its lines of interference or discoloration. Comparatively, the film stock looks crisp and rich. The contrast resonates with the dying Nicholas Ray's declining health, his body a shriveling remainder of the strong form it used to hold.

The contrast within *Lightning* is echoed in a comparison of *Dying* to a later DV film like *The End*. The color 16mm image in *Dying* is vibrant, sometimes even breathtaking, as when warm evening sunlight washes over Bryant and his family as they look for his parents' graves in a southern cemetery. Its quality matches Roemer's positive tone perfectly, emphasizing the vibrancy of Sally or Bryant even in the face of their deaths. *The End*, by comparison, displays the dying with a marked flatness and colors that appear washed out—visual qualities we associate with low-budget DV but also with the space of the hospital and its sterile, clinical feeling. Even in segments that strive for a positive tone, it is hard to overcome the mood created by our aesthetic confinement in drably presented deathbed interiors.[62]

The Return of the Body, and of Spectacle, in *Sick* and *Silverlake Life*

Ontologically, theorists typically associate film with materiality and embodiment, video with immateriality and disembodiment. While these distinctions are technical and not intended to comment on the objects that film and video display on screens, it feels significant, nevertheless, that supposedly immaterial video would be the medium to expose the materiality of dying. That exposure happens most dramatically in the 1990s with *Silverlake Life* (analog) and *Sick* (digital), documentaries that function as a corrective to Roemer's pioneering celluloid film *Dying*, with its absence of bodily scrutiny. Video is the medium that accomplishes this task for two main reasons. First, as discussed earlier, it provided a means for doing low-budget documentary work on difficult subjects that might not attract institutional funding—like dying, especially when the grim decline of the body is a focus. Second, its rise as a viable tool of documentary production coincided with a period of increased discourse on dying bodies in the United States, due to the developing "revival of death" and especially to the massive memento mori the AIDS crisis represented for some Americans. *Silverlake Life* and *Sick* do restore the physicality of death to a place of prominence, but they retain the whole-person orientation of Kübler-Ross. Further, by focusing on dying people with nonnormative sexualities and idiosyncratic ways of coping with mortality, they exemplify the post-1960s exaltation of the individualized death—perhaps at the expense of contributing to a nova ars moriendi or reminding the audience of their own inevitable demises.

Kirby Dick's documentary *Sick* (1997), about his dying friend, is the more explicit of these two in its exposure of the dying body, even though the disease that afflicts Bob Flanagan is mostly invisible to the camera. Cystic fibrosis (CF) is a genetic disease that continually fills the lungs with mucus, causing difficult breathing, coughing fits, and a severely truncated life span. It leaves no external marks, like the visible lesions that HIV would dot across the bodies of *Silverlake Life*'s subjects—an invisibility that frustrates Bob, who has to cope constantly with the hidden physicality of his illness. In response, he customizes a "visible man" model (clear, plastic miniatures used to show the normative work of internal organs) to reveal the way his own body works, mixing concoctions to represent mucus, feces, and semen and rigging the model to dribble these out of its respective orifices. Parallel to Bob's individualized visible man model, *Sick* is structured around a creative strategy of visualizing its dying subject's internal pain, circuitously representing it through the external pain of Bob's s/m sexual practices. With a CF death sentence hanging over him since childhood, Bob learned to cope with the pain he could not control through pain he could master as a sexual submissive—a sort of makeshift, eccentric palliative care. Together with his dom partner, Sheree, Bob turns this interaction between CF and s/m into installation and performance art, displaying his consensually battered body for audiences at both s/m clubs and high art galleries, and for Dick's documentary camera.

Bob's end is foreshadowed after his forty-second birthday and a big solo gallery show in New York, when Sheree shoots a video of him in which he is depressed and refusing a birthday spanking. In another intimate, late-night video from some months later, an upset Bob asserts to Sheree that he is now feeling too sick to submit to her—sexually or even mentally. Soon Bob checks himself back in to the hospital for what turns out to be the last time. Dick and his camera follow, in accordance with Bob's condition of participation in this documentary: that Dick would have to continue the project through Bob's death.[63] The progression toward that "moment," though, is unpredictable, as we see Sheree and nurses tending to Bob in a coma, and then a later time when he has regained consciousness. He tells Sheree he loves her and then wonders aloud, "Am I dying? . . . What is going on? This is the weirdest damn thing . . . the stupidest . . . I don't understand it." A subsequent scene of Sheree comforting a spastically breathing but otherwise unresponsive Bob seems to be leading into impending "moment of death" footage, but the image cuts out as we hear the click of a manual slide projector.

Instead, *Sick* returns to the previous century's popular form of the postmortem photograph with a montage of images Sheree took of Bob's corpse in the hospital, accompanied by the slide projector sounds. We see his body lying in the hospital bed—eyes closed, mouth open—as medical staff check him with a stethoscope. They move him onto a gurney, and his naked body is taken to a new hospital location where Sheree photographs close-ups of his face, chest, and genitals (arranging his hands to touch them). The recourse to still images once Bob's body has stilled concludes the film's saga of embodiment rather poetically. Further, the close-ups of his tattooed and pierced genitals and "S" scar (where Sheree once carved her initial into his chest) reassert Bob's individualism. Even as a corpse, absent of personhood and lying in a sterile environment, Bob—the film asserts—carries his uniqueness beyond the boundary of death.

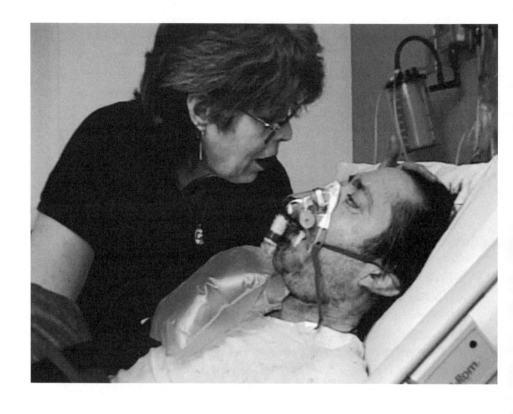

2.2. Bob dying in the hospital (*Sick*, 1997, Kirby Dick, Lionsgate).

Blending a slow process of dying from disease with the prolonged and pleasurable pains of s/m—and doing so in public, through sexually explicit art—certainly qualifies as the unique, post-1960s "death of one's own." By playing Bob's sexual pain and CF pain off each other in *Sick*, Kirby Dick solves the central aesthetic problem of the deathbed documentary, reinvigorating it with the visual spectacle of painful bodily destruction that violent death provides and natural death does not. We do not see bullets piercing flesh or fatal wounds bleeding, as the works in chapter 1 feature, but rather needles piercing Bob's penis, weights suspended from his genitals, letters carved into his chest, objects pushed into his anus, and so on.

Although "moment of death" footage is once again absent, Dick offers two substitutes for this missing piece of Bob's story. The first is a discussion of Bob's *Wall of Pain* art piece. Sheree and Bob had set up a camera with which he took a picture of his own face at each instant that she struck him with a paddle, flogger, whip, crop, and so forth. The resulting large photo collage that displays all these faces shows the same concern for temporal exactness as chapter 1's photographs that pursue the "moment" of violent death, providing a substitute locus of moment-ness in relation to the body within *Sick*. The second substitute is a scene that begins, without an establishing shot, on an extreme close-up of Bob's penis resting on a wooden board. Bob's hands quickly enter the claustrophobic frame holding a nail, which he drives into the head of his penis with a hammer, anchoring it to the board. Shortly, he pries the nail out with the hammer, and *Sick* cuts to an elaborate low-angle shot through which Bob's profusely bleeding penis drips blood onto a clear barrier above the camera. A song called "Hammer of Love" strives to maintain Bob's irreverent, gallows-humor spirit during this challenging scene. The violent penetration of Bob's penis marks the peak of his endurance, the most squirm-inducing performance of suffering the film can display. Thus, while the expected climax of the death story in *Sick* (Bob's "moment of death") is omitted, I argue that a spectacular climax for his sex story is showcased in its place—not temporally in the film's timeline but structurally in its visual and emotional progression.

Silverlake Life, though it does engage in pointed forms of bodily display, does not strive for these heights of spectacle, focusing more on the quieter moments of the dying process—on making newly public its private daily texture. As noted previously, *Silverlake Life* chronicles the life and illness of HIV-positive partners Tom Joslin and Mark Massi. Finding a purpose in the time he has left, Tom becomes determined to make this documentary—carried on after his death in 1990 by Mark (who dies in 1991) and by Tom's former student, codirector Peter Friedman. Where Roemer asserted that his dying subjects "directed the film and gave it its direction," that dynamic is literal in *Silverlake Life* with its dying director.[64] Tom and Mark shoot most of the footage themselves, capturing intimate moments at home, trips to doctors' offices and alternative therapies, arduous errands, two vacations, and visits from friends and family. The variety of events and moods that *Silverlake Life* covers emphasizes the duration of Tom's dying, as do the film's lapses in linearity. Peggy Phelan describes its distinctive temporality as follows: "Dying is not in the future; death is not in the past. Dying is. And this is a film that shows us how long that 'is' is, how many shapes and colors and emotions live and die in it."[65]

At many points in the film, Tom, Mark, or their doctors examine their deteriorating bodies, and the camera does, too, offering clear shots of Mark's back covered with Kaposi's sarcoma lesions or the lesion that grows over Tom's eyelid, sealing it shut. Eventually, Tom's health worsens to the point that he begins receiving hospice care at home—a moment he denotes as starting a grim countdown to death, based on what he says is the average survival time after the start of hospice care (two months). Mark continues recording footage, and for a while Tom is able to keep up his diary-cam entries. Then after we have seen Tom lose all his energy and most of his ability to speak, *Silverlake* cuts abruptly to a shot of his corpse lying in their bed, with Mark informing us that he just died. The documentary lingers with Mark for a while, recording Tom's funeral and some of Mark's grieving. When he receives Tom's ashes (taping the experience with a tripod-mounted camera), the body asserts its materiality one more time: Mark cuts himself while opening the delivery box and then must handle and contain the ashes that spill from a punctured bag.

A sense of political urgency suffuses *Silverlake Life*—a passionate desire to showcase the love between Tom and Mark *and* the lesions that ravage their bodies and signify their coming separation. That urgency emerges from this particular death's integration into the larger casualty list of the AIDS crisis, whose sufferers struggled for support and visibility—but also sought to determine what kinds of visibility would be helpful or harmful to their cause. Activists, artists, and the mainstream media all especially struggled with how to visually represent bodies—like Tom's and Mark's—infected by the disease. Initially, it seemed crucial to display these bodies and raise awareness about AIDS and its physical devastation—a task the mainstream media often avoided. Photojournalist Don McCullin explains part of this resistance: "In terms of photojournalism, the AIDS issue has an enormous problem. It has to appear in print. Yet it's so visually unkind to the eye. It infringes upon the comforts of magazines themselves because it's difficult for the business side to run advertising up against."[66] As the AIDS crisis progressed and its bodies gained visibility, some activists saw a shift in problems of representation, from the invisibility to the exploitation of dying bodies, put on display with little attention paid to the individuals inhabiting them. Protesters outside a 1988 MOMA show of AIDS photography, for example, expressed this frustration through flyers reading, "No More Pictures without Context" and "Stop Looking at Us; Start Listening to Us."[67] Part of Silverlake Life's success, as a film and as a piece of activism, stems from its lesions *and* love approach, from its union of two distinct representational needs during the AIDS crisis: bodies to look at and individuals to listen to. The documentary made public politically volatile sights that had been private, and it did so on two levels: it unfolded on camera the process of an actual natural death (of a highly political type), and it openly displayed love and physical affection between gay men during an era of virulent homophobia.

In the 1980s, the AIDS crisis interrupted the simplified narrative of death in the twentieth century where lives end later, less frequently, and out of public view. The disease brought a return, for some, to the culture of the nineteenth-century epidemic: people were infecting each other and dying on a massive scale. The U.S. public perceived that death was mostly befalling gay men, and while that group was not fully integrated into or accepted by mainstream culture, it was vocal and creative, making its plight known through activism and art. In addition, AIDS challenged the narrative of twentieth-century death by refuting the idea that traditional support systems for the dying had disappeared. As Walter generalizes, dying becomes unmoored in the twentieth century because "community and religion, the two underlying supports of habitual ways of dying and grieving, are in long-term decline."[68] Yet for men like Tom and Mark dying of AIDS, the queer community and the active networks of support it provided were essential. This discrepancy again reveals the bias toward hetero, white, middle-class dying in much scholarship on the subject, which does not seem to count thriving sexual and ethnic communities when assessing the decline of community in the twentieth-century United States. Multipronged strategies for getting the public's attention and sympathy during the crisis emerged from that queer community: activists exposed the scale of the problem through projects like the AIDS quilt, but they also sought to humanize individual victims. This latter approach demanded death stories, and especially highly individualized, autobiographical death stories like Silverlake Life that would distinguish one dying gay man from all the others, making one death "in full detail" matter where abstract thousands might fail to make an impact.

Such a project would have seemed more possible in the early 1990s than a few decades prior because documentary began to yield significant autobiographical work only in the 1970s—at roughly the same time that U.S. death culture began to valorize the individualized death as the good death. Both death culture and documentary in this era were reacting against the sterile, scientific discourses that dominated them: body-focused hospital dying and the objectivity-obsessed direct cinema movement, respectively. Fueled by the influence of American avant-garde filmmaking, second-wave feminism's principle that "the personal is political," and a general inward turn in 1970s American culture, documentarians began to point their cameras at themselves.[69] Joslin himself was part of this trend early on with a documentary about his coming-out process, *Black Star: Autobiography of a Close Friend* (1977), clips of which are shown in *Silverlake Life*. In between his production of *Black Star* and the posthumous release of *Silverlake Life*, an abundance of intriguing autobiographical documentaries had appeared, from filmmakers such as Michelle Citron, Ross McElwee, Su Friedrich, Marlon Riggs, and Sadie Benning. And *Lightning over Water* had pioneered the combination of real death and (partly) autobiographical filmmaking.

By using the machine that has most defined his life, the camera, as a tool in his dying, Tom revives the deathbed customs of previous centuries, in revised forms. Both Ariès and Kübler-Ross trace histories in which the crowd that used to gather at the deathbed suddenly dissipates in the early twentieth century, leaving the dying increasingly alone. They see this dissipation as a problem for two reasons: it deprives the dying of companionship and support, and it prevents the living from witnessing death. With his camera, Tom repopulates his deathbed with virtual witnesses.[70] This act clearly helps alleviate the second part of the preceding problem by exposing audiences to a condensed and mediated version of a dying process. Though these witnesses are temporally and spatially separated from Tom's actual deathbed, the thought of their eventual presence—elsewhere and elsewhen—seems to give Tom strength as he dies, the sense of purpose emphasized in post-1960s death culture that can soothe the pain of endings.

Tom and the other filmmakers who document death also reconnect the process of dying with a nineteenth-century process of grieving: the meticulous production of artworks and craftworks to aid in mourning. These included lockets and frames to hold photographs, as well as elaborate patterns woven from the hair of the dead. Mostly made by women, the primary guardians of memory in that era, such works lingered over the bodies of the departed (directly, through hair, or symbolically through photographs) to cope with their loss.[71] Of these activities, Geoffrey Batchen writes, "No doubt the time spent in crafting such things was part of the period of mourning, a time of contemplation and creative activity that helped to heal the bereft as well as memorialize the dead."[72] Work to make these mementos contributed to a gradual process of *working through*. Those customs and their functions are revived and revised in films like *Silverlake Life, Death: A Love Story*, and *The Andre Show* as loved ones process a death by documenting it—aided by the demanding work of shooting, editing, and distributing. Batchen points out that the duration of labor these crafts required supported the grief function, too: "The labor of embroidery ensures that the act of remembrance would be painstaking, extended through time, deliberated."[73] The process of filmmaking, like the process of dying, is long and multifaceted, allowing this channeling of grief to unfold and evolve over time. In the case of *Silverlake Life*, the healing labor is shared by the dying, put to use by Tom in coping with his own death and by Mark and Peter in grieving for it.

That this labor is done on video rather than film is again significant, and not just in terms of production costs—though the boxes of cassettes that Peter Friedman assesses with his camera, containing Tom's forty hours of footage, make clear the project's economic unfeasibility on celluloid for a filmmaker of limited means. Shot in the late 1980s and 1990 and then released in 1993, *Silverlake Life* is the first deathbed documentary of the home video era, when the American public had affordable access to home video cameras for their own shooting and VCRs for home viewing. Made mostly in the home for an audience who might view it at home (as some did on PBS even before its VHS or DVD releases), *Silverlake Life* exudes the intimacy of home video combined with a professional filmmaker's aesthetic sense and structural intentions. One of the powers of the video camera Tom and Mark exploit is its mobility. With it, a very ill man can still function as a full crew, shooting image and sound with a single, affordable machine, as we see in *Silverlake Life*'s first-person camera sequences. Tom, for example, shoots what he sees as he walks into a store to complete an errand—capturing the exterior, the aisles, and his frustrating effort to pry one plastic tub from a stiff stack of them. The audience's oppressive and disorienting confinement to point-of-view shots in this sequence underscores the pain of confinement in a dying body—another strategy *Silverlake Life* employs for helping its audience access the internal, invisible experiences of dying. The location of the body is emphasized as a confusing and unpleasant place, for the audience in terms of spatial disorientation and for Tom in terms of suffering and progressive debilitation.

Elsewhere, it is the immediacy of video rather than its mobility that becomes important. Some of the footage used in *Silverlake Life* is shot off of a television monitor rather than just edited into the film. That extra level of mediation indicates a deliberate emphasis on the act of viewing, on the everyday primacy of spectatorship. And because video is the medium, image creation and image spectatorship can happen simultaneously. This point is made when Tom and Mark set up a camera, point it at themselves lying in bed, and run it directly through a monitor. We see them looking offscreen at the very same image of themselves that we are seeing, but they are watching it as they create it. The content of the clip is mundane, with the two of them talking about filming themselves, arranging the composition, examining marks their disease has made on their faces, and making funny hand motions to simulate trees. The fact that the content is so understated stresses that the real importance of this clip is not what we see but how we are seeing it, how it is constructed, and the comment it makes on the role of media in our lives. We are seeing the moving image directly realize its dual function as window and mirror, with the instantaneity of video providing for the latter possibility. Michael Renov perceptively makes this point: "Durable, lightweight, mobile, producing instantaneous results, the video apparatus supplies a dual capability. . . . it is both screen and mirror, providing the technological grounds for the surveillance of the palpable world, as well as a reflective surface on which to register the self."[74] *Silverlake Life* carries this dual function through on a large scale, as discussed earlier, providing an informative window on death for the living and a therapeutic mirror of death for the dying individual.

Here, media and life are intertwined, as video is a tool that both records life and shapes it. As we have seen, both aspects are essential to the camera's role in Tom's death, where it both documents and helps him cope with his dying, molding it into a meaningful and individualized process. The interplay between creation and spectatorship in *Silverlake Life* challenges typical power dynamics between moving image producers and consumers. In the early years of an age when nonprofessionals could increasingly cross that line from consumer to producer using video technology, *Silverlake Life* models how to do so—and why to do so. Media producers in Hollywood told Mark that he could close the eyes on a corpse and they would stay shut, as discussed earlier. But Mark has the power to make media, too, and he can use it to announce that Hollywood is lying—about this aspect of death and so many others.

The extent to which *Silverlake Life* could only have existed in its current form on video is demonstrated in the shots of most immediate proximity to the absent "moment of death." The film cuts from Tom in a severely depleted state on his deathbed to Tom's corpse—still lying in bed but with his glasses removed, a sign of an end to his spectatorship and subjectivity. Here, the audience bears witness to an outpouring of grief from Mark, who has been attending to Tom and is also running the camera. Mark records but also speaks, in a quavering voice interrupted by sobs: "[*Moan*] This is the first of July, and Tommy's just died. [*Inaudible*] when he died, and I sang to him. I sang to him, [*singing*] 'You are my sunshine, my only sunshine, you make me happy when skies are gray. You'll never know dear how much I love you, please don't take my sunshine away.' Isn't he beautiful? He's so beautiful. I love you, Tommy. All of us—all of your friends will finish the tape for you, okay? We promise. We promise. Bye! Bye, Tom!"

This scene, full of raw emotion that both draws us in and shakes our resolve to keep watching, illustrates a tension between the dual role people play as documentarians and mourners in such intimate documentaries of natural death. Despite the irrepressible emotion in his voice, Mark begins with a faint attempt at objective reporting. He gives us the facts—"This is the first of July, and Tommy's just died"—but uses a fond nickname for his subject/partner. Mark maintains a third-person report of events for a short while, but after reenacting the way he sang to Tom, he slips back into direct address, speaking directly to the corpse's object as if it were still the beloved subject. The handheld camera—which Mark has operated elsewhere in the film with professional steadiness—shakes uncontrollably, seeming to respond to the tragic stillness of Tom's body with compensatory, frenetic motion. The cause, of course, is Mark's sobbing, as *Silverlake Life* fulfills Sobchack's call for documentary to register its response to death visibly, to offer "signs of the filmmaker's situation and stance" through cinematography.[75]

Silverlake Life builds grief into its very bones, manifesting it not just in what we see but also in how we see it through Mark's fragile point of view. In this scene, the one-man camera crew is himself openly grieving for the subject of his documentary that is also the object of his affection—emoting in a way that a film crew's presence would likely inhibit, and recording in a way a filmmaker from outside the circle of loved ones (like Roemer) never could. The scene also marks an immediate transference of subjectivity within *Silverlake* from the dying person to the closest mourner, once that person becomes a corpse. *Sick* employs the same strategy, when Bob's dying moments are immediately followed by Sheree's intimate photographs of his dead body. This shift of perspective within deathbed documentaries deviates sharply from the conventions of violent death documentary footage—Abraham Zapruder's in Dallas, for example, or Vo Suu's in Saigon—where the perspective of the cameraperson is almost always generic.

Despite the tension between Mark-as-documentarian and Mark-as-partner, *Silverlake Life* itself and the act of documenting at this moment interject a promise for the future into this scene of parting with the past. Mark promises Tom

2.3. Tom before his death (*Silverlake Life*, 1993,
Tom Joslin and Peter Friedman, New Video Group).

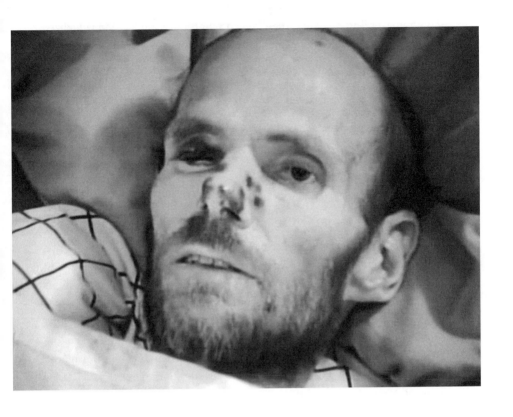

2.4. Tom right after his death (*Silverlake Life*, 1993, Tom Joslin and Peter Friedman, New Video Group).

that he and Tom's friends will "finish the tape for you," fulfilling the meaning-making function the camera brings to Tom's death. The camera helped define the filmmaker Tom's life and then helped him forge a unique, individualized death. Both his life and his death will now be preserved—for a time, at least—on video.

Silverlake Life thematizes the act of preservation it is performing through two moments that begin and end the work. The first comes in the opening moments, situated after Tom's death, just before Mark's comments about trying to close Tom's eye. Mark naps on his couch, and the camera pans right, revealing a monitor on which a videotape from Tom plays. The screen shows what we later learn is the first footage Tom shot for *Silverlake Life*: a close-up of himself with a medium-specific electronic matte laid over it, framing his face in a heart shape with the words "Mark, I love you" written alongside it. Thus, even within *Silverlake Life*, we see footage shot for the project already serving one of its main functions: preserving a trace of Tom to comfort Mark and others after he dies. This function is performed even more poignantly in the final scene, when Tom has (again) died and Mark has just been interviewed about sensing his presence in the apartment. The film closes with a musical number from *Black Star* in which Tom and Mark—younger by more than ten years—do a lightly choreographed dance to the doo-wop song "I Met Him on a Sunday," ending arm in arm looking at the camera. This scratched and dated celluloid, displayed through a full-length video feature, enacts a restoration to health and life for Tom and Mark—both dead at the time of *Silverlake Life*'s release.

These two scenes in which moving images resurrect the dead in *Silverlake Life* reveal the most important way in which video aligns with, rather than diverges from, its technological predecessor, film: it preserves. Video, too, derives from the "mummy complex" that Bazin saw in the roots of the plastic arts.[76] For most who have experienced loss, it matters little how a moving image returns their dear departed—through an indexical process or not, if they are even aware of that difference. It matters only that a camera has "secure[d] the shadow," allowing a partial return across the border between death and life.[77]

Conclusion: Individualism Guards against Identification

In *Sick* and *Silverlake Life*, we see the cultural pendulum recenter—back from the one extreme of body-fixated hospital dying in the mid-twentieth century and the other extreme of overwhelmingly psychological discourse about dying in the post–Kübler-Ross 1970s (including *Dying*). Exploring both physical and emotional aspects of natural death in a documentary mode, these films also exemplify the revised good death, the "death of one's own." Highly individualized stories about dying, they focus on men outside the sexual mainstream finding novel ways to cope—through documentary production or the controlled pain of s/m—with dying slowly at a relatively young age. A notable portion of the small subgenre of American deathbed documentaries share this penchant for eccentric end-of-life stories: *Lightning over Water*, with its celebrity death of director Nicholas Ray; *The Andre Show*, in which the dying party is a young HIV-positive boy who has been adopted by a filmmaker; and *Southern Comfort*, which features a trans man dying of ovarian cancer in rural Georgia.

But in aligning so well with the neoliberal individualization of the new good death, these films sacrifice much of their memento mori potential. The memento mori cautions, "remember you will die," but neither Bob Flanagan nor Tom Joslin dies a widely relatable death. "You" may not feel implicated by seeing two men in their forties waste away from CF and AIDS—diseases that are genetic (and detectable from childhood) or preventable (because many rationalize that they will not catch those). This disassociation appears in the audience responses to *Silverlake Life* that PBS received after the broadcast. From these, it seems that the film prompted viewers to identify with the experience of witnessing a loved one's death rather than imagining their own deaths: the dying Tom reminded some viewers of their own deceased relatives and of the process of watching them die.[78]

Lack of direct identification with the dying also crops up around the edges of *Sick*. Its DVD includes a documentary short, *Sarah's Sick Too*, which profiles a young fan of Bob's with CF. Her visit with him is documented in *Sick*, and the subsequent short updates viewers on her life since the film's release. Born of the disease they share, Sarah's identification with Bob is apparent in both the film and the short, especially when she tapes herself rewatching Bob's death scene from *Sick* at home on VHS. Turning away in tears before it ends, she remarks, "It's really hard to go through life knowing how you're going to die. It's even harder to see it." Her own painful ability to translate this past death preserved on video into her own future death is opposed by the implicit inability that she describes of other viewers to do the same: "Most of the people who have seen this film that I've talked to say that the hardest thing to watch was when Bob nails the head of his dick to a board. And everybody who says that, I always ask them if they really watched the whole movie and did they see the ending. Because I would think that the hardest thing to watch would be him dying." While the highly visible spectacle of genital impalement connects with viewers painfully, the internal and emotional pain of Bob's death does not make their own flesh twinge to the same degree.

As a number of psychological studies have shown, Americans asked to imagine others' deaths and their own deaths offer more realistic descriptions of the former and more idealized descriptions of the latter. This blind spot about one's own death affects even medical professionals who have regular contact with the dying.[79] Viewers of *Sick*, *Silverlake Life*, and the other documentaries about unique natural deaths may thus mourn their subjects at a comfortable distance, sympathizing without identifying. A refusal to frame dying as a generalizable experience is both the strength and the liability of these documentaries in their usefulness to documentary's efforts to make death visible.

In her brief consideration of deathbed documentaries in "Inscribing Ethical Space," Sobchack describes them as "unblinkingly record[ing] the subject's death."[80] As demonstrated earlier, however, the camera's eye *does* blink in these sagas, and always at the same point. Its blink effaces the "moment of death" in *Dying*, *Sick*, and *Silverlake Life* and in every U.S. deathbed documentary I have studied, keeping the focus on the process of dying and avoiding the false sense of climax that such a moment could present. The "moment of death," however, is not just absent because it might steal the show or even because it is so difficult to identify and isolate. It is absent because that recorded sight's "full detail" would likely deflate the idea of death as heroically individualized. Roemer's idealistic belief that "people die in the way they have lived [and] death becomes the expression of everything you are" cracks and breaks apart if brought too close to the biological end of life—the phase in which hospice professionals refer to a patient as, finally, "actively dying." By that time—in an age of modern medicine, with its strong painkillers and sedations—the last vestiges of unique personhood have usually evaporated from the dying body. For the duration of "active dying," the dying party sinks into a state reminiscent of Giorgio Agamben's "bare life": the state of being merely biologically alive, unable to participate in sociopolitical life.[81] While the longer process of dying could possibly evoke "the expression of everything you are," its conclusion in death tends to be an act of bare mechanics—shifting patients from alive to dead in a routine sequence that presents precious few opportunities for individualism. This homogeneity becomes particularly apparent in *Time of Death*, as this episodic documentary television series shows new, unique patients taking their own paths through the dying process but ultimately reaching the same state of hardly living, lost subjectivity week after week.

This darker reason for the "moment of death's" absence becomes apparent in the Canadian documentary *Dying at Grace* (2003, Allan King), which provides a useful counterpoint to the U.S. films discussed earlier. *Grace* uses a strictly observational, direct cinema style that keeps the audience at a greater emotional distance from the dying than the interview-laden and frequently autobiographical American films. King tracks the dying processes of five patients at the Toronto Grace Health Centre's palliative care unit. One seems to draw the camera in a bit more than the others, and her death provides the climactic final scene of the film. Eda Simac has remained warm, upbeat, and even helpful to the other patients in the unit through her long battle with breast cancer. She seems, in most ways, to be dying a model good death of the post-1960s era: doing palliative care rather than accepting painful life-prolonging treatments and maintaining her unique and lovely personality through this difficult experience. Had Roemer been making this documentary, he may have stopped filming around this point, as Dying showed very little footage beyond a certain stage of debilitation. But King presses on with Eda, and her ability to forge a death that is an "expression of everything [she is]" falters as the pain and medications to suppress it overwhelm her. Her resilient smile disappears as she enters a frightening state of moaning distress, then later simple unconsciousness. Not a personal failing, Eda's loss of self is a consequence of modern dying and, ironically, especially of hospice and palliative care, whose mission to provide comfort and suppress pain requires medications that inhibit alertness and eventually consciousness. Interesting moments in Grace reveal this tension, as nurses try to persuade suffering patients to take more pain medications and some patients resist because they fear that they will no longer feel like themselves. Like all of the five patients featured in Grace, Eda's individual personality falls away as she becomes just a (well-cared-for) barely living body in a bed.

The final shot of this two-and-a-half-hour journey delivers what Grace has not shown up to this point and what no U.S. deathbed documentary shows: an attempt to pinpoint and display the "moment of death." Eda appears in close-up, unconscious, with her eyes half open and mouth gaping, her breaths coming as intermittent spasms—until they stop coming. The sheer rarity of this taboo documentary sight on-screen and its placement at the very end of a long and emotionally demanding film give it a certain power, but in other ways this climax does not feel climactic. Eda's body looks almost exactly the same as those of the other four patients King has shown approach the very end. She exhibits what have, by this point in the film, become rote conventions of the last phase of dying: lying in a bed, unconscious, eyes open but staring blankly, mouth gaping, breathing raggedly. In the accumulation of these scenes, one conclusion is unavoidable: an individualized "death of one's own" must be crafted long before the process of dying comes to an end. Natural death's final phase today

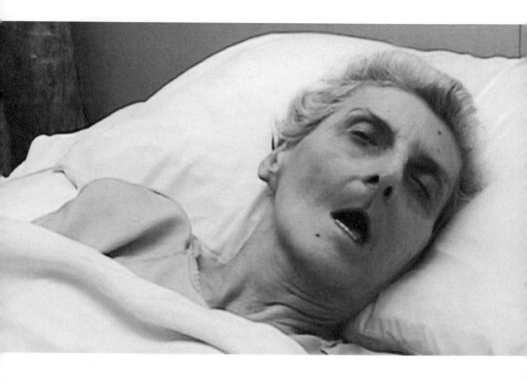

2.5. Eda takes her last breaths as the camera records
(*Dying at Grace*, 2003, Allan King, Criterion Collection).

is, so often, hopelessly routine—an experience of sparse biology common to all those who used to be individuals, and one that would not fit comfortably in documentary stories about individualized good deaths.

Chapter 1's conclusion referenced filmmaker Harun Farocki's troubled reaction to documentary images of violent death—napalm deaths during the Vietnam War, whose brutality and injustice seemed to foreclose any possibility of an "appropriate" response. Farocki chose a gesture of self-injury, burning his arm with a cigarette to endure what he acknowledged to be a hopelessly partial version of the effects of napalm on human bodies. In the face of natural death, less frequently characterized as "unjust," the stakes and requirements of our roles as viewers change. The documentary representation of these deaths generally does not solicit an active response, does not function as a call to arms. As we watch these processes of dying, a simpler reaction than Farocki's seems adequate—one that can be wiped away without leaving a scar. We cry. In this way, the tiny subgenre of the deathbed documentary is kindred to Linda Williams's "body genres," which encourage a physical connection between the bodies onscreen and in the audience through mimicry. Here, we are meant to mimic not the dying but the living who mourn them, perhaps shedding tears alongside Mark in *Silverlake Life*. The act is a cathartic release, one that lets us keep a safe distance from the more difficult revelation implicit in the bodies dying onscreen: that in time we will mimic them, too. As Sally remarks in *Dying*, "All you have to do is wait."

3

"A NEGATIVE PLEASURE"

SUICIDE'S DIGITAL SUBLIMITY

An act like this is prepared within the silence
of the heart, as is a great work of art.
ALBERT CAMUS, on suicide,
The Myth of Sisyphus and Other Essays

In the midst of the classic documentary *Berlin: Symphony of a Great City* (1927, Walther Ruttmann), a strange and significant fictional moment intrudes. The film thus far has been a lively tour of this modern city, capturing all manner of urban sights: the desolate streets at daybreak, masses of citizens pouring in and out of train stations, the briskness of machine labor in factories, weddings and funerals, lunchtime at the zoo. But now the sky darkens, the wind luffs out café awnings and fiercely swirls dead leaves. Offering no establishing shot, Ruttmann cuts to the tightly framed body of a woman leaning precariously far over a bridge railing. A point-of-view shot follows, with a straight-down look at the churning water below, before Ruttmann returns us to the woman with increasingly close shots of her crazed, tormented expression. We see an object drop into the river with a splash that alerts passersby, who swarm at the railing and scan the surface of the water. The woman does not reemerge, nor does any ripple linger. Indeed the water's violent churning has subsided, as it flows lazily past the struts of the bridge.

While other scattered snippets of *Berlin* hint that they could have been staged or reenacted, the bridge jumper scene is the film's only overt departure from a strict documentary mode. It exudes the feeling of a staged event with its impossibly positioned close-ups, the woman's exaggerated performance, its brief shot of the "jump" that does not look like a body falling into the water, and the sheer improbability of capturing this event using available film technology. The jarring intrusion of this conspicuously staged moment within Ruttmann's actuality footage speaks to the strong desire to record "real death" that chapter 1 traced through the history of film and photography. In the particular case of public suicide, the idea that a camera might glimpse the emotional decision to end one's life and the ensuing dramatic plunge was obviously compelling to Ruttmann, as much as it may feel unseemly to viewers.[1] His inability to document an actual suicide and recourse to a fictional mode is also consistent with the technological difficulty of recording such an act in 1927. Because a documentarian could not know when the next attempt would be made, their best option would be to stake out a bridge and keep the camera ever ready to roll when a pedestrian appeared to contemplate the drop. But to burn through pricey film stock monitoring an individual who *might* jump off the bridge would be a costly endeavor. There would be no chance of setting up an unattended camera to run automatically because of the era's short rolls of film and need for manual adjustment with varying light levels and focus settings. To staff and supply this hypothetical operation would, in other words, be prohibitively expensive and impractical.

Advancements in moving image technology since 1927 have radically changed the status of that hypothetical operation. Chapter 2 noted that video and digital video (DV) make newly affordable and practical the act of waiting for a natural death to occur with a camera rolling, and chapter 4 will demonstrate that the saturation of public space with digital recording devices has produced a dramatic increase in documentation of violent death. The case of recording public suicide at bridges where such acts are known to occur straddles these two scenarios of documenting death. Like the former, it involves prolonged periods of waiting for a moment that is bound to arrive, but with unpredictable timing. Like the latter, it depends on camera surveillance of strangers in public space, and on a great deal of contingency. In this case: who will jump, when, how, and how much of the act the camera operator will be able to enframe.

The temporal affordances of DV—its ability to record for long periods of

3.1. A woman contemplates suicide (*Berlin: Symphony of a Great City*, 1927, Walther Ruttmann, Image Entertainment).

continuous time and the practicality of recording great quantities of time via cheap tapes or hard drive storage—helped realize Ruttmann's imagined scenario eight decades later with a documentary called *The Bridge*. Its director, Eric Steel, aggressively put video surveillance to work capturing jumps at San Francisco's Golden Gate Bridge, the world's "most popular" suicide site. Recording on four DV cameras simultaneously during all daylight hours of 2004, the production captured close-up views of multiple suicides—footage of actual deaths that became the film's backbone.

News of Steel's project became public in January 2005 when bridge officials leaked the story to the *San Francisco Chronicle*, and he was quickly embroiled in multiple controversies. The Golden Gate Bridge District condemned him for falsifying permit information (on which he claimed to be making a series of documentaries about American national monuments), word spread that he had not informed his interviewees about his footage of their loved ones' suicides, and media coverage questioned whether Steel had made a "snuff film" at the magnificent landmark.[2] Steel attempted to defend his controversial project against the snuff label by saying that his accusers misunderstood "the difference between filming death for the entertainment of others and filming it for the education of others."[3] Referencing a common ethical dichotomy of death documentary (does such footage provide only ghoulish thrills, or can it be informative and beneficial?), Steel places himself exclusively on the side of education—a position I will challenge in this chapter. The film's release brought polarized reviews. Stephen Holden of the *New York Times*, for example, praised *The Bridge* for "juxtapos[ing] transcendent beauty and personal tragedy as starkly as any film I can recall," while the *Guardian*'s Andrew Pulver wrote, "This could be the most morally loathsome film ever made."[4]

Though this documentary is hardly as unproblematic and straightforwardly profound as Steel professes, it would be a mistake to dismiss *The Bridge* as snuff. In doing so, we would ignore a film that epitomizes cinema's struggle with the limits of representation, its efforts to overcome death's resistance to visibility by seeking spectacular deaths, and the very real ways in which digital technology has changed the means—though not the stakes—of these endeavors. While its attempts to "educate" are less pronounced than Steel claims, its capacity to "entertain" is greater and more interesting than he can safely admit. Despite the film's unsettling lack of self-awareness, its efforts to entertain signal an important break with an established dichotomy in documentary displays of violent death that parallels the entertain/educate split. Before *The Bridge*, there had been disreputable films allowing audiences to enjoy the taboo audiovisual pleasure of actual death and reputable films asking audiences to bear witness to actual death as something terrible (and usually political). My discussions of *Faces of Death* (1978, John Allen Schwartz) and Internet shock sites (in the introduction and chapter 4, respectively) illustrate the reviled variety; the reputable type includes documentaries such as *Night and Fog* (1955, Alain Resnais) or *Hearts and Minds* (1974, Peter Davis). *The Bridge* uncomfortably explores the territory between these poles, perhaps acknowledging that in an increasingly crowded marketplace of documentary death, conventional portrayals no longer command the attention they once did.

That exploration is unquestionably marked by ethical transgression, especially by a failure to meet any conceivable documentary standard of informed consent in depicting either the dead or the living. But a willingness to examine the content of the film itself, in addition to the ethics of its production, underscores the inadvisability of separating ethics and aesthetics. In fact, *The Bridge's* aesthetics as a finished film—*how*, audiovisually, it presents recorded deaths to an audience, beyond the mere fact of doing so—raise as many ethical doubts as Steel's production methods.

The Bridge appears to epitomize the documentary quest to make actual death visible. It exposes (both optically and politically) a type of highly public death that, ironically, had remained mostly unseen (again, both optically and politically), for reasons I will explore later in this chapter. I argue, though, that the apparent visibility of these elaborately recorded deaths is illusory. In a move that renders it politically compromised and ethically dangerous, *The Bridge* covers over suicide's "full detail" through its aesthetic strategies—capitalizing on the aesthetics of the Golden Gate Bridge itself, stylistic techniques associated with fiction film, and the inherent optics of suicide by falling as compared with other methods. Thus enhancing the grandeur of recorded suicide, *The Bridge* slowly trains audiences of mainstream documentary to overcome the impulse to view these jumps as purely horrific—an effort that peaks with its carefully chosen climax. The result is a documentary that returns, shortly after 9/11, to the traumatic sight of bodies falling fatally through space and presents them as a *sublime* spectacle: simultaneously magnificent and terrible. This combination of sublimity and suicide, generative as it may be of arresting images, breaks sharply with psychologists' and sociologists' guidelines for how image-makers can promote suicide prevention—allegedly an important goal of *The Bridge*.

It is this unusually clear and specific intersection of aesthetics and ethics in *The Bridge* that motivates my extended analysis of the film. Singular as this project seems because of its extreme subject matter and production methods, it is in other ways emblematic of the new ethical pitfalls that accompany our expanded capacity to record death with digital tools. Now that it is technologically practical for a documentarian to, for example, record dozens of public suicides, new ethical quandaries emerge (as they will more and more often in the coming years of continued innovation in moving image technologies). How should one judge the curiosity of some viewers to witness these mediated deaths? Does their display demand a political function to be justified, and how directly should that display engage with politics? Through what aesthetic strategies should a filmmaker present such footage, and what are the ethical consequences of his aesthetic choices? In its implications for this final question, *The Bridge* proves most instructive, exposing the ethical danger of mixing evocative aesthetic approaches with tragic lived realities.

How to Record a Suicide in 10,000 Hours or Less:
Logistics and Ethics in Shooting *The Bridge*

To record almost two dozen suicides for *The Bridge*, Steel devised a methodical production plan fully dependent on DV's temporal affordances. He and his crew kept four DV cameras trained on the bridge's pedestrian walkway every day from dawn to dusk during 2004. The cameras were split between two stations overlooking the structure from nearby coastland: one on the northeast side, one on the southeast side. Each station was continually staffed. An operator manually controlled the primary camera fitted with an extreme telephoto lens, which could zoom close enough to track individual bridge walkers. The operator decided whom to follow in these telephoto views, using, as Steel explains, "whatever instincts he or she possessed to try to determine who might climb over the rail."[5] The second camera at each station recorded a continuous, static wide shot of the bridge, only requiring the operator to change its DV tape every hour. The crew recorded footage of most of that year's twenty-four suicides, striving for maximum visibility in their cinematography: they zoomed the cameras in as close as possible and tried to capture the act in its entirety, from the climb over the railing to the splash in the water below. In addition to this elaborate bridge surveillance, Steel shot around 120 hours of interviews with the jumpers' friends and family (and with medical and psychiatric professionals speaking about suicide, though none of their interviews made it to *The Bridge*'s final cut).[6] Rounded out by vivid shots of the Golden Gate Bridge from many angles and in many weather conditions, the production amassed more than 10,000 hours of footage.[7] That gives the ninety-three-minute documentary a staggering 6,500:1 approximate shooting ratio—a ratio demonstrating, among other things, that *The Bridge* never could have been funded as a celluloid project.

During his production phase, Steel went to great lengths to conceal his surveillance of the bridge from the public, and even from his interviewees. As he explains, "My biggest fear was that word would get out about what we were doing and someone that wasn't thinking clearly would see it as an opportunity to immortalize themselves on film."[8] In that scenario, Steel would have become the snuff filmmaker he is accused of being, in a strange way, by capturing actual deaths that were indeed staged for his camera (just not by him). The consequence of his covert operation, though, was that the production recorded jumpers without their knowledge, let alone informed consent—a factor that combines with their impending deaths to give them no agency in their cinematic representation. Steel is by no means the first to bear uninvited witness with a camera to violent deaths in public space and to have to consider how best to represent a victim who can no longer represent himself. But the fact that he *set out* to record such agonizing moments in the lives of others and his initial dishonesty with their grieving loved ones compromises his ethical position.

Moreover, making sure to avoid actively attracting jumpers does not ethically exempt *The Bridge*'s crew from intervening in the jumps that occurred on their own. Unsurprisingly, the intense "fly on the wall" technique that the extreme telephoto lenses enable has attracted a great deal of suspicion from viewers about low-level complicity in the recorded deaths. Crew members all had the bridge patrol's emergency number on mobile phone speed dials and would reportedly call in whenever someone began to climb the railing. By setting rail climbing as the criterion for making a call, though, the production's involvement would usually be too late, as many of the depicted jumpers express little hesitation once they make that climb. This element of intervention exists in tension with the project's larger goal: to get the footage it set out to capture, *The Bridge* must train its cameras on some suicides that the crew cannot or does not prevent.

Here a return to Sobchack's essay "Inscribing Ethical Space" (detailed in the introduction) is beneficial, as Steel's mediated gaze straddles several of her categories for ethical or unethical recording of actual death. His is the "helpless gaze" in the sense that visible distance from the event prevents direct intervention; but Steel chooses his own vantage points and thus prevents *himself* from directly intervening (critics have suggested that if doing so were a real priority, one camera operator would have been walking the bridge). In a rare moment of intentional ethical vulnerability, Steel undercuts his own intervention strategy by including footage in the film of another image-maker on the brink of documenting death whose location *on* the bridge saves a life. An amateur photographer snapping pictures on the walkway notices a woman climb the railing. After a brief moment photographing the event, he leans over and lifts her back to the walkway. Interviewed in the film, he describes his initial hesitation to intervene: "When I was behind the camera, it's almost like it wasn't real, because I was looking through the lens." He reports being fixated on how great the material was but then realizing, "I had to actually get out of that mode of thinking and . . . do something to help her." Unlike this man, Steel and his crew try to both record and act, presumably calling the bridge patrol with one hand and keeping the other on their tripod arm.

Thus, the gaze in *The Bridge* is also the "interventional gaze," visibly evidenced by shots of bridge patrol officers that have been called in and by the shaky camerawork after some jumpers climb the rail, which presumably signifies a distracted operator calling the patrol. But a disturbing parallel observation is unavoidable: the polished camerawork of some other jumper shots (especially Gene Sprague's, discussed later) implies that attention went to the footage rather than intervention. The latter scenario exemplifies Sobchack's "professional gaze"—one that she isolates from the others as being not wholly acceptable. This gaze fails to meet Sobchack's fundamental requirement for justifiable death documentation: the film "must indicate that watching and recording the event of death is not more important than preventing it."[9] In this ethical borderland between interventional and professional gazes, *The Bridge*'s operators implicate themselves every time their tilt downward follows a falling body a little too smoothly.

To accommodate the uniquely digital mode of documenting death that Steel employs, I would propose an addition to Sobchack's list: the expectant gaze. Characterized by the new, technologically enabled ability to simply run a camera and *wait*, the expectant gaze is accompanied by an ambivalent desire for death to occur. The documentarian looking in this way has primarily sought out an opportunity to record a life ending, not an opportunity to save one; it is death he waits for expectantly, not rescue. Gestures to the contrary (such as this crew's calls to the bridge patrol) can be commended, but they must be reconciled with the project's broader aim.

The expectant gaze relies on characteristically digital temporal extremes—on gazing with the camera running for a very long time—in order to capture death, but these extremes are largely erased when the footage is edited for distribution. Neither the feature film format that *The Bridge* adopts nor common Internet formats like the YouTube video can accommodate the protracted stretches of "dead time," in which nothing of apparent interest occurs, that documentarians must record while awaiting brief glimpses of death itself.[10] Given the number of suicides in 2004, the length of each jumper's fall, and the number of cameras *The Bridge* had running, the production could only have captured, at most, about six minutes of falling body footage amid its ten thousand hours. The fatal falls that are the film's primary spectacle of death, for which the camera operators expectantly wait, thus represent about 0.001 percent or less of the project's footage. As inhuman as such calculations can feel when the subject matter is recorded suicide, their implications for the human beings on the recording side of the camera are intense. While some expansive digital projects accumulate their footage through automated surveillance, recall that *The Bridge* dispatched operators to run cameras manually all day, every day for a year. This project's expectant gaze, then, is a human, embodied gaze. Real people spent thousands of hours sitting with cameras employing it, training their lenses on the endless stream of individuals traversing the bridge—any of whom contingency might have transformed into a spectacle of death, but didn't. These sights were instead demoted to the realm of the digital mundane—mostly to what is anachronistically called the cutting-room floor.

At 93 minutes in its finished form, *The Bridge* leaves approximately 599,907 minutes of digital video unseen by its audience, discarding these by-products of its expectant gaze. Documentary in the celluloid era, too, produced and abandoned significant amounts of footage, but the relatively high cost of film stock limited the practice and required greater selectivity about when to run the camera. The expectant gaze's huge quantities of discarded time become practical only in the digital era, bringing these previously unfathomable shooting ratios—like *The Bridge*'s 6,500:1—into being in the service of catching brief, spectacular sights. There is a massive divide between these quick glimpses of falling bodies and the unseen hours of recorded time that undergird them. This divide contributes to my argument that despite failures to capture death "in full detail," when death and digital technologies meet in an attempted recording, they reveal each other's essential qualities. Here, it becomes clear that both have a tendency toward long durations (the long dying process that typifies most deaths in contemporary U.S. culture; the extended hours of footage digital filmmakers can afford to shoot) that get overshadowed by a more visible romance with instantaneity (the fetishized "moment of death," especially in violent deaths; the exhilarating brevity of a YouTube video). In the combination of death and the digital, as in *The Bridge*, these shared traits rise to greatest prominence.

As 10,000 hours of footage were edited down to feature length, the offbeat project took on a fairly conventional documentary shape, typified by its six-minute opening sequence. We begin with our entire visual field obscured by fog, which shifts quickly through a time-lapse effect, intermittently thinning to allow one of the Golden Gate Bridge's towers to peek through. Its thick steel struts ascend skyward, complemented by the narrower vertical and diagonal lines of its support cables, and its red-orange hue gleams in the late afternoon sun. Cars fly down its road with the accelerated frame rate, and a boat's wake streaks the water below. The contemplative score accentuates this beauty and mystery with shimmering gongs and cymbals and with strings holding sustained notes. As fog engulfs the bridge again, the time lapse ends, and a transition introduces a calmer day's activity: birds fly over the bridge, kayaks and a cruise ship pass under it, and many pedestrians cross it. A sparse, plaintive piano part enters the score, inflecting the scene with sadness as the camera lingers on a middle-aged man looking over the edge. Shortly, he swings himself over the low railing, holds on for a few seconds, and lets go. The camera tilts down unsteadily as the operator struggles to anticipate the rate of his fall, his flailing body leaving and reentering the frame before it makes impact in a shower of frothy sea water. A kitesurfer floats through the shot, and we slip into an interview with him and his friend—supplemented visually with a montage of kitesurfing at the Golden Gate, and aurally with a half-lively, half-melancholy indie rock track. The kitesurfer, who saw the splash, explains how strange it was to realize that he was enjoying "a real celebration of life" through sport while "that person was at the lowest of the low of their life."

This opening sequence introduces a structure and tone that are representative of the film as a whole. As we adjust to the daily life of this particular public space, we see its normality disrupted by a shocking event. After a brief moment to absorb it on our own, the event is folded into a narrative frame through interviews, which both highlight its unusual quality and also attempt to contextualize it within the range of "normal" human experience. We're cued to feel sad that the event took place, but also to recognize what a rare and visually interesting spectacle the film is providing for us. If this deeply conventional documentary format feels uncomfortable in *The Bridge*, it is because the ethical and emotional volatility of the film's death footage cries out for some kind of formal acknowledgment of the content's singularity. This disjunction between ordinary form and explosive content is particularly loaded because of suicide's status as a supremely taboo type of death. To elucidate what is at stake in the ethics and aesthetics of sublime digital suicides, I now turn to the rich history of this taboo and its representation.

3.2. The first jumper falls (*The Bridge*, 2006, Eric Steel, Koch Lorber).

"Prepared within the Silence of the Heart":
The Public and Private in the History of Suicide

In discourse on suicide, Albert Camus's book-length consideration of the topic, *The Myth of Sisyphus*, is often quoted for its opening line: "There is but one truly serious philosophical problem, and that is suicide. Judging whether life is or is not worth living amounts to answering the fundamental question of philosophy."[11] *The Bridge*, as I will demonstrate, hesitates to take a side on Camus's "fundamental question," but it does plunge into territory acknowledged more cryptically on the following page of *Sisyphus*: the relation between suicide and aesthetics. Camus writes of suicide, "An act like this is prepared within the silence of the heart, as is a great work of art."[12] He stops short of granting suicide artistic status but proposes an intriguing link between preparing one's own death and an artist's creative process. *The Bridge* expands on that link by documenting one strikingly artful suicide, and by strengthening that death's artistic quality with its own aesthetic interventions. Historically, bold aesthetic interventions in the representation of suicide have been risky. Compared with the types of death considered in previous chapters, representations of suicide tonally depart from both the abrupt injustice of violent death and the routine sadness of natural death because the act itself has been so frequently and thoroughly reviled. Its reviled quality has confined suicide to the realm of the private on many levels: an individual suicide today is typically "prepared within the silence of the heart," committed alone and in secret, and kept largely out of public discourse. But there has actually been a charged interplay between public and private throughout suicide's history in Western society—an interplay that resonates with controversies around this film that makes doubly public the Golden Gate's uncommonly public acts of suicide.

The most famous suicides of the classical era—when the act found its greatest, though not universal, acceptance—were practically social affairs. Socrates and Petronius, for example, are described as taking their lives amid entourages of friends, sometimes grieving, other times reading poetry or sharing a last meal with the man about to die.[13] In another public element, citizens in parts of ancient Greece could request permission from the senate to kill themselves, receiving free hemlock if their reasons were deemed satisfactory.[14] Citizens of later eras and cultures would rarely receive state permission to end their lives, but certain public elements would still characterize what became a much more private act. In the Middle Ages and early modern period, these included intensely public desecrations of suicide corpses, which could be "hung by the feet . . . dragged through the streets on a hurdle . . . burned . . . pierced crossways with a stick . . . [or] buried under five feet of water in the sand."[15] Many of these practices emphasize their performance in public space, often as a deterrent to others in the community. Here the public display of suicide corpses is used, in an extreme and gruesome fashion, to discourage suicide; in a later section, I will argue that *The Bridge* enacts a parallel public display with quite different aesthetics and equally questionable results.

Most pertinent to issues of ethics and aesthetics in *The Bridge* are the public aspects of suicide in the more recent past that center on the role of media. The flourishing of the popular press just before the eighteenth century provided opportunities to disseminate details about individual suicides nationally, beyond the range of a mutilated body hanging in a town square. This technological innovation bolstered a wave of interest in suicide, which had become "a genuine fashion" for European aristocrats to debate in the salons (or even to commit). While the press in this period could have been used in the same spirit as corpse desecration, its role in publicizing suicide seems more sensational, even salacious, than discouraging. At the risk of piquing interest rather than repulsion, British newspapers printed not only suicide rates but also "articles on the most interesting, strangest, or most striking cases of suicide" and fueled the aristocratic fashion for suicide by reporting heavily on the most famous deaths.[16]

Extreme examples appear in Britain's *Illustrated Police News*, which brought the most visually spectacular suicides to public attention in the 1860s and 1870s. One typical illustration, *Suicide on a Railway*, shows a woman's severed head sitting apart from her body in a pool of blood. At the *IPN*'s most macabre, it painstakingly displays the awkward mechanics of self-crucifixion and self-beheading in multiple issues.[17] These bizarre illustrations bring supposedly real suicides before the public eye but at the same time hyperbolically—almost comically—underscore suicide's profile as a private act. The men in these images struggle alone in dark garrets with homemade execution equipment, trying to enact modes of death meant to be *public* spectacles, with attendant staff, as solitary suicides. Elsewhere, the *IPN* serves as a precursor for *The Bridge*'s displays of real suicides in its images of women jumping to their watery deaths from bridges.[18] These engravings share many visual markers with *The Bridge*: a vantage point floating below the bridge and toward one bank, a falling body that dominates the frame's center, and pedestrians who witness the jump without intervening. In the *IPN*, reporting "news" is a transparent excuse for printing lurid displays of death, but it is significant that these illustrations claim journalistic authority.[19] Central to their appeal, it seems, is their grounding in actual events—regardless of the reader's level of credulity. *The Bridge* shares both these qualities of the *IPN*'s suicide representations: an investment in the graphic display of suicide (though with less overt morbidity) and a reliance on the power conferred by these deaths' real-world origins.

While images from the IPN or *The Bridge* can be reviled as distasteful, the debate about whether and how suicide should be represented in public has higher stakes than matters of taste—an assertion whose roots lie in the medicalization of suicide. By the nineteenth century, a growing trend of attributing suicide to insanity and melancholia became dominant, as the main current of discourse on the act shifted from courts and churches into medical journals.[20] Public shaming practices like dragging suicide corpses through the street became inappropriate once those who committed suicide were rhetorically transformed from sinners and criminals into victims of a psychological disorder. The twentieth century continued this trend with intensified study of the problem in psychology and sociology, disciplines that issued new prescriptions for reducing suicide through individual pharmacological treatments and broad societal reforms, respectively.[21] Despite its active scholarship, Georges Minois argues that the era of medicalized suicide has also brought a decreased willingness to acknowledge or examine *individual* suicides in public discourse.[22] This new taboo on the visibility of individual suicides is doubly relevant to *The Bridge*, a work that exposes individual suicides for detailed public examination and one whose suicides are already unusually—even defiantly—public. Leaping from an open-air structure full of tourists in broad daylight is an inherently public act, and that aspect seems integral to the Golden Gate Bridge's appeal as a suicide destination. Its jumpers are willing to be, and perhaps even want to be, highly visible and watched as they end their lives, in contrast to the intensely private manner in which most suicides are conducted. *The Bridge* amplifies that public quality immensely by screening individual suicides for a mass audience, challenging Minois's taboo.

One of the reasons for the recent public silence about individual suicides, and for my claim that the aesthetics of suicide representation have higher stakes than matters of taste, is a resurgent belief in "suicide contagion." This phenomenon occurs when people exposed to an individual suicide—usually through the media—feel compelled to imitate that suicide. An 1845 issue of the *American Journal of Insanity* (!) confidently asserts that "no other fact is better established by science" and continues with a vivid warning against newspaper reports describing individual suicides: "A single paragraph may suggest suicide to twenty persons. Some particulars of the act, or expressions, seize the imagination, and the disposition to repeat it, in a moment of morbid excitement, proves irresistible."[23] More than a century later, Joost A. M. Meerloo's study *Suicide and Mass Suicide* (1962) subscribes to the same belief, asserting plainly,

"Every suicide can start a chain of suicides."[24] Though scholars today are not in full agreement, suicide contagion has been largely confirmed as a real effect by suicide statistics in recent decades.

Dubbed the "Werther effect" by David Phillips, whose 1974 study elevated it out of the realm of myth, one early manifestation of suicide contagion allegedly emerged from the immense popularity of Goethe's epistolary novel, *The Sorrows of Young Werther* (1774).[25] Its title character commits suicide by gunshot when he can no longer endure his frustrated love for a married woman. Conceiving of the act as supremely romantic and beautiful, Werther nevertheless sees his plans go awry when he does not die immediately and must endure many hours of suffering before his painful death. Despite Goethe's attempt with this brutal ending to temper his character's romanticized vision of suicide, many readers still idolized and identified with Werther, publicly speaking and writing in defense of his choice to die. "Werther fever" saw Europeans dressing like the melancholy character and decorating household objects with scenes from his story.[26] It was "a phenomenon that included not just enthusiasm for the novel, but also a desire to emulate its hero," and in the novel's 1775 reprinting Goethe added warnings to the reader not to follow Werther's example.[27] An early example of the alarming power of suicide's representational romanticization, *The Sorrows of Young Werther* also gestures—through its sequential presentation of suicide as grand and then terrifying—at the sublimity that *The Bridge*'s representation of suicide would realize more fully.

The authors of the *Oxford Textbook of Suicidology and Suicide Prevention* (which devotes a chapter to suicide contagion) note, crucially, that there is "substantial evidence that non-fictional media reports on suicides exert a stronger imitative effect than fictional ones" and that the way suicide is represented can impact the rate of imitation greatly.[28] The latter conclusion places the rare burden of life-and-death consequences onto the representational choices of professionals like filmmakers and journalists. Drawing on this research, the American Foundation for Suicide Prevention has published guidelines—which the Centers for Disease Control and Prevention and the American Association of Suicidology have endorsed—that encourage media-makers to discuss suicide publicly, not suppress it, but to do so in a manner that will reduce the likelihood of imitation. Central to these recommendations is the well-supported theory that substantial attention to *individual* suicides can encourage imitation; thus, the guidelines discourage reporting on "a particular death . . . at length or in many stories."[29] They also caution against "inadvertently romanticizing suicide," which another textbook, the *Comprehensive Textbook of Suicidology*, echoes with a warning about "the praise, glorification, or otherwise rewarding of the original stimulus suicide" in its depiction.[30] The guidelines continue, "Research indicates that detailed descriptions or pictures of the location or site of a suicide encourage imitation."[31]

These guidelines seem unable to even conceive of suicide documentation on The Bridge's scale, offering no specific clauses about displaying graphic footage of suicides, but it is not hard to extrapolate and assume that such a display would be discouraged. In trying to humanize and individuate its jumpers, The Bridge engages in precisely the style of representation proven to increase suicide, as it also does with the darkly beautiful shots of the Golden Gate as a suicide venue. Especially problematic is the relentless focus on one jumper, Gene Sprague, whose story structures the film and whose death, I will argue, is romanticized—perhaps not inadvertently.

Suicide's Aesthetics:
The Horrible, the Beautiful, and the Sublime

For all the metaphysical awe and terror we associate with the *experience* of dying, the unstaged *appearance* of death, as I have demonstrated in previous chapters, rarely suggests this sublime mixture of qualities—a reality helpful to acknowledge when seeking precedents for The Bridge's aesthetic rendering of individual suicides. Further, most methods of committing suicide are so visually gruesome that they resist either the romantic or the sublime register, especially in their few documentary recordings. Michele Aaron observes that on the (also rare) occasion that fiction films depict a realized suicide attempt, they typically frame it as "painless or invisible but similarly anti-abject," revealing a desire for softened representations of the act.[32] But Aaron also illuminates the techniques of concealment necessary to create such representations: compositions that leave most of the body offscreen, well-timed cuts away from the act in progress, and so on.

To understand the severity of those techniques' absence in documentary recordings of suicide, one need only watch a news crew's footage of Pennsylvania state treasurer Budd Dwyer's 1987 suicide at a press conference. Using the most favored method of suicide in the United States (by a wide margin), firearms, Dwyer puts a handgun in his mouth and shoots a round upward into his brain.[33] The camera operator records in a medium shot as the gun fires and sprays the back wall with blood, zooms out as Dwyer's body falls to a sitting position against a cabinet, then zooms in to a close-up on his lifeless face. At this point, an astounding volume of blood pours from Dwyer's nose in torrents, and a second stream runs down his face from the exit wound atop his head. This actual suicide is uncompromisingly displayed, and the effect is brutal.

There is no way to fit the aesthetic lens of sublimity over an act like Dwyer's— a sense deepened by other footage of actual gunshot suicides. When Ricardo Cerna shot himself in the head inside a California police interrogation room with a concealed handgun in 2003, for example, a wall-mounted camera recorded his death. The ugly carnage of the gunshot wound, which immediately and unceremoniously pours blood down the front and side of Cerna's body, is reinforced by the drab aesthetic details of the video's mise-en-scène: a claustrophobically small room, bare institutional walls, and the distressed man's grubby sneakers and gaudy T-shirt. Similar qualities pervade the death footage of Daniel V. Jones and Jodon F. Romero, each of whom shot himself in the head during separate confrontations with police that were broadcast on live television in 1998 and 2012, respectively. Filmed in extreme long shot from helicopters, these recordings emphasize abjection, as each man's body flops limply to the ground after the bullets' impact, and Jones's gushes a stream of blood onto the pavement where he falls.

Suicide by gunshot, then, does not lend itself to a sublime documentary aesthetic because it appears too horrific and ugly when made visible by cameras. Other methods effect the body's death with less visible violence and can lend themselves to a beautiful—though not sublime—documentary display, when these suicides unfold in the right medical and ideological context. I am referring here to another subset of death documentaries that depict assisted suicides, typically in the mode of political advocacy for the international right-to-die movement. Sometimes screening theatrically and sometimes airing on television, these include *Death on Request* (1994, Maarten Nederhorst), *The Suicide Tourist* (2007, John Zaritsky), *How to Die in Oregon* (2011, Peter Richardson), and *Choosing to Die* (2011, Charlie Russell). Implicitly seeking to redeem the documentary recording of assisted suicide from its infamous association with Dr. Jack Kevorkian, these films work to link assisted suicides with the contemporary model of the "good death" discussed in chapter 2. They frame terminal patients as courageously individualistic: opposing social norms against suicide, these patients take control over their deaths, making active and commendable choices to die without pain at a time they designate. Employing the right film aesthetics proves key to their framing of suicide as potentially beautiful—a framing essential to the mission of political advocacy. The climactic scenes of the suicide deaths themselves in these documentaries generally employ a gentle score, a warmly lit domestic setting, and frequent cutaways from the dying patient to the emotional faces of her or his supportive family members and kindly doctors. Assisted suicide documentaries thus demonstrate that recorded suicide can be aligned with the aesthetic category of the beautiful. But the calm stasis of these deaths—akin to many from chapter 2's nonsuicide deathbed documentaries—gives a sublime aesthetic little traction here. Emotionally moving but not dynamic, these represented suicides appear neither magnificent nor terrible.

The Bridge uses sublime aesthetics to subvert the suicide act's customary brutality—aided by its choice to document a type of suicide (falling into water) that is visibly dynamic but that renders its external violence invisible. One of the most satisfyingly precise-yet-versatile labels in the study of aesthetics, the sublime emerges from a long lineage of theorizing. Edmund Burke defines it eloquently as "not pleasure but a sort of delightful horror, a sort of tranquility tinged with terror."[34] Building from Burke's writing, Immanuel Kant refines the sublime to "a pleasure that only arises indirectly, being brought about by the feeling of a momentary check to the vital forces followed at once by a discharge all the more powerful. . . . since the mind is not simply attracted by the object, but is also alternately repelled thereby, the delight in the sublime does not so much involve positive pleasure as admiration or respect, i.e. merits the name of negative pleasure."[35] Unlike his tamer categories of aesthetic judgment, the sublime for Kant is a visceral experience—wrapped up not just in the mind's operation but in the movements of the "vital forces." There is a certain disturbing harmony in a "momentary check to the vital forces" in the observer that accompanies the sight of a permanent check to those forces for another human being, as in *The Bridge*.

Beyond Kant's reference to the "vital forces," other aspects of the sublime align well with death, suicide, and even the type of suicide in *The Bridge*. In "The Nuclear Sublime," Frances Ferguson notes that both Burke and Kant conceive of the sublime as emerging from "great"—almost excessive—objects or experiences, quoting Kant's assertion that it affixes to that which is "great beyond all measure." The sublime "specifically elude[s] the apprehension we think ourselves to have of the objects of our perceptions," as Ferguson puts it, also paraphrasing Burke's attitude that "we love the beautiful as what submits to us, but we fear the sublime as what we must submit to."[36] The nuclear weapons Ferguson is writing about certainly fit this description—powerful to an extent that we cannot understand and that demands our submission—but so does death itself as a human experience. The sublime requires submission, but Ferguson emphasizes that it also authenticates our individuality because it is a subjective, aesthetic judgment rather than an inherent trait of objects. It asserts selfhood in the face of powers greater than the self, as does suicide—an act that, however tragically, restores a measure of individual control over the forces of life and death. Perhaps that is why, referencing Friedrich Schiller, Ferguson mentions suicide as "the inevitable outcome of the logic of the sublime" and why Steel infuses the most individualized, tightly controlled suicide he records with the strongest overtones of sublimity.[37] While the sublime can be a densely theoretical concept, I want to emphasize that I do not employ it in my analysis of recorded suicide for esoteric reasons but rather for grounded, ethical ones. As I will assert in my reading of The Bridge, the project's documentary use of the sublime as an aesthetic strategy is inextricably linked to its ethical transgressions and the practical, embodied consequences these carry.

The Bridge is not the first text to combine sublimity and suicide, nor even sublimity and suicide in digital documentary work. Richard Drew's photograph The Falling Man (2001) sparked immediate and intense controversy over its sublime depiction of a man in free fall, after he has jumped from the upper floors of the World Trade Center's North Tower during the 9/11 attacks. This photograph is of special relevance to The Bridge because, as Annette Habel writes, "There is a reciprocal association between 9/11 and the depiction of human bodies falling."[38] It is hard, in other words, to look at bodies falling from a bridge without thinking about the bodies that fell from the towers.

As noted in the introduction, both moving and still images of the jumpers were widely created, briefly circulated by the mainstream press, quickly removed from that circulation, and revived on the numerous Internet sites where journalistic gatekeepers and cultural taboos hold little sway. On a day of invisible mass death hidden behind the crumbling walls of the towers, these images made visible dying individuals, and as such, they provoked both shameful fascination and the anguish of looking. Although many jumped (an estimated fifty to two hundred people) and many of the jumps were recorded, Drew's image of one brief instant in an anonymous man's long, ten-second fall stood out above all others because, in my view, of its improbable sublimity.

It seemed impossible that an image-maker could find grace or awe alongside the terror of this rare and particularly tragic form of suicide—these deaths that were chosen by people who did not desire to die but who exercised their limited agency to select death by falling over death by fire or smoke. But The Falling Man exudes sublimity. The title figure is engulfed by the gleaming surfaces of the towers, which completely fill the photo's background and remind the viewer that both they and the man stand on the brink of destruction—gone within an hour or a few more seconds, respectively. Small as the man is against this imposing background, he dominates the image through the striking pose in which he falls: headfirst, arms resting loosely at his sides, one knee bent, the other leg nearly straight. The sleek lines of the towers thus accentuate the perfect verticality of his descent, imbuing it with greater visual power rather than overwhelming it. His face is small and poorly illuminated, communicating nothing, which leaves the viewer to project only the appearance of his body—controlled but fluid, almost relaxed—onto his mental state. Amid the shot's magnificence, though, its framing makes it hard to forget the terror of its context: the falling man appears in the top third of the image's portrait layout. This composition reminds the viewer that he has a long way left to fall—fatally and gorily, onto concrete.

Hundreds of newspapers printed Drew's photograph on September 12 and saw angry reactions from readers pour in. Many of the complaints purported to be about the falling man's identifiability (though even after exhaustive searches he has never been identified with certainty), but I believe it was the symbolism and aesthetics of this documentary death image that more deeply disturbed the public.[39] Drew defended his photograph partly by denying its status as documentary death at all: "I see this not as a person's death, but as part of his life. There's no blood. There's no guts. It's just a person falling."[40] Photographs of life do not generate letters to the editor the way photographs of death do, though. As Barbie Zelizer puts it, Drew's is an "about to die" image, quite distinct from images of living even if their subjects are not yet dead. It is clear from the tenor of the controversy that viewers saw death in The Falling Man—a picture of awe and elegance in horrific circumstances that alternately comforted and disturbed viewers as a vision of 9/11 deaths.[41] Naomi Halperin, a photo editor who fought to get the picture printed, takes comfort in what it did not show, what it screened out about that day: "I saw grace, I saw a stillness. Even though I know that he was falling, I saw a quietness in that as opposed to a loud, horrible, burning death."[42] Journalist Tom Junod reads it as more existentially frightening: "At a time when the country was desperate for images that were communal and redemptive, Drew gave it a man left to the mercy not of God but of gravity, and dying utterly alone."[43] Sublimity's awe and horror were both present for viewers of The Falling Man, just in different proportions.

Perhaps the photo's most unsettling aspect is the way its aesthetics connote agency. To wrench a graceful death out of the terror of this context implied an exertion of effort and purposefulness, implied that the man falling prepared this suicide "within the silence of the heart," at least in the few minutes or seconds during which he decided to jump. He must have chosen to dive, struggled to make his body fall in this exquisite way. The intentionality of his pose refuses to let the viewer disavow the agency of the jumpers—as heartbreakingly limited

3.3. *The Falling Man* (2001, © Richard Drew/Associated Press).

as that agency was—by imagining that they slipped out or were blown out.[44] It forces the viewer to acknowledge this man's choice to jump and perhaps prompts her to think, unthinkably, of what choice she herself would make in his situation. Little wonder, then, that *The Falling Man* provoked such a harsh rejection. What most of those who saw the image never discovered, though, was the illusory nature of the man's graceful, purposeful dive—lacking, after all, the excess of intentionality it seemed to possess. In comparison with the other eleven frames Drew snapped of the man, this particular photograph's frozen, enduring sublimity comes to reflect only an accidental split-second pose of his body as it tumbled haphazardly through the air. As Junod writes, seeing these unpublished frames reveals that "he fell like everyone else . . . which is to say that he fell desperately, inelegantly."[45]

Capitalizing on the instantaneity of photography, Drew's image fabricated a sublime documentary death from a profilmic event that would be difficult to place in this aesthetic category. Steel's moving image medium offered no opportunities for that manner of deception. To display, in its full duration, the sublime death that ends his film, he would need an (unwitting) artistic collaborator: another falling man who really did pursue a graceful suicide with undeniable intentionality.

Calibrating Sublimity in *The Bridge*

As the previous sections demonstrate, when the generally private act of suicide has entered public space (either physically or through representation), the tone tends to be resoundingly negative. Works that dilute suicide's horror by exploring its potentially positive aspects—grace, nobility, a release from suffering—often meet intense controversy, as did Goethe's *Sorrows* and Drew's *Falling Man*. With the sight of falling bodies inextricably linked to the 9/11 jumpers, the idea of centering a reputable post-9/11 documentary that was aiming for the festival circuit on that visual spectacle risked a particularly strong controversy. This association was not an accident of poor timing for *The Bridge* but rather one of the several origin stories Steel tells about the film. On 9/11, Steel watched the jumpers from his New York office window, recalling in an interview, "I could actually see that from where I sit now. Obviously, that's one of those things that you just can't erase from your mind. . . . Someone jumping off the bridge was making a choice to escape an emotional inferno, perhaps not equivalent, but somehow related perhaps to what I had seen on 9/11."[46] Steel's response to the horrifying sight that he "can't erase from [his] mind" is to seek out, record, and make widely visible more jumpers, following the thin metaphorical connection of the "inferno." One could surmise that Steel is returning obsessively to an experience of trauma. But it is questionable whether the product—perhaps too direct in its return—is therapeutic for a post-9/11 audience. As one unsettled reviewer wrote, "After 9/11, viewers can be forgiven for never wanting to see another soul take a fatal plummet."[47] As I will detail, in Steel's compulsion to repeat this personal and national trauma, he, by chance, encounters one suicide that can repeat the sublime aesthetics of *The Falling Man*, too.

Connotations of sublimity waft through many reviews of the film, which refer to it as "a beautiful, wrenching, horrifying work of cinema" and "an emotional and aesthetic whirlpool of horror, fascination, beauty"; another review observes, "these images of death are grotesquely, irresistibly fascinating; their poetic, vaguely unreal gracefulness contrasts poignantly with the despair they imply."[48] Deadly jumps from a high place, as we witness them in *The Bridge*, have the potential to evoke both of Kant's two categories of the sublime: the mathematical and the dynamic.[49] Experiences of the mathematical sublime overwhelm us with their magnitude—like beholding the expanse of a starry night sky, in nature, or the broad bulk of the pyramids, among human-made objects. Magnitude is a particularly affecting element of jumps off the Golden Gate Bridge. The bodies we see fall traverse a vast, frightening distance—second only to the jumps from the World Trade Center—that truly can influence the "vital forces" when contemplated, as Kant describes. Dynamically sublime sights are those that awe us with their overpowering force rather than their overwhelming magnitude—like a lightning storm or a volcanic eruption. These suicides may affect viewers as dynamically sublime through the crushing force of gravity that drives the bodies downward as they contort, and the powerful impacts with the water that send up breathtaking bursts of white against the bluish-gray bay (a spectacle of impact that documentation of the 9/11 jumps did not, mercifully, display).

The dynamic quality of this method of death is morbidly well suited to cinematic representation, which, as previously discussed, often struggles to visualize the internal bodily process that defines death. Cinema is an art distinguished by its capacity to convey motion, and the jumpers achieve death by motion of a profoundly visible and dramatic nature. Movement itself is the lethal force, in a much more perceptible way than a bullet from a gun. Kant emphasizes that to experience the dynamic sublime, one cannot oneself be in physical danger from the event witnessed but must be "a safe distance" away. Watching a volcano erupt from within the lava's range, for instance, produces not "delightful" horror but just the regular kind. Again, cinema—still a century away from invention at the time of Kant's writing—proves to be an appropriate medium for the dynamic sublime. It offers close-up audiovisual access to the powerful force while maintaining a "safe distance" for the viewer, who is separated by both time and space from the sublime profilmic event.

Documentary death is undoubtedly adept at "repel[ling]" the mind with its horror. In *The Bridge*, it becomes even more taboo when its potential sublimity is acknowledged—when a documentarian demonstrates that the mind can also be "attracted by the object." Death documentaries that either attract or repel, but not both, are the most common variety of their uncommon breed. *The Bridge*'s tenuous balance of the two puts it in relatively unexplored documentary terrain. But, as Kant insists, the sublime is an aesthetic judgment, not an intrinsic quality; it is a particularly difficult judgment for documentary audiences to feel comfortable making about such taboo material. David E. Nye asserts, in agreement with Kant, that "one person's sublime may be another's abomination"—an idea that certainly applies to how reviewers and the public have judged *The Bridge*.[50] Steel seems to understand that difficulty, and he relies on three major tools to make audiences receptive to the sublimity of suicide: the sublimity of the Golden Gate Bridge itself, anesthetization to the shock of seeing death, and stylistic techniques that aim to soften suicide's horror.

In the film's opening sequence, described earlier, the magnificence of the Golden Gate Bridge seems to contrast to the horror of people jumping from its span. Introduced as a majestic site, the Golden Gate immerses visitors in a dramatic intersection of the best that nature and architecture have to offer. It provides recreation, transportation, and an unrivaled vantage point for Bay Area sightseeing. Only the ominous score and the fog prepare the viewer for the death footage, which, in this first instance—preceded by shots of happy tourists and followed by shots of happy kitesurfers—feels like an upsetting and anomalous disruption of normality in public space. Amid the Golden Gate's atmosphere of communal pleasure—one associated with U.S. national identity and the promise of the American West—an instance of such acute, individuated despair is difficult to process. For pedestrians on the bridge, who remain largely oblivious to the jumpers throughout the film, it seems difficult to even *detect* amid the surrounding sensory overload. Thus, the deaths at this site that should feel extremely visible and public—occurring, as they do, in a completely exposed outdoor area full of people and in the light of day—still need the documentary camera to wrench them out of invisibility.

This factor in suicide at the Golden Gate recalls a painting Steel cites as an inspiration for *The Bridge*: Pieter Bruegel's *Landscape with the Fall of Icarus*. Bruegel's landscape is packed with visual information, centered on a brilliant blue expanse of water, bounded by cliffs and a port city, and dotted with islands and ornate ships. The foreground is densely populated by a farmer plowing, a shepherd and his flock, and a fisherman. The sun blazes hot in the background, hinting at the title character's doom, but none of the men in the foreground see him sinking into the blue water . . . nor may the viewer at first, since his figure is so small and de-emphasized, in a dark corner of the scene. Like the Golden Gate's visitors, the men in this painting are too engrossed in the activity and beauty of the day to notice a small pocket of tragedy in their landscape. And through his composition, Bruegel implicates us, the viewers, alongside them. We, too, may have missed the sinking body were it not for the title's prompt to look for it.

With a similar effect, the massive Golden Gate Bridge engulfs those who visit it and juts in all directions, its architectural lines constantly soliciting them to look left, right, up, down, and outward to the bay and skyline. Additionally, every view is filled with motion: cars, bicycles, and people traverse the span, which sways in the wind, while below the water churns and boats pass by. The unrelenting clamor of cars makes the site's sonic environment just as overwhelming. Like death itself, the totality of this place seems beyond the capacity of representation. Significantly, Steel's zoomed-in digital cameras accomplish the opposite: with the overwhelming magnitude and dynamism of the Golden Gate rendered elsewhere in the film, these shots filter it out and isolate individual anguish. They make visible the deaths that are otherwise lost among the stimuli of teeming environments, highlighting what neither Bruegel's laborers nor the Golden Gate's tourists seem to notice.

The first time we see one of these suicide close-ups, it feels like a violation of the site's spirit, evocatively described in Nye's *American Technological Sublime*: "The *San Francisco Examiner* editorialized that the bridge is 'a gateway to the imagination,' noting that 'in its artful poise, slender there above the shimmering channel, it is more a state of the spirit than a fabricated road connection. It beckons us to dream and dare. First seen as an impossible dream, it became a moral regenerator in the 1930s for a nation devastated by depression' . . . 'can do proof' that the nation's 'inventive and productive genius' would prevail. It was, and is, an outward and visible sign of an ideal America."[51] Nye does not mention the estimated sixteen hundred suicides that have occurred at the bridge since its opening in 1937. Their terrible counterpoint to its stunning beauty is a lens through which this optimistic description reads very differently. The "moral regenerator in the 1930s for a nation devastated by depression" appears in *The Bridge* as a reminder of a different kind of depression still devastating that nation. Its beckoning to "dream and dare" connotes its

3.4. *Landscape with the Fall of Icarus*, c. 1555 (oil on canvas),
Pieter Bruegel the Elder (c. 1525–69) / Musées royaux
des Beaux-Arts de Belgique, Brussels, Belgium / Bridgeman Images.

darker lure for those bold enough to kill themselves in such a frightening way. As a sign of a can-do, ideal America whose "inventive and productive genius" could solve any problem, the bridge looks newly frail. This perspective on the structure harkens back to Émile Durkheim's assertion that most suicides stem from society's failure to integrate individuals into a system fully, to give their lives collective meaning.[52] The unseemly suicide pilgrimages to this landmark, this symbol of national pride, that Steel records illuminate its social failure. Documenting the loss of human potential that goes largely unprevented at the site, *The Bridge*'s digital cameras provide the too-visible proof of the gap between America's ideal and its reality.

In the film, suicide adds an element of terror to the bridge's grandeur, but the bridge in turn lends an element of grandeur to the terror of suicide, pulling both into the realm of sublimity. The Golden Gate provides a majestic final view for those about to die, imbuing their deaths with grace, at least as they appear to witnesses: their trajectories trace the vertical lines of the bridge downward, and the mutilation of their bodies on impact is screened out by a splash. This screening out is crucial, as the splash provides another barrier to death's cinematic visibility—much like the strategic framing and editing choices Aaron identifies in fiction film's romanticized suicides—that, in this case, suits *The Bridge*'s aesthetic ambitions perfectly. Seeing the moment of fatal impact in "full detail" or the corpses would pull sublimity back into horror—especially this site's corpses, which are much the worse for wear after their fall. Those contemplating suicide at the bridge often imagine an instant, clean death, but the reality is (as usual) a more painful and durational process. The fall's impact splinters bones that then shred internal organs, and those who survive it drown, either in the water or in their own blood as it fills their lungs. After death, the Coast Guard recovers only some of the bodies, and those not located quickly can have their eyes and cheek flesh eaten off by crabs. *The Bridge*, while making actual suicide deaths visible in some ways, leaves the embodied violence of this method of suicide in the realm of invisibility—keeping it literally beneath the surface, subsumed to the aesthetics of the sublime. Suicide in this documentary, then, misleadingly appears "painless . . . anti-abject," as Aaron observes that it does in most commercial fiction films.[53]

All these graphic details are described in "Jumpers," a *New Yorker* exposé on Golden Gate suicides that *The Bridge* credits as its inspiration, but they are notably absent from or downplayed in the film, communicated to the audience only partially by one young man who survived the drop and describes his injuries.[54] Where Goethe emphasized the physical suffering and gruesomeness of Werther's suicide, Steel seems unwilling to acknowledge the violence of the act he records. He refrains from showing all but one oblique glimpse of a body being retrieved from the water. For a documentary so aggressively pursuing views of public suicide from multiple vantage points, this omission reveals a great deal about its aesthetic priorities. The Golden Gate thus promises to lend grace and a public venue to an act that is usually messy and private, and *The Bridge* cooperates by suppressing any unsettling remnants that resurface.

But just as the awe of the Golden Gate distracts pedestrians from seeing suicidal despair, the initial shock and horror of watching a jumper's descent can mask its appealing aesthetics. To train his audience to look past horror and see something magnificent intermingled with it, Steel attempts a gradual anesthetization through repetition of the fatal jumps. Susan Sontag first wrote about gruesome photographs' potentially anesthetizing effect in *On Photography* (1977) (an idea she revisits in *Regarding the Pain of Others* [2003]): "To suffer is one thing; another thing is living with the photographed images of suffering, which does not necessarily strengthen conscience and the ability to be compassionate. It can also corrupt them. Once one has seen such images, one has started down the road of seeing more. Images transfix. Images anesthetize."[55] Though Sontag is writing about still images, this particular aspect of her photography theory translates well to moving images. During a dense, temporally bound collection of such sights in a single documentary, her numbing process can happen quickly.

The Bridge needs it to, so that a spectacle that seemed horrific in the film's opening moments will feel sublime by its closing scene. Key to this audience transformation is repeated viewing of the difficult sight, which *The Bridge's* audience potentially experiences on two levels: the many jumps they see while watching the film, but also similar images they have seen beforehand (chiefly the 9/11 jumpers). Repeated viewing of a difficult sight is not just a means of anesthetization but also a strategy for comprehending the sublime. For example, Nye gives an account of activist Margaret Fuller's attempts to absorb the sight of Niagara Falls in 1843. Prepared for the experience by drawings and a panorama, Fuller stayed at the falls for a week to view them many times from multiple angles. "Before coming away," she wrote, "I think I really saw the full wonder of the scene."[56] *The Bridge* uses a similar repetition approach to acclimate viewers to the sight of real death and allow its potential sublimity to well up, displaying one very specific variety many times and from multiple angles and distances. Five jumps are shown with zoomed-in closeness, and another four appear in extreme wide shots of the whole bridge.

These wide shots are a notable component of *The Bridge's* anesthetization process because they not only add more jumps to the film but also prompt the viewer to look for them actively. The first of these "postcard" views, as Steel calls them, frames the entire bridge in a wide, static shot that remains on-screen for a long forty-five seconds. Tucked away somewhere in that time and space is the tiniest dark speck falling from the bridge, followed by a small splash. Knowing the film's topic of people jumping off the bridge, the viewer will likely expect that sight in any sustained view of the structure, but Steel pushes her to *want* to see suicide by setting up a challenge of finding it in the shot. One of these postcard shots even begins with two pedestrians who are being interviewed about their encounter with a jumper on the bridge saying, "we didn't see him jump"—an editing choice that admonishes the viewer not to make the same mistake and to look carefully for the splash. Bruegel's *Landscape with the Fall of Icarus* shares this macabre *Where's Waldo?* quality, its title prompting the viewer to hunt through the landscape for Icarus's tiny, sinking shape. Through *The Bridge*'s many iterations of suicide's display, the event we thought of in the opening sequence as a rare spectacle—intruding upon the tranquillity of the bridge's daily life—is thus slowly infused with a sense of typicality. The jumps even accumulate a limited set of conventions through their repeated presentation: people pause to look down before jumping, leap feet first, and flail their arms and legs on the way down.

In planning these repetitions, Steel mimics the structure of genres such as the musical or pornography, both of which are adept at dispensing spectacle. *The Bridge*'s prime spectacle, recorded suicide, becomes the backbone of the film through its editing scheme: all other elements are arranged to complement the jumper shots, the way narrative is arranged around song-and-dance numbers in musicals or around sex acts in pornography. And like those genres' prime moments of spectacle, the jumper shots in *The Bridge* are meted out at regular intervals, so that the viewer never waits long to see another. Given that the project was always so firmly rooted in the aesthetics of visible death, this structure comes as no surprise. Asked if he thought about leaving out the jumper footage, Steel said he had not, "because his whole concept was 'to be able to show what it looks like *from the outside.*'"[57]

As always in documentary, what something "looks like from the outside" is filtered through the filmmakers' choices about how to look at it. Structures and stylistic techniques that we associate with mainstream, fiction film (like the spectacle-emphasizing editing scheme just mentioned) play a major role in how *The Bridge* aestheticizes its documentary footage of suicide. To be clear, the startling thing about this comparison is not that a documentary is employing techniques we associate with Hollywood fiction—a familiar phenomenon—but rather that such techniques are being grafted onto *this* documentary footage, to

3.5. A wide "postcard" shot of the bridge, with jumper
(*The Bridge*, 2006, Eric Steel, Koch Lorber).

death footage, to amplify its suspense and affect. As Andrea Fitzpatrick writes, in reference to 9/11's falling-body images, "Aesthetic values in representations of human suffering [do not] preclude an ethical engagement with them. The goal is not to impose prohibitions on certain aesthetic or formal gestures but to identify what they do to embodied subjects in this unique genre."[58]

An influence in *The Bridge* from mainstream fiction film is best illuminated by contrasting it to another documentary on suicide at the Golden Gate. Far more experimental than *The Bridge*, *Suicide Box* is a thirteen-minute short created by Natalie Jeremijenko and shown as part of a larger installation at the Whitney Biennial in 1996. Like *The Bridge*, it records jumpers at the Golden Gate but with an unstaffed camera triggered by their vertical motion—not by an elaborate, fully staffed, four-camera setup. The results are accompanied by footage of daily life at the site and on-screen text that describes the project with the detached style of a scientific report.

Suicide Box displays footage of fatal jumps, just as *The Bridge* does and ten years before it, but did not seem to generate much controversy. Granted, *Suicide Box* had a limited circulation, confined to high art circles, as opposed to *The Bridge*'s theatrical release and wide availability through DVD and streaming distribution. But another factor causing the disparity in controversy, I argue, is that *Suicide Box*'s footage employs none of mainstream, commercial cinema's stylistic tools for spectacular representation, while *The Bridge* employs many. *Suicide Box* eschews a polished look throughout, diminishing the sensuous beauty of the Golden Gate with its cheap video aesthetic and handheld cinematography, but the jumper shots are particularly ragged. Their brief, mostly black-and-white, static views in extreme long shot make the falling bodies appear just as black specks against the sky. The shots are cut together roughly, one after another, with only the indistinct noise of electronic equipment running on the sound track. The resulting scenes are basically degraded versions (blurry, no color, limited sound) of what we would see if standing where the camera recorded these jumps.

Suicide Box provides another opportunity to expand Sobchack's list of gazes, with its ethics-centered taxonomy of the moving image camera's ways of recording actual death. Jeremijenko's footage employs what I would term the "automated gaze," originating from an unstaffed camera that records everything with a homogeneous, unresponsive aesthetic style. While *Suicide Box*, with its vertical-motion-triggered recording apparatus, presents an eccentric case, the automated gaze at death has become increasingly common in the video and digital era through the explosion of closed-circuit television (CCTV) surveillance of public space. Death footage recorded by these kinds of cameras litters the Internet shock sites I analyze in chapter 4, conveying at once the charged energy of startling sights recorded by chance and also the frustrating optics of conventional surveillance aesthetics. Deaths captured by the automated gaze tend to appear in static, low-resolution, extreme long shots that communicate extremely little of death's "full detail." The fatal action here typically unfolds far from the camera, sometimes even slipping out of the frame that will not move to follow it, and is generally recorded without audio. While it might seem that the automated gaze cannot be ethically judged because of its absent human intentionality, I would emphasize the importance of assessing its ethics before and after the recording is made. Who set up the camera, why, and under what conditions? Who preserved and distributed its death footage, in what form, and for what purpose? Sobchack focuses on the ethics of recording death, but considering how fraught and contested the distribution of such footage has been throughout the history of image technologies, this phase of documentary death's life cycle deserves greater ethical consideration—a task I engage with further in chapter 4.

What makes *The Bridge* so singular and shocking, then, is its implementation of extreme, embodied surveillance that does not rely on an automated gaze. Where *Suicide Box* and other automated recordings display death less clearly than it would appear if witnessed in person, *The Bridge*'s cinematographers intentionally use technology to *enhance* human vision, adding greater visibility, drama, and suspense to how the viewer would perceive its deaths if she were there to see them with the naked eye. These operators zoom much closer, offering clear, full-color shots that "see" from an otherwise inaccessible vantage point, revealing details like facial expressions and nervous fidgeting. The frame is mobile rather than static, directed to follow the jumpers and give us the best possible view of each descent, striving to keep the falling bodies centered and in focus. Music provides audiences with cues for how to feel about the jumps, combining a yearning, minor-key score with melancholy pop interludes. Steel also uses foley effects, adding a postproduction splash sound to accompany each impact on the water. The mise-en-scène does its part, too, as the striking atmosphere of the Golden Gate is used to set the mood for the jumper footage—especially when the editor cuts in shots with ethereal fog, a lightning bolt, or a hopeful rainbow to generate specific emotions.

The accumulation of these techniques is crucial to the final revelation of sublimity that ends the film. Building to a scene of brazen escalation, Steel saves his most spectacular footage until the audience is fully primed to encounter a sublime suicide—primed by the accrued sublimity of the Golden Gate and by the adjustment to watching recorded deaths throughout the film. Then he can enfold magnificence and horror into the suicidal act rather than dividing them between intention and act, as Goethe does. This particular jumper, Gene Sprague, is shown over and over throughout the documentary, pacing the bridge. Appearing at regular intervals, he walks along clad entirely in black with his long, dark hair blown about by the wind.

Because no other jumper's story spans the entire length of the film, one starts to wonder while watching *The Bridge* for the first time what makes Gene's so remarkable. Like most of the jumpers, Gene had a history of mental instability, had talked about committing suicide in the past, and struggled with finances and relationships. Other jumpers in the film are more memorable for the unique content of their stories: one had a friend who fears that she contributed to his death by giving him her prescription medication and cutting short a social visit when he said he was feeling suicidal; another was just twenty-one years old and had direct conversations with his sympathetic father about whether he should kill himself and how; another, Kevin Hines, lived to narrate his journey of despair to and off the bridge, which ends with hope through his survival and newfound direction working in suicide prevention. If the film prioritized suicide prevention and "education" over "entertainment," as Steel claims, Hines's story would have been the optimal focal point (despite the fact that his jump was not recorded and he appears only in talking-head interviews). Instead, *The Bridge* highlights Gene's story, building suspense by teasing it out over ninety-three minutes and ending on his jump. That choice turns him into a protagonist—adopting another convention of commercial fiction—in a film that, ethically, feels like it should not have a protagonist. The way Steel structures his footage and mediates Gene's image implies a disturbing judgment: that Gene's jump is more significant than the others, that his life and death are worthy of greater attention. In short, he is the star of *The Bridge* where the others are supporting players.

When we finally see his suicide, the reason it has been withheld and hyped for so long becomes clear. Unlike the other four furtive jumps seen in close-up, Gene's is uniquely graceful. He sits on the railing with his back to the drop and then smoothly hoists himself into a standing position atop it. For a second, he balances there—his tall frame, clad in black leather, complementing the vertical red struts of the cables. Maintaining his straight-backed stance, he tips his weight resolutely toward the bay and gently falls backward with a high diver's grace. Spreading his arms straight out in the first instant of his descent, Gene does not flail wildly like the other jumpers in free fall; during the drop, he holds his chosen pose remarkably well as his body twists slightly in the wind and lands with a towering splash. Gene's mediated suicide is, in a

3.6. Gene stands atop the railing (*The Bridge*, 2006, Eric Steel, Koch Lorber).

3.7. Gene, midfall (*The Bridge*, 2006, Eric Steel, Koch Lorber).

word, spectacular. It realizes the eerie fantasy that remains illusory in *The Falling Man*, capturing an artful death that can withstand an unblinking, moving image display—that need not be excerpted in a split-second photograph to suggest sublimity. Like "the falling man," Gene is the lone body falling sublimely enough to be fetishized by a documentary image-maker amid a host of more aesthetically unremarkable suicides.

For the compassionate viewer, there is always an element of horror in seeing real people die on camera. While none of the deaths I have studied for this project have been easy to watch, Gene Sprague's is the only one whose aesthetics convey—disturbingly—an undeniable majesty. Significantly, it is also the most skillfully documented. Unlike the other jumps, every visible instant of Gene's, from his climb onto the railing through his splashdown, is enframed. The camera operators (including Steel, who personally filmed Gene for ninety-three minutes) capture the sight from both the north and south recording stations and provide clear views of it from two different angles.[59] With perfect Hollywood style, shots from these two angles are sutured together with a match cut and even maintain the 180-degree line, conveniently visible in the form of the bridge itself. Thus, a serendipitous confluence of aesthetics wins Gene the role of protagonist in *The Bridge*: his jump provides the greatest spectacle, and the crew records it with the most skill.

In its cinematic presentation, Gene's jump is not only shocking and spectacular but also specifically sublime. A brief comparison with mainstream, commercial cinema underscores the sequence's sublime aesthetics and their association with that branch of filmmaking. Hitchcock's *Vertigo* (1958) might seem the most natural match with *The Bridge*: it features a suicidal character who journeys to the Golden Gate Bridge, appears entranced by the site, and leaps into the bay. Further, she seems to have been infected by a hereditary strand of suicide contagion (as we are told that her great-grandmother killed herself and may be possessing her), and, just like *The Bridge*'s subjects, she is unknowingly being watched by a vaguely creepy voyeur. The missing ingredient in *Vertigo*, though, is the spectacle of freefall that is so important to *The Bridge*. Madeleine makes her leap from the shore underneath the structure, at Fort Point, and falls only about ten feet into the water, out of the camera's view (a strange venue choice explained by a later plot twist).

There are precedents, though, in both documentary and fiction film history for the conspicuous stylization of bodies falling through space. In the former, beyond *The Falling Man* in photography, one should recall Leni Riefenstahl's hypnotic high-dive sequence in *Olympia* (1938) and Werner Herzog's awestruck shots of ski jumpers in *The Great Ecstasy of the Sculptor Steiner* (1975). While the threat of a fatal landing pervades Herzog's film, these documentaries generally celebrate the controlled descent of skilled bodies in athletic competitions— a far cry from *The Bridge*'s more controversial display of lethal falls that end unhappy lives. Mainstream, fiction film has more frequently found aesthetic beauty in violent falls, with the seamless realism of new digital effects generating a glut of such scenes in recent decades. Examples include *Cliffhanger* (1993, Renny Harlin); *City of Angels* (1998, Brad Silberling); *Vanilla Sky* (2001, Cameron Crowe), *Lord of the Rings: The Fellowship of the Ring* (2001, Peter Jackson); *King Kong* (2005, Peter Jackson); *Watchmen* (2009, Zack Snyder); *Harry Potter and the Half-Blood Prince* (2009, David Yates); *Dredd* (2012, Peter Travis); and *Les Misérables* (2012, Tom Hooper), to name a sample. These scenes of dramatic descent exemplify what Kristen Whissel identifies as digital cinema's special effects–enabled obsession with verticality, manifesting now in digital documentary without the aid of effects through *The Bridge*.[60]

The final scene of *Crouching Tiger, Hidden Dragon* (2000, Ang Lee) resonates strongly with *The Bridge*, as it depicts suicide via bridge jump and stylistically softens the horror of that event. Like Steel, Lee uses an ornate bridge for his location, shrouded by fog and immersed in an awe-inspiring natural environment. A young Chinese warrior woman, devastated by the emotional destruction she has wreaked upon fellow warriors, has been drawn to this mountaintop bridge by a legend that those who jump from it will float away and have their deepest wishes come true. But there is sadness, not hope, in her eyes as she shares a few parting words with her lover and then springs over the railing. The actress's movements combine with practical and digital special effects to portray this suicidal leap as supremely elegant. Her body strikes an open pose, her hair and clothes flow in the wind, and the camera swoops around her to provide multiple views of her slow-motion descent, eventually losing sight of her in the thick fog. An evocative score plays under the event, and we are even guided in how to react by an on-screen witness: her lover, who appears saddened but also deeply moved.

Many of these techniques for amplifying spectacle reappear in *The Bridge*'s finale of documentary death. Gene himself begins this appropriation, as the lone suicidal individual at the Golden Gate paying attention to aesthetics. With a touch of flair, he arrives at the bridge in a kind of costume—his outfit an expressionistic signifier of his dark thoughts—and deftly choreographs and performs his graceful jump. With its back-to-the-drop positioning, slow and dramatic tilt, and calm maintenance of the body's straight, vertical pose, Gene's jump feels unquestionably *cinematic* in its conception and execution. Exuding aesthetic intentionality, his jump's fluid and expressive motion primes it to register well in a moving image medium, regardless of the fact that Gene did not know he was being recorded. His choreographed jump so closely aligns with the aesthetic qualities of commercial fiction's dramatically-falling-body trope, described earlier, that this trope may have directly shaped it. In other words, I suspect that Gene Sprague was thinking about some film scenes when he planned how, exactly, to fall from that bridge. Like Mark in *Silverlake Life* and so many others steeped in U.S. death culture, Gene may have "known" what death looks like primarily from fiction film. Implicitly shaped by cinema, Gene's death—enfolded into a work of cinema without his knowledge or consent—now plays its own role in shaping the medium's depiction of death and in shaping death culture at large.

Gene's consideration of appearances aligns not only with cinematic representation but also with the intensely public quality of this suicide venue, where an estimated 76 percent of jumps are witnessed by someone on the bridge.[61] Prevention advocates comment that this location may be chosen by people who want to be stopped, to be talked back over the railing. But a more uncomfortable possibility those advocates might not want to consider is that, as mentioned earlier, it may also be chosen by people who want to be *seen* killing themselves. Unbeknownst to Gene or the other jumpers, *The Bridge* would amplify that public quality by recording and displaying their deaths for a theatrical film audience. Whether Gene planned his exit for his potential witnesses at the Golden Gate or for his own satisfaction—a parting gesture of success and control in a life that seemed to lack those qualities—he gave his audience a true performance.

The audiovisual mediation of Gene's already-striking suicide in *The Bridge* strives to elicit a sublime interpretation. To amplify awe and give his respectable target audience extra assistance in getting past the horror of recorded suicide, Steel relies heavily on his audio track. The last spoken words in the film, played over Gene's image just before he stands up on the railing, are from his older friend Caroline, who has been a source of calm and well-articulated wisdom throughout her interviews. Speculating on why Gene chose the bridge, she says, "Maybe he just wanted to fly one time." No longer dark and brooding, the score now lets its string instruments rise to higher and higher notes, bolstering this connotation of flight, before fading out to silence with Gene's fall. Familiar elements from fiction fare like *Crouching Tiger* recur here: the euphemistic framing of a deadly fall as "flight," environmental elements that conceal the violence of landing (fog or a splash), the inspirationally swelling music, the survivor who is both saddened and moved. With them, *The Bridge* strives to create an environment in which viewers can finally embrace the "negative pleasure" of sublime suicide—a sight whose educational value remains stubbornly abstract in what Eric Steel claims is an educational, suicide prevention documentary.

This closing sequence demonstrates that despite exploiting powerful digital technology, *The Bridge* ultimately owes much of its shape to chance—a factor that has always been integral to the documentary capture of life as it unfolds, to the magic of this cinematic form. Chance survives even in a production like Steel's, with its punishing shooting schedule that endeavors to master contingency through the unblinking gazes of its digital cameras. The film is able to build to such a sublime release only because its crew happened to witness this one immaculate jump and to record it with more skill and better camera coverage than others. Even with two people training four cameras on the bridge all day every day for a year, the odds that they would capture a performance like Gene's seem slim. With documentary death's mystique somewhat dulled by the many contributions of video and DV to its archive, Gene's jump restores a feeling of "I can't believe they caught that on camera" reminiscent of Robert Capa's *The Falling Soldier* and Eddie Adams's *Saigon Execution*.

A "False Romantic Promise":
The Bridge's Reception and Gene's Posthumous Fame

A documentary that records and displays the suicides of real people certainly breaks taboos and raises ethical issues, as its vocal detractors have noted. But as I have argued earlier, *The Bridge* is an even more volatile work than its surface-level public controversy acknowledged. By uncovering its sublime aesthetics beneath the mere fact of its displays of suicide, I seek a more sophisticated understanding of its ethics and potential effect on audiences—and, by extension, of broader questions about aesthetics and ethics in an era of burgeoning death documentary.

When documentarians enhance the potential for aesthetic pleasure in their death footage, they risk consignment to the ethically condemned "death porn" category, alongside films like *Faces of Death* and Internet shock sites that stream gruesome actuality footage (analyzed in the introduction and chapter 4, respectively). Aware of the ethical quagmire he creates by showing lush close-ups of actual suicide, Steel is eager to disassociate his deployment of this footage from any unseemly fascination with the sight of death. He asserts that *The Bridge* will disappoint viewers who crave graphic death scenes: "I don't think it's used or incorporated in a way that will satisfy someone's voyeuristic urge to see it. . . . If it were exploitation, I could have put together a clip-reel of people jumping off the bridge and sold it on the Internet."[62] Here, Steel references death porn and fights to avoid that label for his film.

As noted previously, linking documentary death to activist or humanitarian causes can often secure the type of respectability Steel seeks. To show death as sublime without having his documentary dismissed as lurid trash, Steel's strongest option is to forge such a link between *The Bridge* and suicide prevention. He could have aligned his project easily with a ready-made source of "redeeming social importance": several local organizations had been lobbying the Bridge District for years to erect a suicide barrier at the site. In fact, Bay Area filmmaker Jenni Olson was completing her own documentary, *The Joy of Life*, advocating for this suicide barrier during *The Bridge*'s production phase. As with *Suicide Box*, this film is more experimental than *The Bridge*: its first twenty-seven minutes are contemplative shots of San Francisco locations with voice-over narration about a butch lesbian's sexual escapades, then its concluding section on suicide is a very legible advocacy piece. There, Olson accompanies static 16mm shots of the bridge (without anyone jumping off it) with narration about its history of suicide: the number of jumpers, the duration of their falls, the fatality rate, the bridge's design history, and the decision to build such a short guardrail.

Having firmly established a problem, Olson's script then details a solution: a suicide barrier. The narrator deflects the claim that people prevented from jumping would just kill themselves elsewhere (citing a sociological study that demonstrates otherwise), scolds the Bridge District for continually resisting a barrier project, and describes how other former suicide landmarks have been fitted with effective barriers.[63] Olson has said about the structure of this activist segment, "I wanted to attack it without being gruesome or exploitive, which a lot of the material about the topic is."[64] Beyond designing its content as activist, Olson proactively put her film to work: she adapted its script into an op-ed for the *San Francisco Chronicle*, collaborated with the Psychiatric Foundation of Northern California in its pro-barrier efforts, and sent DVDs of *The Joy of Life* to the Bridge District's board of directors.

While I found no evidence that Steel himself took the kinds of advocacy measures Olson did, *The Bridge* was certainly put to political use by established barrier advocates after its release. And despite its tremendous and perhaps unforgivable ethical lapses, *The Bridge* did produce unprecedented material results in this cause, becoming one of the primary forces that pressured local government into approving a suicide barrier proposal for a safety net beneath the walkway (though, at the time of this writing, construction on the project still has not begun). Olson herself acknowledges that *The Bridge* "brought an enormous amount of attention to this seemingly intractable issue. It was an absolute tipping point I think. The fact that he was making the film became like this PR nightmare for the Bridge District."[65] Olson's film exposed the facts, but Steel's got the headlines with its falling bodies. *The Bridge* bluntly made visible the long-ignored suicides at the city's signature landmark in living color and queasy close-up, essentially embarrassing voters and the local government into taking action.

To the press, Steel has often emphasized *The Bridge's* major impact in the barrier campaign, but, significantly, the film itself scrupulously avoids any barrier advocacy.[66] In fact, confined strictly to the world of the jumpers and their loved ones, it makes no mention of a potential suicide barrier at all. This absence coexists uncomfortably with the film's purported ambition of suicide prevention and Steel's claim that *The Bridge* shows death to educate, not to entertain. A related absence of interviews with experts—in psychology, sociology, or suicide prevention—puts an undue burden on grieving loved ones to educate the audience about suicide and severely limits the type of knowledge that can be presented. The effect of these absences is palpable in records of the film's reception, such as comments from Steel's most eager pupils on *The Bridge's* official message board. Many there express sympathy for the jumpers and a wish that something could be done to solve this problem of suicide at the bridge. But in my examination of all 960 entries on the board, I found that only 23 made any mention of a suicide barrier—and a number of these wrote about a hypothetical barrier idea, without awareness of the actual barrier campaign.[67] In one of her wisest insights about the "education" provided by images of suffering and death, Sontag argues, "To designate a hell is not, of course, to tell us anything about how to extract people from that hell, how to moderate hell's flames. . . . moral indignation, like compassion, cannot dictate a course of action."[68] *The Bridge* does not dictate a course of action, either for Golden Gate Bridge district officials or for viewers anywhere who might need guidance in how to prevent a suicide. Suicide prevention—regardless of whether one believes it *should* be the documentary's goal—thus feels like an afterthought for *The Bridge*, a defense to trot out against ethical criticism more than a demonstrably pursued educational effort.

Despite the controversy it generated, *The Bridge* also achieved a surprising measure of respectability, playing at major film festivals.[69] Assigning the documentary a label Steel worked hard to avoid, but modifying it to fit that new target audience, one viewer wrote about it as "*Faces of Death* for the Starbucks crowd."[70] In arguing that suicide prevention and barrier advocacy were an afterthought for the makers of *The Bridge*, my intention is not simply to diminish their benevolence but to emphasize that the film itself has different ambitions—ambitions that perhaps are worth the price of these attacks for Steel and for its fans. By analyzing its aesthetics and not merely its fraught ethics, I have taken seriously Steel's ambition to show what death "looks like from the outside," examining how he turns suicide into a sublime spectacle that even "the Starbucks crowd" can watch without shame.

The end results of those aesthetic ambitions—Gene's ascent to star status in the documentary, and the amplification of sublimity in his death—have indeed had a powerful effect on the film's reception. Their impact on the viewing public resonates with comments from an interviewee in *The Bridge*, who speaks about the "false romantic promise" of a Golden Gate Bridge suicide and laments about her friend Daniel, "I think it drew him with this idea of being famous." Daniel did not become famous, but Gene Sprague has become more famous than one would expect for a man posthumously portrayed in a limited-release documentary. He stands as something of a modern-day Werther figure, on a much smaller scale than Goethe's protagonist. In addition to the large percentage of comments devoted to Gene on the film's Internet message boards, he is also elaborately memorialized on two different websites that receive intimate RIP messages and virtual flowers from strangers who have only seen him in *The Bridge*. One of these sites reports that a third site used to exist, but its owner closed it down "because of the over zealous people who saw the film and glorified his suicide."[71] A number of singers and bands have recorded songs based on Gene's appearance in the film and posted them online, including one titled "Maybe He Just Wanted to Fly One Time." And Gene's image has been duplicated many times as clips from *The Bridge* are posted to YouTube and tagged with his name.

To forge a celebrity out of suicide footage, and to infuse the act itself with the awe of the Golden Gate Bridge, is to dramatically disregard the aforementioned media guidelines for depicting suicide and the research about suicide contagion. Through the language of those guidelines, Gene's suicide in *The Bridge* is "a particular death [that] is reported on at length" and is "romanticized" through Steel's presentation of it—effectively so, as evidenced by viewer responses. Eighteenth-century commenter J. J. Engel worried that readers of *The Sorrows of Young Werther* would "take the poetic beauty for moral beauty," a fear that applies equally well to this twenty-first-century film.[72] The threat posed by *The Bridge* exposes a categorical difference between documentary displays of war death and of death by suicide, and it also exposes the error of applying the former's justifications to the latter. Most displays of war death implicitly rely on the axiom that broadcasting the visible horrors of war will promote peace—

that actually seeing the human bodies that war rips apart will galvanize a naive public into active opposition. While seeing displays of war death is believed to diminish war, seeing certain displays of suicide is proven to *multiply* suicide through the effects of suicide contagion. In this context, when Eric Steel is asked why he could not tackle his topic without the death footage, his reply takes on a disturbing new resonance: "Once there's an actual film of someone jumping off the bridge you can't just forget it; the image won't disappear."[73]

While aiming to enlighten an apathetic public that pays little attention to suicide, Steel's campaign to implant "the image [that] won't disappear" also reaches suicidal people. For some of them in viewing *The Bridge*, the aforementioned 1845 warning from the *American Journal of Insanity* seems to apply: "Some particulars of the act, or expressions, seize the imagination." Tangible traces of that impact appear on the film's official message board, where a large number of commenters evocatively describe being "mesmerized," "entranced," or "haunted" by the sight of the jumpers, often repeating the phrase "I can't get it out of my mind." Though some there credit *The Bridge* with convincing them *not* to kill themselves, at least ten describe its spellbinding effect as fueling suicides or suicide attempts. One man writes, "I hope I can find the courage to do what those tormented souls did—take control of their own destiny. Barring the use of another method, perhaps someday I too shall join their ranks." Others mourn the loss of loved ones to the Golden Gate, whose recent viewing habits they describe: "After my friend spent hours obsessively watching this movie, she made the leap. Draw your own conclusions." Another woman writes, "My daughter jumped from the Bridge on August 1, 2008. She had watched the movie over and over for months. . . . I believe it became in a sense, hypnotic to her." Such stories migrated from Internet message boards to the national news when reporters revealed that eighteen-year-old Kyle Gamboa—whose 2013 jump from the Golden Gate Bridge became a high-profile case—had repeatedly viewed *The Bridge*'s trailer before his suicide.[74]

To pioneer the documentary display of sublime suicide, as Eric Steel has done, is also to take great ethical risks with viewers' emotions, and even their lives. But the specific risks and rewards of a project like *The Bridge* are complex and wholly entangled with aesthetics. To extract them requires a willingness to critically analyze documentary death footage rather than dismiss it as obscene at the outset—even if analysis still elicits a negative verdict in the end. Such dismissals carried low stakes in André Bazin's era, when documenting death on film was a seldom-realized fantasy. But as the digital age matures and the public gains access to real death "on demand"—in theaters, on DVD, streaming, downloadable—media scholars must fully address these multiplying texts.

Conclusion: The Diver in Reverse

In his richly articulated condemnation of documenting death, described in my introduction, Bazin at one point moves from generalities to a hypothetical example of the act he so detests: "I imagine the supreme cinematic perversion would be the projection of an execution backward like those comic newsreels in which the diver jumps up from the water back onto his diving board."[75] For all the stylistic manipulations Steel uses in *The Bridge*—and for all of its politically disengaged, ethically suspect, dangerously romantic aspects—one cinematic tool he selectively rejects is a manipulation of time, like the manipulation Bazin describes. Time's flow is not decelerated, frozen, repeated, or reversed at any point during the jump footage, despite the use of such techniques elsewhere in the film. There is no mystical slowing down of the moment of death, nor will any of these "divers" be returned "up from the water" to their points of departure. Temporally, then, death unfolds routinely and irreversibly in *The Bridge*, in contrast to its depiction in other falling-body film scenes mentioned earlier, *all* of which use slow motion. Unlike their descents, often filtered through composite effects and CGI in addition to the slow motion, the falling bodies of *The Bridge* defy the much-discussed immateriality and ephemerality of digital technologies. True, they are transferred to the screen algorithmically instead of indexically. But for viewers—in a less theoretical, more experiential sense—these individuals still plummet with the heavy weight of their embodiment, pitched downward with unattenuated speed. As an audience, we sense their materiality. We believe in it, in a practical, painful way.

And yet, theorists of the digital also write that its images are infinitely malleable, never fixed as a final product that will remain untouched. *The Bridge* has not remained untouched, and its remixing in a few YouTube videos yields one particularly interesting example that defies Bazin's notion of "the supreme cinematic perversion": a music video from metal band Seether cut together with footage from *The Bridge*. The original Seether video includes a narrative about a young man contemplating suicide from a rooftop. Halfway through, he makes the leap—tipping backward just like Gene, but in slow motion. By the end, though, the band's belted-out determination to "rise above this" has the power to reverse his descent, propelling him back up from the ground to the rooftop unscathed. The YouTube remix, as comments from its author make clear, is an earnest (if perhaps distasteful) attempt at a suicide prevention video. In it, the roof jumper's shots are replaced by footage from *The Bridge*, including some of the death footage.[76] Gene appears most prominently. He makes his jump, and by the end is restored to his starting point by rolling the video clip backward—like Bazin's newsreel diver coming "up from the water back onto his diving board."

This amateur editor's optimistic revision of *The Bridge*'s irreversible suicides, however naive, speaks to something deeply rooted at the intersection between death and documentary, to a quality that unites celluloid film and digital video: cinema's illusory promise to preserve what it records, to hold onto what would otherwise be lost and return it to us anew with each viewing. In the face of actual death, this promise is achingly seductive—even when the only moment that gets preserved is a person's last, as in *The Bridge*. Its footage of suicide at the Golden Gate, like *all* documentary images of death, is rife with cognitive dissonance. A rare memento mori in a death-denying age, it is also a simultaneous pledge that some spectral form of immortality is possible—that we can hoist the dead back over the railing through a video clip played in reverse.

4

STREAMING DEATH

THE POLITICS OF DYING ON YOUTUBE

Photographs of an atrocity may give rise to
opposing responses. A call for peace.
A cry for revenge. Or simply the bemused awareness,
continually restocked by photographic
information, that terrible things happen.

SUSAN SONTAG, *Regarding the Pain of Others*

There is an axiom that threads through the history of documentary media, a belief that each new generation of image-makers reaffirms. To discard or doubt it,
perhaps, would shake the form's foundations too dramatically. The belief is in
the ability to decrease war and violence through the documentary representation of war and violence—that if a photograph, say, can perfectly communicate
"the horrors of war," then its viewers will come to oppose war and promote
peace. In the documentary *The Devil Came on Horseback* (2007, Annie Sund-
berg and Ricki Stern), an ex-marine turned military observer, Brian Steidle,
carries that belief with him as he journeys to the Darfur region of Sudan in
2004. There, he documents the genocide raging in the area as the Janjaweed
militia tears through villages, burning homes and killing and raping residents.
Unable to capture graphic shots of fatal attacks as they happened, Steidle none-

theless trains his camera on countless corpses. With the razor-sharp visuals digital photography provides, he documents the corpses of young and old alike in painful detail, bodies felled by gunshot, beating, burning alive, and so on. Deliberating about what to do with his images, he expresses a confidence that, "if these photos were released to the public, there would be troops in here in a matter of days."

Once the horrors of war he records have emotionally worn him down, Steidle returns to the United States, allows his photos to be published in the *New York Times*, does interviews with major news channels, and goes on the road to present on the crisis in Darfur. On this circuit, he brings with him several huge binders filled with the photographs—page after page of grisly corpses, evidencing the atrocities that the photos themselves endeavor to halt. But the images he spreads do not make the impact that Steidle *knew* they would; as he sees it, they fail to inspire tangible action on behalf of Darfur. Instead, many of their viewers appear to absorb only Sontag's "bemused awareness . . . that terrible things happen." The documentary thus draws to a downbeat conclusion as Steidle arrives at a similar insight: "I definitely look at the world differently now. I knew that bad things happened; I didn't know that people would stand by and allow them to happen. I honestly thought as I wrote an email home that if the people of America could see what I've seen there would be troops here in one week . . . That's not true at all. They've seen it now and we've still done nothing." The credits roll soon after his statement and nudge the viewer toward action with a URL and the message: "There is a growing movement to end the crisis in Darfur. You can make a difference." Considering the way *The Devil Came on Horseback* has documented the dissolution of Steidle's own faith in this sentiment, the earnest words scrolling by on-screen convey an unintended irony.

Steidle tried to deliver what new technology promised at the turn of the previous century: the "soul-stirring pictures of actual, grewsome war" that so excited a *Leslie's Weekly* author in 1900 and that Steidle hoped would mobilize a response to genocide in 2005.[1] The intervening century, however, brought so many "pictures of actual, grewsome war" that new entries into that realm need to meet a higher threshold of vividness to stir the soul—to drive home more than just a fortified awareness "that terrible things happen." While Steidle's binders full of photos are certainly gruesome, the images are ultimately too familiar in their subjects and aesthetics to make the impact he wants. They bring the Rwandan genocide to mind most immediately, but they also share broad conventions of corpse photography, recalling the camps of the Holocaust and even the battlefields of the American Civil War. Because the period of history spanned by camera technology is so crowded with atrocities, corpses and their documentary traces have become almost clichéd signifiers of the terrible things that happen in the world. Their effectiveness in political causes in centuries past—perpetrator photographs appropriated for antilynching pamphlets, concentration camp images that evidenced genocide by the Nazis—has lost potency in the twenty-first.

Further, as discussed in chapter 1, the corpse photograph can feel like an image made "too late": a still representation of a still object that can only gesture toward the final moments of the person who once inhabited it—moments conspicuously absent from the photo. As Vivian Sobchack writes, in these images, "Our sympathy for the subject who once was is undermined by our alienation from the object that is."[2] The corpse's missing subjectivity, its sense of suffering already past, seems to dilute the photo's activist potential. The most legendary entries in the U.S. annals of death images that have "made a difference," after all, are not corpse photographs. They are the photo and film footage of General Nguyễn Ngọc Loan executing handcuffed prisoner Nguyễn Văn Lém in Saigon in 1968. The paragon of the "moment of death" image fantasy described in chapter 1, Eddie Adams's photo of this event, *Saigon Execution*, offers a long, hard stare at this sight, playing out in the contortions of Lém's face as he is shot point-blank in the head. The publication of *Saigon Execution* has a popular reputation as a major turning point in the Vietnam War, shifting public opinion more sharply against American involvement there. Despite evidence from historians that media coverage of that war *followed* rather than precipitated this change in attitude, the legend persists that Adams's picture played a large role in ending the war.[3] Clint Eastwood's *Flags of Our Fathers* (2008), a film whose very premise argues for the importance of images in war, includes a monologue to this effect in its opening moments: "The right picture can win or lose a war. Look at Vietnam: the picture of that South Vietnamese officer blowin' that fellow's brains out of the side of his head—[*motions gunshot*] 'Blammo!'—that was it. The war was lost. We just hung around trying to pretend it wasn't." As this scene exemplifies, popular history seems to have rendered a verdict on *Saigon Execution*: this documentary image of death in progress—not coming soon or already past—"made a difference."

In their use by activists, images of actual death best satisfy the challenging questions that haunt their very existence: Why should we make and look at them? What right have we to do so? While I have endeavored to frame all my previous case studies through their political implications, this chapter examines the explicit activist use of documentary death in conjunction with digital media. To do so, I consider shifts in the production, distribution, and exhibition of such material, as well as longtime characteristics of politically effective documentary death that remain constant (and, indeed, become more apparent) in the digital age. On the production side, mobile phone cameras represent a massive technological shift not so much in kind but in scale: these easy-to-operate digital recording devices travel around in the pockets and purses of billions, vastly increasing the likelihood that a death in public space will happen in a camera's vicinity.

Distribution and exhibition changes have been equally dramatic, both in kind and in scale, as the Internet allows these mobile phone users to circulate what they capture fairly easily and at no cost (or, rather, at the start-up cost of a phone and Internet access). In a social and technological context where more and more videos from billions of recording devices vie for the public's attention, "it is not enough to have a camera," as Leshu Torchin notes. "The question of how images are presented, circulated, and put to use remains."[4] This distribution revolution is underscored by its surprisingly minimal role in *The Devil Came on Horseback*, a digital documentary about digital photography. As mentioned earlier, when Steidle goes to speaking engagements, he lugs around huge binders filled with prints of his photographs, inviting the audience to flip through them after the presentation for more evidence. While the bulk of these binders helps visualize the extent of the violence in Darfur, they also register as a curious anachronism in this twenty-first-century story. They sit there, heavy and sedentary on the table, awaiting one viewer at a time to walk over and look at them. This image of the literally bound photographs signifies their physically bound limitations within the fluidity of the digital age. Videos shot on mobile phone cameras are not at all bound in this manner but rather can become viral, bestowed with all the rapid and unfettered movement that word implies. Or, if one prefers, they are "spreadable media"—a phrase Henry Jenkins uses to counter the connotations of autonomous proliferation in an unchanged form associated with the term "viral."[5]

If activist videos of death are "spreadable," then YouTube, the Internet's most popular worldwide destination for streaming video, is the primary place where people try to spread them. Launched in 2005, YouTube quickly became a hub for participatory culture and the notion of interactivity so central to new media theory and Web 2.0. In terms of activist videos, and especially activist videos of death, that notion of participation is especially charged. Writing on the Holocaust and twentieth-century media, Barbie Zelizer makes an assertion that is important to reexamine in relation to YouTube in the twenty-first: "It may be that the act of making people see is beginning to take the place of making people do, and that witnessing—even if it involves a narrowed representation of atrocity and little real response—is becoming the *acte imaginaire* of the twentieth century."[6] Studying activist videos of death on YouTube reveals the extent to which "witnessing" in that space can facilitate "doing," but also the very real limitations of the actions that emerge in that scenario. Jodi Dean delivers a digital-age update to Zelizer's sentiment, noting how the Internet seems to promise that we can witness and then take action immediately through interactive commenting, reposting, petition circulating, and so on—measures some have disparagingly categorized as "slacktivism." Along these lines, Dean writes, sites like YouTube make us surprisingly passive: "Discussion, far from displaced, has itself become a barrier against acts as action is perpetually postponed. . . . It's easier to set up a new blog than it is to undertake the ground-level organizational work of building alternatives. It's also difficult to think through the ways our practices and activities are producing new subjectivities, subjectivities that may well be more accustomed to quick satisfaction and bits of enjoyment than to planning, discipline, sacrifice, and delay."[7]

Further, despite its wide accessibility that welcomes nonprofessional media producers and provides new ways to consume, too, YouTube is hardly a digital utopia even as a space for just witnessing. As Torchin notes, the traditional documentary format on which activists have often relied finds little traction on the site, especially because its users are so accustomed to very short works.[8] YouTube tends to present raw video without the context often necessary to understand what is being depicted, and at the same time it creates another kind of context that feels awkward and insensitive: that of seeing somber activist videos posted alongside clips of skateboard stunts and pets being tickled. In her innovative video-book *Learning from YouTube*, Alexandra Juhasz puts it bluntly: "[YouTube is] a context that is not ideal for activism, analysis, or community."[9]

Nevertheless, relatively early in the histories of mobile phone footage and of YouTube, two sets of mobile phone death videos that were fully integrated into activist causes circulated heavily on the site. Never removed by YouTube's administrators, despite activists' fears that they would be because of their violent content, these videos depict the 2009 killings of Oscar Grant in Oakland, California and Neda Agha-Soltan in Tehran.[10] Although we generally do not give much thought to aesthetics in raw video shot by nonprofessionals on mobile phones, I want to highlight their importance here; both sets of videos make politically charged deaths metaphorically visible to the public, but one set's greater success in making death optically visible (among other aesthetic features) gives it wider exposure and more activist power. Through these aesthetics, I argue that an audiovisual resemblance to the vision of death presented by mainstream, commercial cinema is most likely to generate audience sympathy and media attention via YouTube (ironically, since the site achieved its initial popularity by offering user-generated alternatives to that mode). Further, I argue that the tendency of most streaming video to strip away an event's context greatly shapes the way viewers understand the depicted deaths—but not always in a decidedly *negative* sense, as some have claimed. Grant's and Agha-Soltan's recorded deaths provide an illuminating challenge to scholars' and activists' claims that YouTube's lack of context makes it a deficient and even dangerous venue for political content.

"Not a Shock Site": Streaming Death on and off YouTube

As the Internet's highest-traffic and culturally dominant video streaming site, globally, YouTube is essential to digital-age attempts to make death visible through its documentary recording. But understanding the nuances of how this kind of footage circulates online—both in general and in relation to the two case studies that are presented in this chapter—requires explorations both of YouTube's corporate policies about graphic content and of the wider network of social media and other streaming sites in which YouTube is situated. On YouTube itself, users trying to distribute death videos face a challenge from the site's "Community Guidelines," which limit graphic content: "Graphic or gratuitous violence is not allowed. If your video shows someone being physically hurt, attacked, or humiliated, don't post it. . . . YouTube is not a shock site. Don't post gross-out videos of accidents, dead bodies or similar things *intended to shock or disgust*."[11] But as the latter rule hints, YouTube judges graphic clips by (somewhat) specific criteria rather than excluding all such content. The expanded guidelines elaborate on these criteria: "If a video is particularly graphic or disturbing, it should be balanced with additional context and information. For instance, including a clip from a slaughter house in a video on factory farming may be appropriate. However, stringing together unrelated and gruesome clips of animals being slaughtered in a video may be considered gratuitous if its purpose is to shock rather than illustrate." Here, YouTube adopts the spirit of Supreme Court justice William Brennan's definition of obscenity, offered during the case *United States v. Roth* in 1957: that which is "utterly without redeeming social importance." The site avoids harboring "death porn" by requiring some plausible intention for the material beyond shock, sensationalism, or disrespect, and by banning "unrelated and gruesome clips . . . [strung] together."

Statements about the role of context on the site are especially interesting here. YouTube suggests that graphic material "should be balanced with additional context and information," seeming to recognize the tendency of its own format (favoring short, user-uploaded videos) to omit adequate context. YouTube's expanded guideline on sex and nudity reinforces this call for context and highlights another dimension of the site's philosophy about censorship: "Most nudity is not allowed. . . . There are exceptions for some educational, documentary, scientific, and artistic content, but only if that is the sole purpose of the video and it is not gratuitously graphic. For example, a documentary on breast cancer would be appropriate, but posting clips out of context from the documentary might not be." The discouragement of "clips out of context" favors professional, fully edited documentary material, despite YouTube having made its reputation through nonprofessional raw video.

As activist videos of death on YouTube illustrate, the malleability of these guidelines and their dependence on human judgment allow the site to distribute death videos in many circumstances—when YouTube administrators decide they are educational or, indeed, when they could "make a difference" in a cause deemed worthy.[12] This chapter will analyze two such sets of YouTube videos, but the site does remove the majority of death footage posted there. That removal process begins with the unpaid labor of YouTube users who press the "Report" button on videos they find inappropriate (for any reason); it continues with the underpaid labor of professional content moderators, who must view each flagged video and individually judge whether it should be removed (or have warnings and age restrictions added to it). Most content moderation for U.S. sites is now outsourced to low-wage workers, especially in the Philippines, increasing the extent to which the streaming video experience of U.S. audiences is globally inflected—even with domestically posted videos. Not incidentally in relation to this book's topic, content moderation jobs have a high turnover rate, and those who perform them sometimes require psychological counseling, developing a PTSD-like condition from spending full workdays evaluating an endless stream of mediated horrors.[13]

Even this labor-intensive system with its high human cost, though, cannot actually adequately keep graphic content off of YouTube. Despite increasing pressure from worldwide governments to fend off propagandistic content from ISIS and other violent extremist organizations, YouTube has continued to rely on this imperfect, post-uploading system of censorship, and its officials have stated that the company could not possibly prescreen the volume of videos posted to the site (roughly three hundred hours of content per minute).[14] The gap between posting and removal that this structure creates is what largely enables the continued circulation of graphic death videos online. During that gap, social media often enter the network of distribution, as YouTube video virality depends on off-site actions (especially given YouTube's limited realization of its internal social media affordances). YouTube users embed a video to their Facebook and Twitter feeds—where the video begins a separate process of content moderation for each of those sites—sharing it with wider circles of friends and followers, any of whom can share it further. By the time YouTube (or any similar site hosting streaming video) actually removes a video, it has often already been seen by vast audiences both on and off the site. In an instructive example, gunman and ex-journalist Vester Lee Flanagan recorded his 2015 murders of two former colleagues with his mobile phone as he committed them and then engineered the distribution of this death footage for maximum virality. In the hours after the incident, Flanagan seeded his Facebook and Twitter accounts with a steady flow of justifications for his actions. Only when his name was released as a suspect and journalists began scouring the Internet for information on him did Flanagan post the death video, giving it maximum exposure before Facebook and Twitter could react and suspend his accounts.[15]

During the window in which a fated-to-be-removed death video is still accessible, it is not only shareable but downloadable (through any number of free and easily accessed programs online). Now housed on the hard drives or in the clouds of other users, these videos can be freshly uploaded—back to the same places in a whack-a-mole style saga of posting and removal, or to sites with less stringent censorship policies. Thus, despite the swift removal of Flanagan's video by Facebook and Twitter, anyone can still watch it today on LiveLeak or TheYNC, two sites that form end points on a spectrum of respectability for "death porn" websites.[16] While LiveLeak does post news stories in addition to its graphic images and videos, TheYNC typifies the more extreme mode of marketing documentary death footage to an unabashedly morbid audience—an audience seemingly disinterested in its possible "redeeming social importance" and focused solely on its grim audiovisual attractions. When YouTube asserts in its "Community Guidelines" that it is "not a shock site," these are the shock sites from which it is distancing itself.

Death porn sites have regular users who come to browse such material, but the sites can also be the final destination for a viewer who has first tried to find a particular death video on YouTube and eventually concluded that it is not allowed there. I say "eventually" because many YouTube posters—from individuals to news organizations—capitalize on others' desire to find these forbidden clips, titling their videos to imply access to what they never actually display. A YouTube search for "james foley beheading" provides illustrative examples. As far back as 2004 and Nick Berg's recorded murder, terrorist execution videos have polarized the U.S. public between the revulsion that many people feel at the idea of watching a recorded beheading and the undeniable draw these sights have for others—freshly evidenced in search engine data that reveal how often Internet users tried to access these videos.[17] In the aforementioned example search term "james foley beheading," one may click on small-time news channel You Spot's video titled "ISIS Militants Behead Abducted American Journalist James Foley [Real Video]" but discover that the "real video" is a one-minute excerpt that ends before the beheading itself. Other search results use a thumbnail preview of Foley's killer pressing a knife to his neck in the moment just before its penetration, despite the fact that the previewed video contains neither the beheading footage nor even that thumbnail frame.[18]

Any actual footage of Foley's 2014 beheading that appeared on YouTube has been removed, but this and other ISIS execution videos abound on death porn sites, constituting a large portion of the sites' uploads during the group's highly active period of executions. These perpetrator videos often appear on the sites in an edited form that retains their gore and cuts the surrounding propaganda—as was the case when, for example, ISIS burned Jordanian pilot Muath Al-Kaseasbeh alive and TheYNC posted a 1:24-minute excerpt of the group's 22-minute video.[19] But such posts, I would assert, still bolster one of the primary goals that motivates the very existence of these highly political snuff films: to spread fear, in the most vivid and immersive form possible. The apparently symbiotic relationship between ISIS and the death porn sites that host recordings of their murders reveals the sinister potential of a digital media environment with an unfettered circulation of images and few gatekeepers— an important caveat to my support for such an environment elsewhere in this chapter.

One death porn site, TheYNC (which is representative of others such as Goregrish, Rotten, and BestGore), hosts graphic actuality videos in categories such as "Accident," "Gore," "Murder," "Suicide," and "War & Conflict." Lacking any "About" page where a website's owners typically explain its purpose, TheYNC and its users nevertheless communicate the site's worldview through the sensationalistic titles of its video posts, through the lack of contextual information with many videos, and especially through the site's sponsors. As one scrolls through the home page's dense grid of violent offerings, highly explicit video ads for hard-core pornography from sites like PunishTube.com—often violent in nature—autoplay in the page's right sidebar, suggesting a profitable crossover between visitors to death porn sites and visitors to sexually pornographic sites.[20] I emphasize these ads not to condemn the consumption of pornography but rather to note the viewing mode for death footage that their prominent presence encourages: actual death is made visible here for titillation, with no pretense of an interest in education, activism, or even an apolitically existential curiosity about the end of life.

Of all the research I have done for *Dying in Full Detail*, browsing death porn sites has been the most distressing—not because this footage is the most explicit (though it is) but because of the brutally unsympathetic environment these sites foster for watching people lose their lives, because of the palpable aura of inhumanity and disrespect that hangs in the virtual air there. As much as I might like to dismiss death porn sites as outliers, little-trafficked places in some dark corner of the Internet, their troubling popularity demonstrates a fairly widespread desire among today's Internet users for documentary death in its most graphic and unethical forms. LiveLeak is ranked 696 globally and 522 in the United States among the world's most-visited websites, and even the far less reputable TheYNC logs view counts in the millions for its top videos.

More striking even than their popularity is these sites' sheer volume of death footage, documenting lives ending from all manner of violent causes and from all corners of the earth: a male attacker chases a woman down in the street and stabs her to death, two men rob a gas station and gun down its attendant, an angry crowd beats a man to death inside a church, a woman on a train platform stands too close to the edge and is fatally struck, a motorcyclist plows into a car making a sudden turn on a busy road. Most of these sites' videos are shot from a distance—overtly gruesome in their subject matter, but revealing little of the death's violent detail. Some appear to come from CCTV cameras, others from mobile phones. Some are direct uploads; others are recordings of computer or television screens playing the footage from elsewhere. Some imply a geography, with on-screen Hindi characters from a news report or onlookers speaking Spanish; others occur at completely generic locations. In the absence of further details about these deaths from their postings, such contextual clues within the videos themselves feel significant—seldom as they lead the viewer to any concrete information. Usually many questions remain: When, where, and to whom did this death happen? What motivated a violent attack? Was the perpetrator apprehended? Is there a chance the victim actually survived and recovered? And, hauntingly, who recorded this death and for what purpose did someone distribute its recording? Most videos that end up on death porn sites never prove newsworthy enough to garner significant media exposure and, with it, answers to these questions. Instead, they gather on death porn sites in a steady stream, testifying to the unsettling banality both of violent death and now, in the digital age, of its documentary recording.

"The Whole World Is Watching" . . . Online:
Activist Videos of Death

YouTube's policy against "gratuitous" violence aims to distance it from the atmosphere of shock sites, but it also requires YouTube to make judgments about what recorded violence *should* be widely seen. In 2009, the site deemed two sets of death videos worthy that became integrated with activist causes. The videos of Oscar Grant III show the death of this twenty-two-year-old African American father at the hands of transit police in Oakland, California. In the first few hours of 2009, Grant was returning from New Year's Eve celebrations when Bay Area Rapid Transit (BART) police stopped his train at Oakland's Fruitvale station. Responding to reports of a fight that allegedly included Grant, four officers detained him and his friends on the platform as a train full of passengers watched the scene—and in some cases recorded it. After officers Johannes Mehserle and Tony Pirone pushed Grant facedown on the ground and attempted to handcuff him, Mehserle drew his gun and shot Grant fatally in the back. Mehserle later claimed that he thought Grant might be reaching for a weapon and had mistaken his own gun for his Taser in his effort to subdue Grant. In fact, no one in Grant's party was armed.

Footage has been made public from six cameras that captured parts of this event; some of the videos aired on the local news and on YouTube within days of the shooting, and others emerged during Mehserle's criminal trial.[21] The mounted security camera at Fruitvale station was directed at the tracks and the outer edge of the platform, recording only the train's arrival and departure, its passengers watching the arrest, and some peripheral movements from officers. In a figurative passing of the torch from one surveillance technology to another, handheld digital cameras and mobile phone cameras vastly outperformed this mounted security camera in documenting Grant's death, reinforcing a sense of the latter as yesterday's model of the Panopticon. Five of these portable cameras recorded the arrest from different angles, and three of those had Grant in frame when Mehserle fired his fatal shot. The quantity and density of cameras watching the police on that night register in Margarita Carazo's footage, in which Tommy Cross Jr.'s digital camera, also recording, hovers at the corner of the frame, displaying a miniaturized duplicate on its LCD screen of the arrest we are watching. None of these witnesses, however, were able to get very close to the action, and the three who did enframe the shooting could present only an obscured view—Pirone, holding Grant's head down on the platform and kneeling on his neck, blocks the line of sight.

Neda Agha-Soltan's death occurred several months later on the other side

4.1. YouTube synchronization of six recorded views of Oscar Grant's death. Posted by streetgangs, July 4, 2010.

of the world. In Iran, many had taken to the streets in massive protests against the reelection of President Mahmoud Ahmadinejad, widely considered to be fraudulent. Among them on June 20 was Agha-Soltan, a twenty-six-year-old woman protesting peacefully in Tehran, accompanied by her music instructor, Hamid Panahi. As the two left the crowd and attempted to return to their car, Agha-Soltan was struck in the chest by a rifle bullet and died moments later. Witnesses on the scene reported that she was shot by a member of the government-allied Basij militia, who was apprehended and identified by the crowd but never prosecuted. As in Grant's case, several bystanders with mobile phone cameras shot footage of this public killing.

The first video of Agha-Soltan posted to YouTube and the most widely viewed shows the anonymous camera operator approaching her as Panahi and Dr. Arash Hejazi, a bystander, lay her on the ground and press their hands to her chest, trying to stop her bleeding. As the operator circles past them to get a clear shot of Agha-Soltan's face, she appears to look directly at the camera just before blood begins to pour from her mouth and then nose. More people gather and begin to scream as she continues to bleed and as attempts to save her become more frantic, at which point the forty-second video cuts out. Another begins with an anonymous operator's thumb blocking the lens—a reminder that these are images captured by nonprofessionals in a chaotic situation. The operator approaches Agha-Soltan and the puddle of blood she is lying in, then passes over Panahi's shoulder to enframe her face, already covered with blood that is pooling in one of her eyes, the other open and staring blankly.[22]

This startling close-up was widely reproduced as a still image by the Green Movement and its international allies for use at protests and in online efforts to gather support for its cause. Understanding the risk the videos posed to those behind and in front of the cameras, their anonymous makers sent them out of Iran to friends who distributed them online and to news outlets. The first video described here, for example, was sent by its author to a friend, who then sent it to an Iranian expatriate friend in the Netherlands, who then posted to YouTube and Facebook and sent it to the BBC and the *Guardian*.[23] YouTube's administrators refrained from removing the videos (despite their violent content), and as they made waves in the site's "attention economy"—where audience engagement is the sought-after commodity—major U.S. news networks also aired them. All this took only hours, with Agha-Soltan's death streaming online and televised on the news on the very day that she died. The videos even spread within Iran, where the government tried—with moderate success—to cut off public access to social media sites such as Facebook, Twitter, and YouTube. Iranians saw the videos on nonstate television channels accessed via satellite

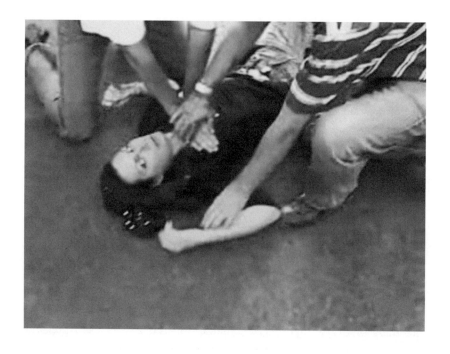

4.2. Neda Agha-Soltan appears to look directly at the camera that records her.

4.3. Neda Agha-Soltan's dying face, covered in blood.

dishes or sent them from mobile phone to mobile phone using Bluetooth connections.[24]

My intention in discussing Grant's and Agha-Soltan's deaths together is not
to equate them but rather to show *differences* in their circumstances, how they
were recorded, and how those videos circulated, as well as the impact of those
differences on activist responses to each death. Nevertheless, both sets of videos were united by their shared aim to publicize deaths that would usually remain politically invisible, using their newly achievable documentary mediation
(with the affordances of mobile phone cameras and streaming video distribution) to command public attention. In other words, their makers and distributors hoped that literal visibility would translate to political visibility and the
greater viability of associated activist movements. Death's expected invisibility
in these two cases is not attributable simply to an atmosphere of death denial
or other such broad factors but rather is quite culturally specific. Grant's death
would likely have remained politically invisible because of the U.S. public's
customary indifference to the unjust deaths of Black men at the hands of law
enforcement, demonstrated time and again in the decades preceding Grant's
killing. Without its documentary capture, Agha-Soltan's death would likely
have been suppressed rather than ignored, as the Iranian government worked
to prevent accurate domestic and international reporting of its violence against
protesting Iranian citizens.

Digital video (DV) secured visibility, to at least some degree, for both deaths,
but when the videos were quickly posted online, they became filtered through
the exhibition conditions of streaming sites—especially YouTube. Here they
entered an environment of death's limitless repetition in time and multiplica-
tion in space. Users could watch the signs of death's finality register in each
video, then return instantly to that video's beginning, reviving the dead and
watching it all again. This mode of viewing is the sort André Bazin so passionately decried in "Death Every Afternoon": the casual repetition of a temporally
sacred moment that, he asserts, should remain unrepeatable.[25] At the time of
his writing in 1958, such an act would have required the physical rolling back of
a celluloid reel, or if death footage were televised, a perhaps fruitless wait for it
to reappear in the medium's flow. In the ensuing decades, VHS would introduce
a rewind function, but viewers would still be made to wait through the abbrevi-
ated duration of the event as it manually reversed and to approximate the right
moment to press play and resume the scene's repetition. YouTube, though,
makes this act of repetition instantaneous, easier than ever, and explicitly encouraged through the "Replay" icon on each video's control panel. And because
Grant's and Agha-Soltan's deaths were each recorded on several cameras—with

the footage from each posted and reposted in many forms by many users—Bazin's sacred moment multiplies not just in time but also in (virtual) space. That expansion is visualized whenever one finishes watching an Agha-Soltan selection, for example, and is then inundated with suggestions of other videos that YouTube's algorithms determine may be of further interest, including more or identical footage of the same incident. Thus, if "Replay" does not appeal, one can instead select from the many little thumbnail images of Agha-Soltan's bleeding face to see other angles or alternate postings of the same video.

The YouTube viewing experience I have just described seems to invite a certain callousness, and yet the act of watching these streaming videos—likely more than once and from more than one angle—helped fuel political responses and actions by or on behalf of the Green Movement. Theorists such as Dean and Juhasz, quoted earlier, express justified skepticism about these progressive powers of new media, but it is hard to deny that the Green Movement put social media—especially Twitter and YouTube—to work for large-scale political actions, as would participants in the Arab Spring revolutions two years later. Within Iran, activists used them to come together in the streets and navigate through government opposition, fully engaging in the "ground-level organization work" and the "planning, discipline, sacrifice, and delay" that Dean sees being phased out by low-investment virtual actions. Outside Iran, people did take to the streets to demonstrate in solidarity (having learned about the Green Movement online, in many cases), but they also used new media tools not just to spread awareness but to interfere actively with the Iranian government's assault against the protesters. Western Internet users provided proxy servers to keep open lines of communication with the protesters in the face of government attempts to cut them off. And many on Twitter changed their location and time zone settings to make it seem as if they were in Tehran, thus making it harder for government agents to find and persecute actual Iranian organizers through Twitter.

That agents were looking for the protesters on Twitter exemplifies the dark side of new media's political potential. As scholars have regularly noted since the 2009 protests in Iran, these media have been wielded by activists against governments *and* by governments against activists, as the powers that be adapt and learn the technologies. This reversal occurred during Iran's protests in general and even with the Agha-Soltan case in particular. For example, one of the men providing medical attention to Agha-Soltan in the videos, Dr. Arash Hejazi, fled the country once they went online because he was clearly identifiable in them and feared reprisals. More strangely, an Iranian woman named Neda Soltani with no connection to Agha-Soltan or her death was also compelled to flee. In the mad rush to supply information about the woman whose recorded death was suddenly being seen around the world, media sources mistakenly published Soltani's Facebook profile picture as Agha-Soltan. Soltani received threats from the regime—which, in this case, had its digitally enabled surveillance done (incompetently) for it by the media. Having no way to correct an error with such global reach, Soltani left and sought asylum in Germany. Even doing Internet searches for Agha-Soltan today, one finds many images of protest signs and shrines that pair the living Soltani's face with the dying Agha-Soltan's—tragically mistaken before-and-after displays that speak to specific perils of the digital age.

Stories from Iran in 2009 or many countries in the Middle East and North Africa in 2011 demonstrate that we must temper excitement about the good that new media can do for activists with an awareness of the evil it can do for oppressive regimes.[26] But it is unwise to *disregard* the former in light of the latter—particularly after the Green Movement and the Arab Spring and even contemporaneous actions within U.S. borders through pro-union protests in Wisconsin and the Occupy movement. Though very different in scope and stakes, these events all demonstrate that activists, not just the governments they protest, have a learning curve with new media: they are still discovering how material and virtual forms of resistance can be mutually supportive and need not be exclusive.

With Grant and Agha-Soltan, digital technology made visible, in mediated form, deaths that fueled political causes. "Citizen journalists" in both situations were on hand and technologically equipped to document brutal killings that the press did not capture—or could not in Iran because of the ban on nonstate media. Digital distribution plays a key role with the Grant and Agha-Soltan videos, as well. Long before such distribution was an option, Abraham Zapruder sold his 8mm film of President Kennedy's death to Time, Inc., which locked it away in vaults for twelve years before it was shown on U.S. television (illegally). By contrast, footage of Grant and Agha-Soltan streamed online within hours or days of their deaths, much less constrained by the power of governments or news corporations' gatekeepers. Both deaths pose dangers to the governments they reflect so poorly on, signifying racial discrimination and police brutality in the United States and politically repressive violence in Iran. Yet no government or corporation could shut away a DV clip in 2009 the way one could an 8mm film in the 1960s. Such clips can be uploaded to YouTube in seconds, often directly from the phones that recorded them, where they can be played, replayed, and downloaded freely—a system that provides the public with unprecedented access to raw actuality footage. Even in Iran, where the government tried mightily to deprive protesters of the digital communication channels that so aided their cause, such channels proved impossible to fully block. They provide, as journalist Youssef Ibrahim puts it, "a new wrinkle for autocratic regimes experienced at quiet repression"—a wrinkle that played a key role in both the Green Movement in 2009 and the Arab Spring of 2011.[27]

Amateur footage of newsworthy events, even of death, is a phenomenon with roots deeper than the digital era, as exemplified by Zapruder's 8mm film of the Kennedy assassination. His footage of Kennedy—along with other 1960s death images, such as *Saigon Execution*—has a sheen of "I can't believe they caught that on camera." Today, however, the recording of public deaths feels almost inevitable. While Kennedy's celebrity status justified Zapruder's decision to carry his 8mm camera to work that day and roll pricey film as the president's motorcade went by, there were plenty of people on the Oakland BART train equipped, trained, and willing to record officers detaining Grant, an anonymous stranger. And Iranian protesters had mobile phone cameras that they drew quickly as they flocked to Agha-Soltan's side.

Intentionality is a key difference between Zapruder's film and the videos shot by bystanders in the Grant and Agha-Soltan cases. The individuals recording Grant did so for the purpose of documenting whatever injustice and violence would emerge from the confrontation between passengers and police—even at the risk of having their cameras confiscated. Those recording Agha-Soltan seem similarly motivated to gather evidence of a deadly injustice, given the personal danger they faced in creating and circulating the footage (a reason they still remain anonymous). The Zapruder film, by contrast, provides a textbook example of Vivian Sobchack's "accidental gaze." His recording of actual death is unexpected and inadvertent, intruding into a casual home movie of the president's visit to Dallas and exempting Zapruder from the ethical problems of the "professional gaze." Sobchack reserves this gaze for professional journalists who pursue death footage intentionally and at the expense of intervention. This gaze is "marked by ethical ambiguity, by technical and *machinelike competence* in the face of an event which seems to call for further and more humane response."[28]

As professional journalists and "citizen journalists" are, to some extent, converging in their documentary activities, it may be tempting to apply the professional gaze label and its attendant burdens to nonprofessionals, like those who recorded Grant's and Agha-Soltan's deaths. But such an application would ignore not only economic factors (citizen journalists are, for the most part, not tracking down good news stories to make their livings) but also social and technological ones. Unlike the intrepid reporters Sobchack quotes in her section on the professional gaze, the creators of YouTube death videos have usually had a singular experience: the right-time, right-place opportunity to record *one* death by chance rather than a career investment in pursuing dramatic images for the news. Though Sobchack's categories of the "endangered gaze" or the "humane stare" might apply to the Grant and Agha-Soltan videos, I believe that a new term is needed to account for the shift in recording practices that digital technology has prompted since Sobchack published "Inscribing Ethical Space" in 1984. I propose an additional category, to be paired with the expectant gaze category I suggest in chapter 3 to describe *The Bridge*: the ubiquitous gaze.

This category connotes the sense in which death's recording has become common, often accomplished by multiple cameras in a single case—a ubiquity evidenced earlier in my discussion of death porn websites. It also connotes the increasing extent to which the public now presumes that a camera will be present and recording when public death occurs. Sobchack's categories were written for a media environment where every once in a while, an individual with a camera—usually a news employee or professional documentarian—would encounter a death and have to decide whether and how to record it. Acknowledging the sharp increase in camera-equipped encounters with death in the digital age, my category of the ubiquitous gaze is not conceived as an isolated and individual ethical judgment. Instead, it addresses the social norms that have begun to solidify in the course of rapid technological advancement.

In situations where violence and death are expected, such as the Green Movement's protests, citizens now tend to be in quick-draw mode with their cameras—always ready to record. This shift is apparent in the bits of death footage that circulated during the Arab Spring, but even more so in those uprisings' iconic metaimages: those of protesters holding their mobile phone cameras aloft and recording en masse. The salient point, these images suggested, was the now-ubiquitous act of recording itself—a new force of surveillance rising up to challenge the centrally controlled Panopticon (though its footage is still subject to exploitation by those in power). As Libyan activist Mohammed Nabbous optimistically envisioned this technologically enabled new reality in 2011, "At least if we die, many people can see it and protest from everywhere!"[29]

The ubiquitous gaze is not just employed in environments where fatalities are expected from the outset; it is also activated in everyday life when the first signs of looming public violence appear. Once the blood is in the water, so to speak, there is now a societal expectation that anyone with a recording device—and they are *many*—will pull it out and use it. This was certainly the case on the night that Oscar Grant died, and the evidence that such a sensibility is becoming a broad social norm abounds on YouTube, where the norm suggests that the products of this ubiquitous gaze should be distributed.[30] The ubiquitous gaze's compulsion to record and distribute documentary footage of death, driven by these emerging social norms and bolstered by YouTube's lack of a rigid gatekeeping system, pushes farther to the sidelines the process of ethical judgment that is so important to Sobchack. Identifying this ethical shift within journalism's history of picturing individuals "about to die," Zelizer observes, "Journalists often avoid depicting what they think is most problematic, but as recent events involving citizen journalists show, nonjournalists may have no such reticence."[31] This diminished role of ethics may perturb us very little when the images evidence injustices, as Grant's and Agha-Soltan's do. But the plentiful clips of violent death uploaded to death porn sites raise sharper concerns about ethics and the ubiquitous gaze.

Helped into existence and brought before the public eye via digital technology, the Grant and Agha-Soltan videos propelled some into political action and generally drew tremendous attention to these deaths. For the Agha-Soltan videos, this was visibility on a global scale, but the Grant videos traveled significantly less beyond U.S. borders. This disparity is evidenced by the statistics YouTube publicly provides on some videos' circulation. For two of the most popular Grant and Agha-Soltan videos, Grant's receives the vast majority of its views within the United States, also making small inroads in Canada, Australia, and northern Europe. The Agha-Soltan video garners equal attention in the United States and Iran but also accumulates more significant view counts in Canada, Australia, and northern Europe than Grant's and has noticeable visibility in countries such as Brazil, India, South Africa, and Algeria.[32] In fact, though the Grant case was discussed nationally in African American and activist communities, its mainstream media coverage and the public's general awareness of it remained mostly regional—occurring, as it did, several years before the Black Lives Matter movement focused widespread attention on deaths like Grant's. The *New York Times*, for example, did not report on the Grant shooting until more than a week after his death, when large protests occurred in Oakland. Agha-Soltan's death, by comparison, received immediate, in-depth coverage by media outlets worldwide.

While unjust treatment of African Americans by law enforcement is perceived as a commonplace among Oakland residents, the existence of clear video evidence that a white transit officer fatally shot a Black passenger lying prone on the ground galvanized locals and brought masses of protesters into the streets on more than one occasion. The videos made visible the previously invisible suffering of this community. Indeed, the protests began not in the immediate wake of the shooting itself but following the broadcast of the Grant videos several days later on YouTube and then on local news. While a small number in Oakland participated in looting and property destruction, most protested peacefully, calling for justice, brandishing photographs of Grant, and sometimes lying down in the street in bodily mimicry of the nonthreatening position Grant was in when he was shot. Grant's supporters closely followed the trial of his killer, Johannes Mehserle, over the ensuing two years and were generally outraged at the leniency of his conviction and sentencing: two years in prison for involuntary manslaughter, of which he ultimately served only eleven months before his June 2011 release on parole. Though Grant's supporters wanted (and deserved) a different outcome, the fact that an officer was convicted of any criminal charge in an on-duty shooting was nearly unprecedented—a result of the political pressure and authoritative evidence the videos helped provide.[33]

The racial dynamics of Grant's death in 2009, the fact that it was recorded, and the palpable outrage it inspired in a major urban area brought comparisons to the Rodney King case of 1991 (though King survived his beating by police). The magnitude of response from the media and the public is, however, not comparable between Grant's case and King's. King's became a major national news story, and the acquittal of his police assailants prompted massive riots in L.A. on a scale well beyond the protests inspired by Grant's shooting. Reactions to Grant's death were comparatively muted. My interest here is not to propose any hierarchy of injustice or suggest that Grant's case was more worthy of attention than King's—or than the string of other unjust deaths of Black men at the hands of police that would follow in the coming years, discussed later in this chapter. Rather, my intention is to think through the ways in which *specific* intersections of racialized violence and digital media impact political discourse in the United States—in this case, to consider what type and magnitude of responses the YouTube videos of Oscar Grant's death produced and why.

In the Agha-Soltan shooting, Internet broadcast of her death videos made Neda, as she is always called by supporters, an instant rallying point for the Green Movement within Iran and elicited an explosion of sympathetic messages and gestures from its international allies (among them, many diasporic Iranians). Her name was yelled on Tehran streets during protests and from residences into the night. She became a fixture of protest signs and a centerpiece of shrines and memorials in Iran and across the globe, as well as a literal "icon" on Twitter. There, supportive users adopted thumbnail photos of her bleeding face as their avatars. Bloggers and posters on YouTube comment boards frequently expressed how deeply the videos shocked and saddened them, adding pleas to spread them and promises to "never forget." One YouTube user conveyed a common reaction from the West in the simple statement, "This is the most terrible thing I have seen in all my sheltered and quiet life."[34] Significantly, the comments on the Agha-Soltan videos contrast with those on Grant's, which emphasize legal and moral debate more than a sharing of grief. Even as the Green Movement sputtered under government pressure in the months that followed, Agha-Soltan still commanded attention. Iranians risked their safety to mourn her publicly, PBS and HBO aired documentaries about her, *The Times* in London named her "Person of the Year," and an Iranian factory was shut down for mass-producing Neda statuettes.[35]

How Death Goes Viral: The Role of Aesthetics in YouTube's Attention Economy

So how did the Agha-Soltan videos from Iran generate such broad interest among the Western public while the Grant videos remained more nationally, and even regionally, bound? Part of the former set's ability to go viral stems from its integration within the larger news story of Iran's election protests and the political factors intertwined with its coverage. In the United States, where relations with the Iranian government are generally hostile, there was a palpable eagerness to support the Green Movement among media outlets and citizens—some of whom framed the movement's purposes in tandem with U.S. efforts to spread "freedom" and "democracy" in the Middle East. I also suspect that the videos achieved so much exposure because many Americans believed they could bear witness to Agha-Soltan's brutal death with few feelings of culpability—unlike images of suffering and death from Iraq or Afghanistan (or, for that matter, *Saigon Execution*). Furthermore, the usual impetus to "do something" that accompanies activist videos—sometimes alienating viewers who would rather do nothing without guilt—was, in some analysts' views, mitigated in this case. These analysts feared that too much U.S. intervention in Iran would only strengthen the government's claims that the unrest was a Western plot and not the true reflection of the Iranian people's wishes.

Alongside these political dimensions of the videos' popularity, I argue that audiovisual elements played an equally crucial role. Specifically, the ubiquity and versatility of DV allowed for a representation of Agha-Soltan's death that mirrors conventions from the West's mainstream, commercial cinema. As described in chapter 3, Eric Steel grafted such conventions onto death footage in *The Bridge* largely in the postproduction process—a calculated artistic choice that many saw as inappropriate. Here, the conventions appear in the raw footage itself, seeping in during a chaotic recording situation that did not facilitate much aesthetic intentionality. Striking among them are the multiple camera angles, which audiences of Hollywood death scenes have long been treated to, but which have become newly practical for documentary in the digital age when more cameras are likely to be on the scene.[36] The difference between these angles in fiction film and in the Agha-Soltan videos is that the latter remain raw shots that we watch sequentially rather than simultaneously—as if we had full access to multi-angle (and likely multi-take) coverage of a single scene in a fiction film, seeing shots that would later be condensed and intercut.

The most ironic convention that aligns the Agha-Soltan videos with mainstream fiction is shaky, handheld cinematography. Such cinematography was less a stylistic choice than a practical necessity for documentarians in the 1960s direct cinema and cinema verité period when it became a visual trademark of the documentary form. It was a style largely prompted by a technological shift, as maneuverable 16mm cameras and synchronized sound equipment allowed for a more spontaneous documentation of events as they happened, without tripods and careful setups—a scenario now extended to nonprofessionals with mobile phone cameras, like those who recorded Agha-Soltan's death. But since its documentary heyday in the 1960s, shaky camerawork has overrun fiction film and television—especially in the twenty-first century. Directors use it intentionally to overlay a gritty, documentary roughness onto fiction for a more real, more authentic feeling. This stylistic adoption is so widespread in fiction that it weakens the link with documentary that the technique is meant to evoke. Where once watching a handheld shot in a fiction film called up associations with documentary, now, I believe, the shakiness of the Agha-Soltan footage calls up associations with fiction film. The unsteady frame that approaches her is very similar to "camera subjectivity" horror films such as *The Blair Witch Project* (1999, Daniel Myrick and Eduardo Sánchaz) or *Cloverfield* (2008, Matt Reeves) and is only a tad more extreme in its jolts than recent war films. Two separate scenes in *Flags of Our Fathers*, for example, feature a shaky, handheld camera and on-screen soldiers approaching a wounded comrade from approximately the same angle as the Agha-Soltan footage. These lives slip away in front of the camera, like hers, amid bleeding and suffering and despite medical intervention from desperate witnesses to the deaths.

The videos also provide clear close-ups of the streams of blood that pour from Agha-Soltan's mouth and nose—blood flow so dramatic that it would be a challenge for an effects makeup artist to simulate convincingly. In fact, the extreme "realism" of Agha-Soltan's bleeding in these videos has been a safeguard against politically motivated accusations that her death was staged. Viewers seem to understand that simulating such a scene well, with simultaneous coverage from several cameras, would demand expensive and elaborate practical and digital effects. Synced to the pace of her escalating bleeding is a crescendo of shouts and wails from the gathering crowd, which audibly register the tragedy, providing the type of immersive soundtrack that makes death scenes more evocative.

Agha-Soltan's Iranian identity also plays a major role. Image distributors and consumers in the West have long proven that they are comfortable watching the bodily destruction of the ethnic other.[37] In particular, the scenario of Americans watching an Iranian woman die at the hands of her own government resonates with the U.S. media's dominant discourse about the Islamic Republic in Iran: that women are the primary targets of its oppressions and, furthermore, are disempowered, helpless victims. This common lens through which U.S. audiences and news outlets viewed Agha-Soltan's death ignores both her personal demonstration of political awareness and power as a protester that day and Iranian women's long history of feminist activism.[38] More broadly, as Evelyn Azeeza Alsultany has argued, a trope of the Muslim woman victimized by her culture has emerged in post-9/11 U.S. media. While this figure does generate sympathy, in contrast to the also-common figure of the Islamic terrorist, it has been deployed most often to reinforce the claim that the recent U.S. wars in the Middle East were invested in the "liberation" of Islamic women.[39] Agha-Soltan's death potentially functioned this way for some viewers, affirming U.S. interventions in Iran's neighboring nations as—perversely—feminist acts.

Extending this comparison to casting and costuming, Agha-Soltan embodied a particular type of Iranian womanhood ideally suited to command sympathy from an international audience. Like Hollywood's favored murder victims—exported around the globe—she exudes the innocence associated with being young and a woman. Her feminine beauty allows for her objectification, too, in the risqué blend of sex and death these films trade in—a viewing mode disturbingly evidenced by numerous lewd YouTube comments on her death videos. Beyond displaying youth and beauty, though, Agha-Soltan in these videos is visually coded as a modern, Westernized Iranian woman and was read as such by the U.S. media and by many within the global Iranian diaspora—regardless of whether this appearance aligned with her actual beliefs and values.[40] As she lies on the pavement, her blue jeans and sneakers are prominently visible below her *hejab*. The *hejab* itself is a *roopoosh-roosari* combination ("as sexy a version of the Islamic covering imposed by law as is possible to wear in Iran") that signifies resistance to the Islamic Republic—not to most Western viewers, but to Iranians in Iran or the diaspora.[41] Setareh Sabety explains the cultural specificities of Agha-Soltan's appearance as such: "Her thin figure, perfectly plucked eyebrows, and signature Iranian nose job also suggest the kind of woman she was: one of the thousands of young, beautiful women who try to look as Western as possible, despite or in outright defiance of the imposed *hejab* and thirty years of Islamist indoctrination."[42] These visual details in the videos were supplemented in ensuing media coverage by a highly circulated family photograph of the beautiful Agha-Soltan wearing no *hejab* at all.

Multiple angles, dramatic blood flow, immersive audio, and the subject's appearance—these audiovisual details make it easier to understand why the Agha-Soltan videos received such disproportionately massive attention from the international community amid all the footage coming out of Iran that summer. Even other graphic videos of fatal violence failed to generate anywhere near the amount of exposure for the Green Movement that her death did.[43] Addressing the ways in which mainstream, corporate media aesthetics drive exposure on YouTube, Juhasz quips, "Like high school cheerleaders, the popular on YouTube do what we already like, in ways we already know."[44] Though their attention and intentions must have been focused elsewhere, the makers of the Agha-Soltan videos achieved a familiar and already-popular aesthetic form.

That Agha-Soltan's death looks like a gritty Hollywood war movie is especially important in connecting with U.S. audiences—the dominant users of YouTube—(and, to some extent, also to global audiences acclimated to U.S. media).[45] Many Americans respond to these representations of death not because they are necessarily callous and entertainment-oriented but because Hollywood has been their primary guide to what death looks like for much of the past century. As discussed in the introduction, while previous generations had ample firsthand exposure at deathbeds, the twentieth century brought both lower death rates and a rapid medicalization of the dying process that replaced its visibility in the home with sequestering in the hospital. There it was kept mainly out of sight, soothing a society that no longer welcomed familiarity with the physical transition from life to death. Fictional, filmic representations partially assumed the role of exposing people to that process, but with an unsurprising preference for spectacle, favoring the most dynamic and dramatized types of death.

The same appetite for spectacle also dominates YouTube, despite the site's high concentration of actuality footage. YouTube's attention economy is "based on the slogan: pithy, precise, rousing calls to action, or consumption, or action *as* consumption," and here the brief, spectacle-oriented video is king.[46] Its dominance curtails documentarians' options for displaying death's duration, its frequent resistance to spectacular visibility, or its context. Sam Gregory, program director for the activist video organization WITNESS, notes the difficulties human rights videos face in attracting attention on YouTube because "much human rights material is not immediately powerful performance, and may not be most effectively or honestly presented in that mode."[47] Agha-Soltan's recorded death has achieved viral status globally because it *is* "immediately powerful performance." It embodies the temporally condensed spectacle of YouTube, plus documentary's poignant stamp of authenticity—the alluring promise that one is seeing the taboo sight of "real" death unfolding before the camera.

Comparatively, the videos of Oscar Grant have the look of courtroom evidence, not of a dramatic death scene—a perfectly reasonable quality that nevertheless deflates their power in YouTube's attention economy. Though more people recorded Grant's death than Agha-Soltan's, the multiple angles offer less to choose from: several use very similar vantage points, and none secure the close-ups that make the Agha-Soltan videos so striking. Those who recorded Grant's death lacked the proximity and mobility of their Iranian counterparts because the BART officers had confined them to the train cars. In the bystander videos, Grant himself becomes a small and obscured collection of pixels, reminiscent of (but even less visible than) Kennedy, who died in miniature and awash in 8mm film grain in Zapruder's recording of his assassination. Bay Area news programs underscored the difficulty of seeing Grant's fatal shooting within the videos by adding a familiar annotation when airing them: a bright circle around Grant and Mehserle that tells us where to look for the obscured action in the frame.[48]

Within this little circle, Grant suffers a lethal injury when Mehserle's bullet pierces his lungs, but one that remains invisible to the camera—unlike, say, the nonlethal kicks and baton blows on dramatic display in the Rodney King video. Grant's dose of police brutality affectively fails to project its actual *brutality* in its video documentation. With this aspect of the Grant videos, we can recall the challenge described in chapter 1 that death documentary shares with genres and movements as varied as melodrama, pornography, and German expressionism: the necessity of externalizing internal states for the camera. Robert Capa strove for and eloquently attained the external visibility of death by gunshot in staging *The Falling Soldier* in 1936. What he achieved with a faux actuality image, the citizens who recorded Agha-Soltan's death managed with legitimate actuality footage, but those who recorded Grant's failed to attain it. This failure of the visible is a particular problem because of the extraordinary expectations twenty-first-century viewers (and juries) have for video evidence—brought on by the expanding camera coverage of public space and the technological fictions spread by television crime dramas. Investigators on shows like CSI and *Law and Order* often manage to obtain clear footage of a crime that cracks their case. Even if this footage is initially distant or blurry, they just push a few buttons to sharpen the image or zoom in on a detail—operations that tend to be technologically impossible or financially impractical for actual investigations.

The limited proximity and mobility of Grant's recorders align their footage more with the distant, fixed positions of surveillance cameras than with the omniscience and omnipotence of the camera in most fiction films. Agha-Soltan's bystanders, like Hollywood cinematographers, knew exactly where the action was and what the viewers would want to see. The bystanders recording Grant, however, sometimes lack that awareness because the Oakland shooting played out in a more chaotic way than the one in Tehran. Karina Vargas, for example, disobeys police orders and exits the train to better record the arrest. But just as she approaches Grant and Mehserle, she suddenly pans left to catch a young man being tackled right next to her. As she does, Mehserle shoots Grant offscreen, and Vargas misses the scene's most important feature.

Considering the challenges of this recording situation, YouTube viewers are wildly unsympathetic to Vargas. Her turbulent camerawork and inability to enframe the action demonstrate what Juhasz calls the "bad video" aesthetic on YouTube, derided by users for its failure to achieve "the conventional norms of quality, particularly in relation to form (lighting, framing, costume, make-up, editing, sound, recording and mixing, performance, etc.)."[49] A comment from Pirate48153 typifies the harsh, misogynistic feedback Vargas receives: "Bitch next time learn how to 2 fukin record b4 u go postin shit up on youtube u stupid hoe." Lest it appear that Pirate is an outlier: forty-six more YouTube users gave this comment a thumbs-up than gave it a thumbs-down—making it quantitatively the most approved-of comment of all 3,357 posted on that video.[50] As this intense outrage implies, details in the Grant videos like Vargas's ill-timed pan disrupt the fantasy of ocular power that mainstream fiction and the Agha-Soltan videos provide, reading as frustrating moments when the contingencies of documentary interfere with desire for "maximum visibility."

The audio track is one element that does push the Grant videos' impact beyond that of automated surveillance footage. In concert with the handheld camerawork, which grounds the footage in human subjectivity, the increasingly clamorous passengers give a sense of immersion that partly compensates for the lack of visual detail. Almost never localized to visible individuals, the comments from onlookers gradually blend together as the coherent, collective will of the 2:00 AM crowd. The camera itself, and thus our viewing position, is sonically and symbolically located as a part of this crowd, whose shouts are loud and close, while those of the officers sound distant. The videos begin with snippets of conversation unrelated to the still-tame encounter between passengers and police—reminders of the event's apparent banality when it began. An offscreen passenger in the Vargas video, apparently talking on his phone, says, "Hey, we're in Fruitvale right now. *Fruitvale*, with a fruit! Where you guys at?" Daniel Liu takes an early break from holding his camera aloft to record the scene and sits down next to a female companion, whose body he absently tapes as she says, "Thank you, baby." As the tension of the arrest escalates and the BART police push Grant to the ground, though, the crowd's attention becomes audibly fixated. Their remarks grow louder, more frequent, and more impassioned, including: "That's fucked up," "Protect and serve, protect and serve," "Fuck the police!," "Get their badge numbers," and, perceptively, "Put it on YouTube."

Although these words suggest a viewing position allied with Grant rather than the officers, they also reinforce the subtle framing of the footage as most notable for the questions of legality and ethics it raises, not for its tragic loss of life. This dynamic is understandable considering that most of the Grant footage precedes his shooting, while the Agha-Soltan footage follows hers; also, witnesses reported that even after the shooting many passengers assumed Grant had been tased or otherwise failed to realize he had been fatally shot with a pistol. The protesters surrounding Agha-Soltan when she is felled by a bullet also provide a cacophony of voices but in a more overtly emotional way: they tell her not to be afraid, plead for her to stay with them, or simply scream. For the majority of Western viewers who do not speak Farsi, the audible emotion of the soundtrack likely feels especially prominent in the absence of linguistic comprehension. In terms of both image and sound, the case I am making is that aesthetics drive exposure for Internet video and that this is true even for documentary, activist material. There, it seems as if political content should trump audiovisual form, but the reverse is more common—as exemplified by the wild virality of "Kony 2012," a slickly produced, deeply problematic work that became the most-viewed activist video in YouTube's history.

"I Never Thought the World Could Be So Small": Identifying with the Dying

In the preceding details, a sense emerges of how greatly audiovisual elements shape the emotional reactions and political actions that individual deaths generate in an era when they are recorded and displayed more and more frequently. What's at stake in that shaping process is the extent to which lives are "grievable," as Judith Butler describes. In *Precarious Life*, she writes about how certain types of death have been ignored or suppressed in public discourse, such as the deaths of gay men during the AIDS crisis or the victims of U.S.

bombings in Iraq and Afghanistan. While Butler draws the borders of grievability based on identity and causes of death, the Grant and Agha-Soltan videos demonstrate that aesthetics, too, can contribute powerfully to Butler's uneasy truth that some lives are "so easily humanized" and others not.[51]

While shot distance and audio play key roles in the relative humanization of the dying Grant and Agha-Soltan, I assert that the primary distinction here is the inclusion of Agha-Soltan's face, in close-up. Intimate facial close-ups are a rarity in documentary death but they are a fixture of death in fiction film—a tool for forging sympathy and identification between audience and character. Facial close-ups like Agha-Soltan's seem also to promise the clearest window on the mystical "moment of death" that mainstream, commercial cinema obsessively displays. The archetypal shot is a close-up of the dying character as her or his expression slackens and eyes close or slip into a blank stare. I described this type of shot in my discussion of Douglas Sirk's *Imitation of Life* (1959) in chapter 2: wealthy actress Lora sits at the bedside of her African American housekeeper, Annie, and listens as the dying woman utters her last words, "I'm just tired, Miss Lora—awfully . . . tired . . ." Annie's head and eyelids droop in close-up as her speech trails off. Many YouTube viewers perceive a similar process unfolding in the first Agha-Soltan video, as her eyes seem to meet the camera's stare and then roll back in a loss of consciousness, soon obscured as blood runs over them. As evidenced by user comments, the apparent visibility of this dying process gives the Agha-Soltan videos an emotional charge beyond the power of documentary's more common images of corpses. As Sobchack, quoted earlier, reminds us: when cameras roll on the dying rather than the dead, identification is more likely.

Beyond close-ups, the Agha-Soltan videos even offer the illusion of eye contact—a feature of documentary images prized by Roland Barthes in *Camera Lucida*. Lamenting his boredom with a recent catastrophe, he writes: "Trying to make myself write some sort of commentary on the latest 'emergency' reportage, I tear up my notes as soon as I write them. What—nothing to say about death, suicide, wounds, accidents? No, nothing to say about these photographs in which I see surgeons' gowns, bodies lying on the ground, broken glass, etc. Oh, if only there were a look, a subject's look, if only someone in the photograph were looking at me! For the Photograph has this power . . . of looking me straight in the eye."[52] Though Barthes then denies its power to fiction film, a look "straight in the eye" is within the repertoire of documentary, and Agha-Soltan's death provides a striking instance. Many bloggers and posters to YouTube's comment boards wrote about this detail and the haunting experience of Agha-Soltan's look as she dies.[53]

Between Oscar Grant and the cameras that record his death, there is no eye contact, nor even many clear shots of his face. The Grant videos portray a victim who is decidedly not "faced," who often becomes a flat representative of a demographic group ("young Black men")—hence the extreme ubiquity of Grant's face in the protests, used by supporters to individuate and humanize him. Renderings of his face—uniformly based on one smiling photo that local newspapers ran in the case's aftermath—appeared as posters, at public memorials, on protest signs, on T-shirts, as masks worn by demonstrators, and even as large-scale murals.

Tellingly, when Grant's shooting was reenacted for the feature film *Fruitvale Station* (2013), director Ryan Coogler focused the scene's cinematography on getting *closer* to Grant's face than the cameras that witnessed his death—a visual contrast the film itself signals by opening with documentary footage of the incident in long shot. *Fruitvale Station* draws its audience figuratively and literally closer to Grant as he is fatally shot: the former through a detailed and sympathetic account of his last day of life, the latter through an evocative close-up of his face reacting to the precise moment that Mehserle fires. Framed sideways, as Grant's head is pressed against the pavement, his face registers the gunshot with widening eyes and a look that cycles subtly through reactions of shock, disbelief, and pain. Maximizing the sense of heart-wrenching emotion and injustice in this close-up, Coogler capitalizes on actor Michael B. Jordan's expressive face, which carries the accumulated associations of Jordan's previous, typecaste roles as other disadvantaged but fundamentally good young Black men (in the television shows *The Wire*, *Friday Night Lights*, and *Parenthood*). This proximity of Coogler's camera to the dying—so easily attained in fiction filmmaking and so elusive in actuality footage—affords the face's humanizing display of suffering that Agha-Soltan's footage showcases and Grant's obscures.

In Oakland, there was a localized outpouring of grief for Grant in the wake of his death, but if public response to the Grant and Agha-Soltan videos generally frames the latter's death as more widely, globally "grievable," it is also because a broad swath of viewers felt able to *identify* with Agha-Soltan as they watched her breathe her last breaths. The political actions that arose from both deaths bear this out in their different deployments of "I am Neda" and "I am Oscar Grant" declarations. "I am _____" or "We are all _____" is a common template for activists whose actions center on an individual. It is also a template that deserves closer examination for its bold (and usually uncritical) declaration of not just support for that individual but direct identification with them.

Grant supporters in Oakland shouted this slogan at marches, spray-painted

4.4. Mural of Oscar Grant in Oakland, California (© Noah Berger/Associated Press).

4.5. Michael B. Jordan as Oscar Grant, at the moment he is shot
(*Fruitvale Station*, 2013, Ryan Coogler, Anchor Bay).

it around the city, and inscribed it on protest signs. The individuals declaring this shared identity were largely (though not exclusively) those who indeed shared with Grant all or most of the identity attributes that were seen as crucial to his death: being a person of color, male, and young. San Francisco filmmaker Kevin Epps, for example, explained at a protest, "I'm angry because [Grant] could have been me. . . . We're guilty until proven innocent."[54] The "I am Oscar Grant" declarations demonstrate one way in which a shared vulnerability to violence can be, as Butler claims, a unifying force—a force she posits as crucial in this post-9/11 world. She writes, "From where might a principle emerge by which we vow to protect others from the kinds of violence we have suffered, if not from an apprehension of a common human vulnerability? I do not mean to deny that vulnerability is differentiated, that it is allocated differently across the globe."[55] In its culturally specific deployment among young African American men, "I am Oscar Grant" evokes that uneven allocation of vulnerability. Compared with members of other demographic groups in the United States, these citizens are implicated somewhat less by the trend posited in chapter 2 wherein a fixation on violent death helps us avoid contemplating the natural deaths we expect for ourselves. Natural death is statistically still far more likely for African American men, but the Grant case demonstrates why violent death may justifiably loom larger in their psyches.[56]

The parallel "I am Neda" declarations seem to follow Butler's principle, too, but ultimately elide her clarification that vulnerability is "allocated differently across the globe." Unlike the mostly Bay Area–based "I am Oscar Grant" statements, which remained situated in a specific social and political context, annunciations of "I am Neda" again achieved global reach. In addition to the phrase's appearance in international protests, it was used to generate personal photos and messages online in solidarity with Agha-Soltan. Amnesty International launched one such campaign, called "Neda Speaks," for which 2,760 users submitted photos.[57] The site's explanation of the campaign grounds its use of the phrase in the local and culturally specific, explaining, "People in Iran yell 'I am Neda' into the street after lights out as a sign of defiance since the government has made it illegal to mourn for her. We want you to join us in support of this fundamental stand for human rights by uploading a photo of yourself holding a sign that says 'I am Neda.'" What is not explained is *why* that powerful phrase should be exported out of its local and specific context—why the declaration of identification "I am Neda" is the best way to make "this fundamental stand for human rights." Nevertheless, thousands of people of diverse ages, genders, ethnicities, and nationalities have posted pictures of themselves with "I am Neda" scrawled on paper they hold, on visible body parts, or on their clothing. As earnest and well-meaning as these individuals probably are, many of them seem to exemplify Jodi Dean's disappointed digital-age principle, "React and forward, but don't by any means think."[58]

While African American Bay Area resident Kevin Epps can say "I am Oscar Grant" because "[Grant] could have been me," there is little credibility in the idea that many of the "I am Neda" declarers would feel like "Neda could have been me." These supporters are able to identify with the woman dying so dramatically in intimate close-up and looking them "straight in the eye," but their sharing of human vulnerability lacks nuance. Their good intentions are dampened by the missing acknowledgment that vulnerability is "allocated differently across the globe"—that a white teenage boy posting from his home in Connecticut, for example, will very likely avoid being shot by his government or dying by any violent means.

One example that is both moving and fraught comes from another, smaller-scale "I am Neda" photo project started by a Tumblr user who "wanted to make a point that Neda became the face of the uprising because we could all see ourselves in her."[59] Responding to that user's call for photos of people wearing homemade "I am Neda" apparel, a U.S. soldier serving in Iraq posted a photo of himself in full military gear, holding open his unbuttoned camouflage shirt to reveal those words, inscribed in marker on his T-shirt. However earnestly and emotionally this soldier describes his feelings about Agha-Soltan's death in his accompanying text, there remains a certain incongruity between the words he has written on his shirt and his visibly signified participation in the U.S. war in neighboring Iraq—a lingering gap between the capacity to sympathize and the right to claim a shared identity.[60] Perhaps the American song "Neda"— recorded and made into a music video by the band the Airborne Toxic Event for Amnesty International's "Neda Speaks" campaign—best expresses the power *and* naïveté embodied in "I am Neda." Collapsing space in a familiar cliché and eschewing the spirit of Butler's assertion that vulnerability is "allocated differently across the globe," the song's repeating chorus about how Agha-Soltan's death affects the American songwriter ends with the deliberately pronounced words, "I never thought the world could be so small."

The Promise and Peril of Context

The qualities of the Agha-Soltan videos that enable this broad, even strained, "I am Neda" identification—their universalizing communication of suffering and death, encapsulated in short, dramatic, and aesthetically familiar clips— are the same qualities that exclude cultural specificity. While useful for drawing attention to an activist cause, such videos reduce complex events to spectacle and strip away cultural and political context—a characteristic of YouTube that worries scholars and activists. Sam Gregory points out that "most human rights situations are embedded in contexts of structural complexity, long histories of repression and reaction and many actors with different agendas."[61] This problem is especially prevalent in raw footage distributed online, where it can be re- or decontextualized when taken from its original site and embedded elsewhere, and where it is often accompanied by uninformed and even misleading user comments. As described earlier, a lack of context troubles YouTube's administrators, as well, forming one of the criteria under which they may remove graphic videos from the site. Even as the Agha-Soltan videos expose conditions in Iran during the protests, they also exclude aspects of Iranian culture and history enmeshed with this murder. Most important, the raw footage itself cannot explain the context of martyrdom's resonance for Islam and for Iran.

Distinct from looser applications in the West, martyrdom in Islam is more codified, and the title can be bestowed or denied officially by legal and religious authorities. At the core, an Islamic martyr (*shaheed*) is one whose death creates a powerful testimony to his or her faith. Martyrdom has been a truly formative concept for Iran, specifically because its population is predominantly Shiite—a sect of Islam for which the martyr Hussein is a key figure—and because the 1980s Iran-Iraq War forged countless martyrs who were revered by the Ayatollah Khomeini and the government.[62] Indeed, Iran remains today "a nation actively promoting the culture of martyrdom."[63] The concept and history of Islamic martyrdom in Iran provided a frame through which many there and in the Iranian diaspora discussed or interpreted Agha-Soltan's death—a set of common cultural reference points familiar to even the secular elements of the Green Movement, whose conception of her martyrdom would not be a religious one. While Agha-Soltan was being embraced as a martyr for the protesters, Iran's government was—rather astoundingly—attempting to reverse that move by making her a martyr for the Islamic Republic. The government offered her parents the pension entitled to an official martyr if they would go along with the story that she was killed by protesters. They would not; as her mother explained, "Neda died for her country, not so I could get a monthly income from the Martyrs Foundation. If these officials say Neda was a martyr, why do they keep wiping off the word 'martyr,' which people write in red on her gravestone?"[64] Understanding the danger that Agha-Soltan's martyrdom could (and did) fuel the Green Movement, the government launched a long and multifaceted campaign to either co-opt or defuse its power, making this offer to her parents and also spreading all manner of counternarratives to explain what viewers saw in the videos.[65]

In a further testament to the Agha-Soltan videos' global appeal, they can accommodate both the complex narrative conventions of Islamic martyrdom in Iran *and* a simpler "innocent victim" story in the West. Her Iranian family and supporters integrated the tropes of Islamic martyrdom into descriptions of her death: pure intentions, fearlessness, a premonition of her death, and a holy corpse that remains beautiful.[66] In her look at the camera, some even saw a variant of a final exhortation—an Islamic martyr's effort to impart truth to the living with her or his final words.[67]

These qualities not only went unsignaled on YouTube but also were generally ignored in the Western news media's coverage of Agha-Soltan. In some cases, their coverage actively (if inadvertently) disregarded the values associated with martyrdom in Iran. One such value crucial to the function of martyrdom's *re-cording* is that graphic representations of martyrs' deaths cannot be lumped in with the so-called gratuitous violence in Western media that inspires so much hand-wringing. Numerous online comments attacked the Agha-Soltan videos as insensitive and violent—aligning, it must be noted, with those of some diasporic Iranian feminists—but as historian David Cook notes in *Martyrdom in Islam*, "In the end martyrdom is *about* blood and suffering."[68] Blood, suffering, and death are essential, not gratuitous, components of martyrdom and its representation—components that give the act such emotional and persuasive power. The Green Movement and its worldwide supporters understood that immediately, making images of Agha-Soltan's bloodied face an ever-present feature of their protests.

Yet these components were suppressed in initial airings of the Agha-Soltan videos on major U.S. news networks. Rachel Maddow on MSNBC played only a small portion of one video, cutting it just before Agha-Soltan began to bleed from her mouth and nose, and accompanied even this snippet with profuse warnings and justifications.[69] Fox News and CNN both blurred out her whole face—a common practice in U.S. television journalism intended to show respect for the victim and family. These channels reversed the digital annotation KTVU put on the Oscar Grant videos, adding a circle that denies access to one portion of the frame rather than a circle that calls attention to one. In doing so, they erased Agha-Soltan's identity, her bleeding and suffering, her charged look at the camera, and the emotional power of the video in general. To suppress Agha-Soltan's identity and the violence of her death in this manner is to neutralize a martyr's most powerful means of bearing witness, converting nonbelievers, bolstering the faithful, and honoring the dead.

In these examples of how news networks integrated the Agha-Soltan videos, an uncomfortable insight becomes apparent: calls for simply *more* context and attacks on YouTube's lack of context fail to recognize the abuses contextualization can inflict upon footage. Here, the bare encounter with raw footage in the supposedly noncontextualized space of YouTube can provide a clearer and more illuminating engagement with recorded death. I argue that the Grant footage presents another instance of the dual promises and perils of context. Part of the reason that Grant's shooting quickly inspired such passionate protest in Oakland was that the widely accessible videos of his death seemed to be plainly legible, with no further context required: a Black man lying facedown with his hands behind his back and posing no threat to anyone is shot at close range by a white officer. As police procedure consultant Mark Harrison elegantly put it, "If they were kids from [the wealthy suburb] Orinda being rowdy on the way home from a Raiders game, I don't think it would have gone down the same way."[70] The videos provide visible evidence of extreme white-on-Black police brutality, the sort that many Oakland residents have felt besieged by for decades.

As the saga of Johannes Mehserle's criminal case got under way, however, his supporters and the press heaped on additional context, details YouTube did not offer that—these sources implied—were necessary to interpreting the videos correctly. For example, the *San Francisco Chronicle* printed detailed diagrams of how BART officers' Taser holsters attach to their belts, the process for changing the holster's configuration, its position on Mehserle's belt, and how that position could have confused him about whether he was pulling his gun or his Taser.[71] A video expert, Michael Schott, hired by Mehserle's defense lawyer testified that the footage shows Mehserle struggle to unholster his gun and that this action suggests he thought he was handling his Taser.[72] Most disturbingly, the news media opposed Mehserle's squeaky-clean record as a BART officer to Grant's five prior arrests, attempting to justify Mehserle's readiness to use force, even though he was not aware of Grant's record during the arrest.

This move exemplifies a lamentable pattern wherein the media aggressively publicizes the past criminal records of Black victims of police brutality. As activist Shaun King wrote on the day video of Alton Sterling's 2016 killing by police hit YouTube, "Now, you know and I know that we will soon learn what Alton Sterling's farts smelled like in the third grade. They'll reach as far back as they need to find a way to degrade and dehumanize him."[73] Arguing for the primacy of one's encounter with the raw, uncontextualized streaming video footage of Sterling's death, King continues, "Please don't fall for that. What you need to remember is how you felt when you first saw this man killed." In the Grant case, the aggressive inclusion in the news of contextual information that favored Mehserle did send one message loud and clear, a message already legible in the way that Grant died: that this young, African American man with a police record was not living a "grievable life" by U.S. cultural standards. His supporters (and sometimes the media, too) circulated a different set of biographical details in an effort to counter this one, emphasizing his role as a father, his very publicly grieving mother, and his friendship with the traumatized men who awaited arrest with him on that train platform.

By contrast, every piece of personal information about Agha-Soltan that the media promoted seemed to bolster her grievability in the West: her university education, close ties with her family and fiancé, love of travel outside Iran, ambition to be a singer, and oft-alleged love of freedom rather than politics (as if dying in protest of a fraudulent election could somehow make sense as an apolitical act). Seldom mentioned in this coverage were details like her divorce or her Islamic religious faith. Thus, in the Grant case, the context provided by Mehserle's supporters and by news media mostly obscures as it claims to clarify, asking the viewer to doubt what initially seemed clear in the raw videos. Instead of spreading lies and conspiracy theories as Iran's government did for the Agha-Soltan videos, Mehserle's supporters cast doubt on the Grant videos by spreading superfluous detail—information framed as highly relevant that should not have overshadowed many of the more basic truths on display in the videos.

Here we might recall a parallel process of dubious contextualization that occurred in the Rodney King case, with which Grant's case is so often associated. Bystander George Holliday's footage of King's beating, shot with a home video camcorder, became key evidence in the trial of LAPD officers. Unable to ignore this seemingly damning video, the defense instead presented it to the court in a way that "distorted and dehistoricized" the beating, as Elizabeth Alexander argues: "The defense in the Simi Valley trial employed familiar language of black bestiality to construct Rodney King as a threat to the officers. The lawyers also slowed down the famous videotape so that it no longer existed in 'real time' but rather in a slow dance of stylized movement that could as easily be read as self-defense or as a threat. The slowed-down tape recorded neither the sound of falling blows nor the screams from King and the witnesses."[74] Such a presentation of Holliday's video pursued advantages for the officers: anesthetizing jurors to the shock of the beating by playing the footage many times, dulling its horror by eliminating the audio, and temporally expanding the short video to create time for lawyers to elaborately narrate it. In doing so, they added their own favored context, providing arguments for why each blow or kick King suffered on-screen was justified by the situation.

The same techniques were used in Mehserle's trial, where the videos of Grant's death played many times on the courtroom's TV monitors. There, they sometimes provided visible evidence for the prosecution to counter inaccurate witness testimonies, but they were also subjected to a series of slow-motion and freeze-frame replays narrated by experts testifying for the defense, as coverage of the trial in the *San Francisco Chronicle* describes: "Running images in slow motion, [Michael] Schott said Grant's right hand had been forced against his back by a second officer, Anthony Pirone, a few seconds before the shooting. Grant's left hand was nearby, though according to Schott it was moving 'up in the air' at the time of the shot. As Schott toggled back and forth between images, Grant was shown being shot over and over again. His mother, Wanda Johnson, watched for a while but then dropped her head against the back of her seat and closed her eyes, crying."[75] Here in the continuous back-and-forth replay of the gunshot are echoes of Bazin's 1958 objection to the documentary capture of death and his sense that the mechanical repetition of a singular "moment of death" would be a desecration (though the moment of fatal wounding rather than the "moment of death" is the one repeated in this case).[76] The repetition prompts an emotional reaction from Grant's mother—one person in the courtroom, at least, who does not seem at risk of becoming inured to this sight, regardless of how often it is replayed.

For many, the Grant case itself felt like a replay—an anxious return to the brutal violence of the King beating and, some feared, the different sort of violence that followed the officers' Simi Valley trial. But the differences are also striking: the public could at any time access raw video of the Grant shooting online, without any framing from news anchors or lawyers, in a way that they could not access raw footage of the King beating; and the Grant videos show, from many angles, police brutality that ends in *death* rather than hospitalization. Yet there is no doubt that they made less impact on the public in 2009 than the King video did in 1991. Like the disparity in attention between the Grant and Agha-Soltan videos, reasons for the greater exposure of the King case than the Grant case are complex, but three suggest themselves strongly.

First, aesthetics are important, once again. Although Holliday was the only witness who taped King's beating and was physically farther away than those who recorded Grant's death, he was able to provide a clearer depiction of an attack that itself was more clearly visible than Mehserle's attack on Grant. The officers in Holliday's video stand back from King, who lies on the pavement in the ample illumination of headlights, and move in only when they deliver their blows. Their attack on King is undeniably more visually dynamic than the gunshot Mehserle inflicts on Grant. Unlike its appearance in the Grant videos, police brutality looks truly brutal on Holliday's tape—even though the attack on Grant was fatal. As Mamie Till understood in 1955 when she exposed her lynched son Emmett's mutilated corpse for mourners and news cameras alike, making visible the *spectacle* of brutality or its physical aftermath—absent from the Grant videos—is often the only way to make the U.S. public pay attention to the death of a Black male. Indeed, instances of Black male suffering consumed as spectacle have been such a consistent feature of U.S. media and public life—from the beating of Uncle Tom in nineteenth-century literature to the beating of Rodney King on twentieth-century TV news—that viewers may expect and even feel entitled to that graphic display when they click on a YouTube video purporting to show a Black man die on camera.[77]

Second, the recorded violence against King is horrifically protracted, exceeding the blink-and-you-miss-it gunshot in the Grant videos. Both recordings show a long altercation, but they distribute spectacle differently within these durations. In the King video, the officers' blows rain down at a consistent pace with no particular climax. The Grant videos are dominated by a long preamble of the officers struggling to get him handcuffed. These thirty seconds are fairly static and uneventful, providing only anticipation of when the gunshot will happen. The anticipation heightens the potential anticlimax of an event we can barely see in the videos, unlike the more sickeningly dynamic kicks and baton strikes against King. Here again we see the feature film version of this event, *Fruitvale Station*, seek to fill in for an absence in the documentary footage, as it did by adding a close-up of Grant's face as he gets shot. To reinfuse Grant's story with durational suffering, the film stays with his character on the platform through the aftermath of the gunshot—which the witnesses recording the actual attack were not permitted to do—showing him struggle with the wound's physical pain as he and the officers wait for paramedics to arrive.

Third, the shock of the King beating in 1991 was accompanied by another shock: that someone had actually recorded the event on video. By 2009, the "I can't believe they caught that on camera" feeling had been diluted by the massive spread of digital recording devices. We now *can* believe it when notable happenings in public space are recorded (by six cameras, no less). We even expect it, as I assert through my digital-age addition to Sobchack's taxonomy of ways that camera operators can record death: the "ubiquitous gaze." In the age of the ubiquitous gaze, the aesthetic quality of a death recording becomes the best measure for its activist potential, but the years since Grant's case have proven that an overwhelming *quantity* of such footage can also command attention. Grant's recorded death, in retrospect, feels like the muted beginning of a heartbreaking trend. It was soon joined by widely circulating mobile phone footage documenting the killings of Eric Garner and Walter Scott, as well as the corpse of Michael Brown, the accumulation of which fueled much larger protests across the United States and the powerful Black Lives Matter movement.[78]

Though none of these incidents were recorded with the six-camera coverage that Grant's received, each possessed qualities that helped make visible—optically and politically, and more so than Grant's—a kind of death that usually remains invisible because of the victim's social positioning. Eric Garner is decidedly faced, and voiced, in the 2014 video documentation of his death, filmed at close range and preceded by several minutes of Garner's pleas for police to stop what he perceived as his constant harassment. Pressed to the ground in a choke hold, Garner gasps over and over again, "I can't breathe"—a clearly audible refrain on the video that became a rallying cry for protesters. Footage of Walter Scott's shooting from 2015 bears closer resemblance to the Rodney King video, as its strength is its unobstructed rendering of violent action. With only the briefest exceptions, bystander Feidin Santana keeps both Scott and Officer Michael Slager within the frame from the moment that Scott turns to run, through the series of eight shots that ring out as Slager shoots Scott in the back, to the sight of Scott's body dropping to the ground. Michael Brown's 2014 shooting was not recorded, but its aftermath was captured by multiple bystanders. Here the unexpected power of a corpse video over a corpse photo becomes apparent, as the shock of these videos is not violent death's frenetic movement, but the significance of stillness as Brown's body lay out in the road for four hours—uncovered for much of that time, exposed to the summer sun and the neighborhood's mostly Black residents.[79] The videos documenting his unmoving body reinvigorate the corpse image and give it new political power precisely through the recorded duration of its stillness—a sign of disrespect from law enforcement who neglected to move or otherwise attend to it.

Although many unarmed Black men like Garner, Scott, and Brown have been killed by police since 2009, many had already been killed in this manner at the time of Mehserle's trial. Yet this context—the larger record of U.S. law enforcement's unjust treatment of Black citizens—was often ignored by defense lawyers and the news media, who preferred to focus on Grant's criminal record.[80] Acknowledging this larger context, Grant family attorney John Burris said in 2011, "I've been involved in ten [similar] cases since Oscar Grant. The only difference was that his was caught on camera."[81] These are acts of contextualization that happened far too seldom in Mehserle's trial or in mainstream coverage of the Grant shooting. Indeed, the racial dimensions of this shooting seem to have been discussed little in the Los Angeles court where a jury without any Black members determined the ex-officer's verdict.

Of course, warnings from activists and academics about a lack of context on YouTube must also contend with the form of context YouTube videos *do*, in every case, provide: the comments of viewers. In the case of the Grant videos, YouTube comments offered a context far more important to understanding Grant's death than the details of Mehserle's Taser holster. The comments contain elaborate, brutal, and persistent articulations of racism against African Americans, a context too raw and ugly to be fully printed in the paper or aired on the local news but that YouTube can display. Overtly racist comments filled with derogatory terms and offensive opinions appear often, from many users on many different postings of the Grant videos. Their presence and quantity provide an important reminder about one aspect of activism on YouTube: that high view counts measure only exposure, not political alignment. The *x* million viewers a video attracts do not translate to *x* million supporters of its apparent cause.

On a broader level, the racist comments illustrate the way in which YouTube and social media sites are havens for hatred at the same time that they are progressive tools, muddying the early image of the Internet as a democratizing, utopic force. As Jason Sperb notes, "The Internet may be the most efficient textual universe for any scholar wishing to prove that racism is alive and well today, and much more rampant than many will admit."[82] Though it is not the site's intention, YouTube creates a public forum where racists can gather and connect. Videos that depict graphic violence against people of color become nodal points for such gathering. They solidify shared attitudes in a manner similar to the lynching photographs of a previous era, discussed in chapter 1, that circulated among racist whites in the United States. Although racist YouTube comments on the Grant videos were usually decried by many other viewers' postings, they expose a cultural context for his shooting that does not match the claims about postracial America elicited by Barack Obama's inauguration in the very same month that Grant was killed, January 2009.

Conclusion: "To Rescue Some Type of Meaning"

When Brian Steidle returned from Darfur to the United States with his binders full of corpse photographs in *The Devil Came on Horseback*, he naively hoped those photographs would have an immediate, concrete, and large-scale impact, leading to U.S. military intervention in Darfur. Earlier in the film, he had longed for an act of transformation: for the camera through which he watched trucks of Janjaweed killers to become a weapon's scope, for what he saw as passive observation to become active intervention. A related act of transformation underlies his fantasy about the photographs, as the dead bodies he preserves in page after page of documentation promise to summon troops who will rise up in their stead and save those who can still be saved. In the face of tragedy as vast and brutal as Darfur's, Steidle can hardly be blamed for desiring a swift and heroic response from his national audience. Though it does not come, his disappointment likely ignores the smaller-scale responses his efforts must have generated: a few hundred or a few thousand minds changed about the situation in Darfur, some significant donations to aid groups and human rights organizations, more citizens drawn to rallies and protests on the issues, and maybe even a politician or two inspired to advocate for Darfur.

In the activist use of documentary death, we hope—as Steidle does—to see clear victories but are inevitably left with partial successes that require too many qualifiers. Agha-Soltan's recorded martyrdom empowered Green Movement protesters in Iran and shed light on their plight for global audiences, but it did not lead to a new election or a government overthrow. Successes feel even more scant in relation to the Grant videos: Mehserle was convicted but on a lighter charge and with a much shorter sentence than Grant's supporters wanted. Further, the narrow media focus on Mehserle's individual culpability and his trial drew attention away from the flawed policies and attitudes in the BART police force that precipitated this tragedy, the structural inequities of law enforcement in the United States, and even more broadly, the persistent racist perception of all Black men in public space as violent threats. Just a few years later, the similarly anemic response from the legal system and policy makers to the death of Trayvon Martin—though its circumstances were different in many respects from Grant's—provided another grim layer of confirmation for how little concrete change the Grant videos had precipitated.

In fact, rather than take a hard look at their own tendencies toward racial profiling or their use of force guidelines, several Bay Area law enforcement agencies considered other policy changes in the wake of Grant's shooting that indicated they had learned a disappointing lesson from the case: get control of the documentary images. Some in the region made plans to equip their officers with over-the-ear (or chest-mounted) cameras to record point-of-view shots of what the officers see, in what has become a nationwide trend in the years since. Though such a system could help make officers accountable in their use of force, that is not the tone with which Bay Area police framed it. San Jose's Sergeant Ronnie Lopez, for example, explains: "We live in a YouTube society where people have the ability to record us. We firmly believe officers do the right things for the right reasons, and this is a way to show *our side*."[83] In this aftermath, it is painfully clear that the technological wonders of new media have very limited power against systemic racism and, in fact, can be mobilized in support of racist power structures as well as against them. These technologies' interventions can only go so far in securing justice for lives that are still not fully grievable in our country.

In addition to qualifying the successes of the Grant and Agha-Soltan videos, I must also note that for the great majority of individuals shown dying on YouTube, no organized political response will emerge to "do something" about their deaths. No users will even make the easy promise to "never forget." These videos will fall into a limbo Juhasz calls NicheTube: "the vast sea of little-seen YouTube videos that are hard to find given YouTube's architecture of ranking and user-generated tags."[84] Faced with these mitigating factors in the efficacy of documentary death, one understands the strangely nostalgic appeal of Adams's *Saigon Execution* photograph as it exists in collective memory. Here, legend has it, is a documented death that *stopped a war*—even if actual evidence suggests that it, less dramatically, bolstered an already-surging antiwar sentiment. But it is possible to think that it stopped a war today partly because the accumulating dust of historical distance covers over those nagging qualifiers that we see more clearly in deaths from the digital age's very recent past.

Whenever I stumble upon one of those seldom-viewed deaths on YouTube, I recall David Cook's powerful insight: "Ultimately, martyrdom is an attempt to rescue some type of meaning and dignity from death."[85] A similar attempt is made by the YouTubers who post those obscure videos, by those who did so for the more heavily circulated Neda Agha-Soltan and Oscar Grant videos, and by most documentarians representing death, whether of martyrs or not. The act of watching an actual death cries out for justification, some reassurance that it has not merely provided a momentary diversion—just another YouTube offering viewed in between music videos and cute kitten montages. We want these images to *communicate* something clear and vital, to effect some change in ourselves and in our world. The Grant and Agha-Soltan videos, especially the latter, did so more than most. But like all documentary records of lives ending in front of a camera, they remain difficult to absorb, perched precariously at the edge of representation.

CONCLUSION

The Nearest Cameras Can Go

— — —

. . . The nearest friends can go
With anyone to death, comes so far short
They may as well not try to go at all.
ROBERT FROST,
"Home Burial," in *Poems by Robert Frost*

Frost's words bookend those of a fellow poet, Rilke, that began this project with the notion of "dying in full detail"—a phrase whose alluring possibilities I have applied to digital documentary, describing a view of death it seems to offer. I am likewise transposing the assertion in "Home Burial" to the context of representation, as well, broadening its "friends" to consider the documentary camera and the audiences that camera serves. Paired, these quotations form two ends of a spectrum of answers to the question this book has ultimately considered: not about the extent to which it is right to record actual death but about the extent to which it is useful. The access cameras in the digital age might grant to "dying in full detail" offers to help us understand a shared human experience that is urgent and complex; but the persistent discourse on death as unknowable threatens that even digital cameras undertaking its representation will "[come] so far short / They may as well not try to go at all."

What I have endeavored to demonstrate in this book is that the promise of seeing death's "full detail" can never be fulfilled by any image technology. "Friends" cannot absorb deaths they witness, and cameras have little chance to communicate the totality of this experience. As machines that thrive on the visible and the audible, the best they can hope to do is inscribe the external signs of death onto celluloid or magnetic tape, or translate them into the binary code that underlies digital video. Those signs, however, can convey a great deal—enough that we cannot say that cameras approaching death "[come] so far short / They may as well not try to go at all." Although death remains a process that, as Bazin says, "must be experienced and cannot be represented"— its "full detail" always out of reach—that does not make the grasping efforts of documentarians futile.[1] As Susan Sontag herself—long a skeptic about the value of documenting human suffering and death—conceded, late in life, "Even if [such images] are only tokens, and cannot possibly encompass most of the reality to which they refer, they still perform a vital function."[2]

Indeed, the preceding chapters have shown undeniably partial and fragmentary images of documentary death doing cultural *work* in various forms, some more ethically comfortable than others. These images have engaged the public's curiosity about the elusive "moment" of violent death, and they have destabilized the notion of death as a moment through chronicles of dying as a process. They have exposed the ugliness and brutality of death in war, and they have framed death as an emotionally or aesthetically inspiring experience. They have helped dying individuals who participate in the filmmaking find meaning in their last months of life, and they have recorded, without consent, fatal attacks or anguished decisions to commit suicide. They have mobilized activists when their dying subjects have the right characteristics and are recorded with the right aesthetics, and they have gone largely unnoticed when failing to meet these conditions. To access this cultural work that documentary death performs, I have looked closely at the images themselves—analyzing the content and circumstances of death's recording rather than condemning or praising the mere fact of it.

Just as I have argued against this knee-jerk reaction of ethically condemning documentary death footage, I have also tried to approach the makers and viewers of these images generously. From my experience researching this book, I have come to believe that the act of recording an actual death is more often characterized by empathy than callousness. And for most viewers who seek out such images, the motivation to look seems to emerge more from a frightened curiosity than a cynical morbidity. Being curious about the nature of death is not inherently morbid. The rare truly universal human experience, dying is a process of momentous consequence in each of our lives—and one for which many people have found few models, through their lived experience or through realistic media representation. Good intentions do not exempt these makers and viewers from the damage their practices might inflict on others, but we will come to misguided conclusions about documentary death if we imagine soulless profiteers creating the bulk of this material for a leering, lascivious audience.

Although the works examined in this book do not exist *because* of digital technology, most would not exist without it. The affordability, versatility, and durational capacities of digital production and distribution have had a tremendous impact on what is possible in the documentary realm—an impact starkly revealed when death is the documentarian's subject. And death's study by digital cameras has, in turn, brought some of its complexities to light: its status as a complicated and variable process, both physically and psychologically, in which the transcendent "moment of death" we might imagine becomes a tiny fragment that resists identification.

Digital technology takes us nearer to death than film technology ever could, but perhaps in the end the idea of proximity is less important to understanding these images' appeal than the idea of control. From the early days of the daguerreotype, image-makers and consumers seemed to comprehend the psychological allure of *capturing* death—of freezing its visible traces in a material picture, one that could stop the relentless progression of time and that the living could hold in their hands. If photography can thus arrest death, the moving image can manipulate its temporality—especially on digital video, when viewers may have nothing to hold, but their hands can instead tinker with time's flow. With a push to the buttons of a remote control, the click of a mouse, or the tactile slide of a finger on a touch screen, the living can tailor death's progression to their whims—repeating, fragmenting, reversing, slowing, or freezing it. As Frost implies, there is a point in the dying process past which the dying cannot bring along the living—a hard truth that makes this affordance of the digital moving image all the more poignant. Through it, we can traverse the mortal boundary between alive and dead as many times as we wish just by pushing a button, with the ease of hopping to and fro across a small stream. Thus, we gain a modicum of control—however slight—over our inevitable fate, to die, that offers so little of it.

Alongside control, the other lure of the digital in relation to death is its vaunted immortality, which is tied to its alleged technological immateriality. The label "immaterial" often feels like a dismissal of digital media as less impactful, less *real*, than a medium like celluloid film. But digging deeper into these comparisons, the assertion of the digital's immateriality is sometimes less of a rejection than an anxious hope. For materiality ensures mortality. The luminescence and rich grain of projected celluloid that cinephiles so love spring from the surface of a physical strip of film, which will slowly and inexorably decay. Its frames, at least in their original form, will eventually die, despite even the most well-funded efforts of preservation. The best approach to the "necessary mistake" of film preservation, writes archivist Paolo Cherchi Usai, is for the preservationist to behave "very much like the physician who has accepted the inevitability of death even while he continues to fight for the patient's life. . . . The real question is, are viewers willing to accept the slow fading to nothing of what they are looking at?"[3]

Digital video promised to sweep away that awful question, capturing eternal youth and eternal life as an unchanging virtual file rather than a buckling, crumbling reel of celluloid in a canister. Mary Ann Doane expresses this function of digital immateriality when she writes, "Digital media emerge as the apparent endpoint of an accelerating dematerialization. . . . [Their] information or representations appear to exist nowhere and the cultural dream of the digital is a dream of immateriality, without degradation or loss."[4] As Doane notes, though, this immortal immateriality is just a dream. Digital files, too, will degrade, disappear, or be abandoned by their guardians at some point in the exhausting, expensive, and ceaseless cycle of content migration to evernewer formats.

Although, as I have demonstrated, digital video's durational capacities have allowed us to record long processes of dying, digital images themselves usually die quick, violent deaths rather than enduring celluloid's slowly decaying "natural" deaths. A digital file is deleted, it gets lost in a server crash, or the last program that can play its file format becomes obsolete in a software upgrade— all these are causes of death for digital images. Sometimes these violent deaths are partial, as a video file may still exist on a hard drive somewhere, but its circulation—its chance to impact audiences—is terminated when, for example, its YouTube uploader (or YouTube itself) removes the file. When documentary death footage disappears this way, the private sight that digital technology had once made public now becomes private again—living on for a time, perhaps, on just one individual's computer. Nothing drives home the illusory nature of digital immortality, the *loss* that pervades this "lossless" culture, more than loading a bookmarked YouTube URL and seeing a black screen with the words "This video is no longer available."

The digital recordings of death I have examined in this book, then, will eventually die, too. As difficult as watching these recordings may have been for those who cared about the dying person depicted, they could also be comforting in their promise to immortalize that loved one, to extend their memory and power to affect the world of the living. This second death, then—the death *of* the video rather than *in* the video—renews the pain of the first. It is the death of memory, of a technological memory that may have outlived the embodied, human memory of those who knew the dying person in life.

A few lines further in "Home Burial," Frost continues, "Friends make pretence of following to the grave, / But before one is in it, their minds are turned / And making the best of their way back to life / And living people, and things they understand." Having virtually followed so many to the grave in the course of writing this book, I feel compelled to close by saying, simply, that the lives I have seen end on camera have had a profound effect on me—on an emotional level as much as an intellectual one. Like the experience of death, this one is difficult to express. Instead of trying, I will come to the end of this work on endings and make the best of my way back to life, and living people, and things I understand.

NOTES

Introduction

1   Bazin, "Death Every Afternoon."
2   Rilke, *The Notebooks of Malte Laurids Brigge*, 17. This passage came to my attention through Friedman, *Fictional Death and the Modernist Enterprise*, 57.
3   Vogel, "The Ultimate Secret," 263.
4   I will use the term "natural" death to refer to deaths we attribute to disease or age, but I make this choice between two terms that are both unsatisfying. Is there anything that feels either "natural" or "nonviolent," for example, about a death in an intensive care unit that is accompanied by forceful chest compressions, jolts from defibrillators, and the frenzied atmosphere of a "code" (when a patient's deterioration prompts CPR or intubation)?
5   Bazin, "Death Every Afternoon," 30.
6   Bazin, "Death Every Afternoon," 31.
7   Bazin, "Death Every Afternoon," 30.
8   Bazin, "The Ontology of the Photographic Image," 9.
9   Dyer, *White*, 104.
10 Bazin, "Death Every Afternoon," 31.
11 Zelizer, *About to Die*, 43–48.
12 Qtd. in Zelizer, *About to Die*, 301.
13 Manovich, *The Language of New Media*, 300, 302 (emphasis in original).
14 For influential discussions of digital immateriality (not all of which frame the digital as simply immaterial), see Mitchell, *The Reconfigured Eye*; Rosen, "Old and New"; Hansen, "Between Body and Image"; Doane, "The Indexical and the Concept of Medium Specificity"; Rodowick, *The Virtual Life of Film*.
15 Editing a digital documentary is, of course, a form of digital manipulation, but here I am referring to major changes to the mise-en-scène.
16 Gunning, "Moving Away from the Index," 30–31.
17 Torchin, "Mediation and Remediation," 39.
18 Halverson, Ruston, and Trethewey, "Mediated Martyrs of the Arab Spring."

19   He Huifeng, "Shenzhen Introduces Good Samaritan Law," *South China Morning Post*, August 1, 2013, http://www.scmp.com/news/china/article/1293475/shenzhen-introduces-good-samaritan-law.

20   Andile Mngxitama, "Tatane's Death Underlines Need for Government to Deliver," *Sowetan*, April 19, 2011, http://www.sowetanlive.co.za/columnists/2011/04/19/tatane-s-death-underlines-need-for-government-to-deliver.

21   Kastenbaum, *On Our Way*, 44.

22   Lundgren and Houseman, "Banishing Death," 226. Lundgren and Houseman clarify that while sanitary conditions in rural areas also welcomed disease, death rates outside the cities were significantly lower (225–26).

23   Lundgren and Houseman, "Banishing Death," 227. A nineteenth-century young man's diary entry about cholera expresses the terror these threats brought: "To see individuals well in the morning & buried before night, retiring apparently well & dead in the morning is something which is appalling to the boldest heart" (Rosenberg, *The Cholera Years*, 3). For more on death in the Civil War period, see chapter 1 and Faust, *This Republic of Suffering*.

24   Ariès, *The Hour of Our Death*. Ariès claims that this model of death spread even to the frontier in the mid-nineteenth century, as letters from that period to loved ones back East indicate (449).

25   Ariès, *The Hour of Our Death*, 448, 473.

26   Ariès, *Western Attitudes toward Death*, 92.

27   Gorer, "The Pornography of Death," 195.

28   Lundgren and Houseman, "Banishing Death," 229.

29   Post, *Inquiries in Bioethics*, 83. To nuance this history, I will note that there are twentieth-century and twenty-first-century Americans for whom the sight of death remains common: medical professionals, care workers in nursing homes, police, and military personnel, for example. The sight of death is thus not hidden from everyone but rather has been increasingly restricted to professionals whose jobs necessitate significant exposure to death.

30   Ariès, *The Hour of Our Death*, 570. Lundgren and Houseman show a major growth period for hospitals between 1873 (178 U.S. hospitals) and 1909 (4,359 U.S. hospitals) ("Banishing Death," 231).

31   Lundgren and Houseman, "Banishing Death," 232.

32   Ariès, *The Hour of Our Death*, 587; Walter, *The Revival of Death*, 59.

33   Lundgren and Houseman, "Banishing Death," 237.

34   Post, *Inquiries in Bioethics*, 86; Lundgren and Houseman, "Banishing Death," 236.

35   Ariès, *The Hour of Our Death*, 614.

36   Halbert L. Dunn, *Vital Statistics of the United States 1950, vol. 1, Analysis and Summary Tables with Supplemental Tables for Alaska, Hawaii, Puerto Rico, and Virgin Islands* (Washington, DC: U.S. Government Printing Office, 1954), 171. Heart failure—as opposed to heart attacks—often kills in a long and unpleasant process.

37   Ariès, *Western Attitudes toward Death*, 88–89.

38   Ruby, *Secure the Shadow*, 12.

39   For an analysis of how death functions in this important documentary (from a more theoretical than ethical perspective), see Jeong and Andrew, "Grizzly Ghost."

40 Qtd. in Hansen, "Schindler's List Is Not Shoah," 301.

41 Williams, *Hard Core*.

42 Gorer, "The Pornography of Death," 197.

43 The infamous film spawned several direct sequels and many derivatives in other multipart series such as *Facez of Death*, *Death Scenes*, *Traces of Death*, and *Banned from Television*.

44 This widespread eagerness survived the shocks of documentary death images from the 9/11 attacks and the wars in Afghanistan and Iraq that followed them, limited as the impact of the latter images may have been. Indeed, the public's continuing drive to see recorded death became newly evident in the first decade of the twenty-first century with data on online image and video searches (e.g., Internet users trying to watch Nick Berg's beheading video in May 2004 made it the most common search engine query in the week it was released) (Zelizer, *About to Die*, 286).

45 Myriad articles and blog posts have debated the value of trigger warnings; I recommend Elizabeth Freeman, Brian Herrera, Nat Hurley, Homay King, Dana Luciano, Dana Seitler and Patricia White, "Trigger Warnings Are Flawed," *Inside Higher Ed*, May 29, 2014, https://www.insidehighered.com/views/2014/05/29/essay-faculty -members-about-why-they-will-not-use-trigger-warnings; Jack Halberstam, "You Are Triggering Me! The Neo-liberal Rhetoric of Harm, Danger and Trauma," *Bully Bloggers*, July 5, 2014, https://bullybloggers.wordpress.com/2014/07/05/you-are -triggering-me-the-neo-liberal-rhetoric-of-harm-danger-and-trauma/; Karen Swallow Prior, "'Empathetically Correct' Is the New Politically Correct," *Atlantic*, May 23, 2014, http://www.theatlantic.com/education/archive/2014/05 /empathetically-correct-is-the-new-politically-correct/371442/.

46 Ensuring that a rape survivor about to watch a film for class knows that it has a graphic rape scene is a widely palatable trigger warning example scenario. But the potential efficacy of such warnings, even in this seemingly clear-cut case, is not easy to predict. Survivors of traumatic events can have highly idiosyncratic triggers—like a sound or a color they associate with the event—rather than intuitive ones like seeing a rape scene in a film. Further, the benefit of a trigger warning may depend on how the warned individual reacts to it. Current psychological research on treating PTSD asserts that controlled exposure to the traumatic memory and its associations is more effective than avoidance. While a college classroom—however thoughtfully managed—is no substitute for a trained exposure therapist's office, research suggests that we may be harming rather than helping our students if we encourage them to avoid assigned material on the basis of a trigger warning. The best use of such warnings, then, may be to prepare students who have lived through trauma to actually encounter potentially triggering material that is curated and taught with care, not to avoid it. *Treatment of Posttraumatic Stress Disorder*, 8.

47 The most publicized instance of extreme trigger-warning culture on a college campus came from a quickly withdrawn document that administrators circulated to Oberlin College faculty advising them to "be aware of racism, classism, sexism, heterosexism, cissexism, ableism, and other issues of privilege and oppression" in choosing what content to teach, to make that material optional where possible, and to favor alternatives. Jenny Jarvie, "Trigger Happy," *New Republic*, March 3, 2014,

http://www.newrepublic.com/article/116842/trigger-warnings-have-spread-blogs
-college-classes-thats-bad.

48   Sontag, *Regarding the Pain of Others*, 7.

49   See especially Barthes, *Camera Lucida*; Sontag, *On Photography*; Sontag, *Regarding the Pain of Others*; Berger, *About Looking*; Renov, *The Subject of Documentary* ("Filling up the Hole in the Real").

50   Sobchack, "Inscribing Ethical Space," 249–55.

51   Sobchack, "Inscribing Ethical Space," 252.

52   Sobchack, "Inscribing Ethical Space," 255.

53   Although her assessment of documentary ethics prescribes close reading as a necessary tool, Sobchack herself does little of it in "Inscribing Ethical Space." Her intentions seem to be broad and theoretical, and her ambitious coverage of an extensive topic in eighteen pages leaves little room for detailed analysis of actual footage. Additionally, far less of that footage would have been available and accessible to a scholar writing on this topic in 1984 (or even revising such a work in 2004) than to one writing on it today.

Chapter 1. Capturing the "Moment"

1   The twentieth-century trends toward death from prolonged ailments continue in the twenty-first, where at least seven of the ten leading causes of death in the United States forecast a slow withering rather than a sudden end (Centers for Disease Control and Prevention, "Deaths: Leading Causes for 2012," 17, August 31, 2015, http://www.cdc.gov/nchs/data/nvsr/nvsr64/nvsr64_10.pdf). These ten causes are based on the CDC's 2012 study, the most recent year for which public data were available. The seven-out-of-ten figure also holds true within each racial category that CDC statistics include, though variance of a few percentage points exists between racial categories when measuring by total annual deaths rather than leading causes. Even the top cause, heart disease, does not always provide a sudden death from a heart attack. Heart failure often kills in a long process accompanied by painful swelling, difficulty ingesting food, and a sensation of drowning when the lungs begin to fill with fluid. Though the following additional statistics do not signify a period of "dying" in the sense of immanent terminality, the average American is debilitated for five (for males) or eight (for females) years before death (Hardwig, "Going to Meet Death," 37).

2   Acknowledgments to Scott Combs, who uses Williams's "Film Bodies" to discuss the temporality of staged death scenes in melodrama—a use that partly inspired my extended comparison between Williams's modes and documentary death. See Combs, *Deathwatch*, 71–73.

3   Williams, "Film Bodies," 713, 703.

4   Barbie Zelizer provides an alternative temporal framing to mine in *About to Die*, arguing for the primacy of the "about to die" moment caught on camera (one that occurs earlier than the "moment" of death I am discussing). For Zelizer, it is less the spectacle of death or the allure of its precisely timed capture that draws viewers in, but rather the way "about to die" images restore a subjunctive "as if" state where the ensuing death or destruction may still be avoided.

5 Williams, "Film Bodies," 713.

6 Barthes, *Camera Lucida*, 92–95; Sontag, *On Photography*, 70; Bazin, "The Ontology of the Photographic Image," 15.

7 Sontag, *Regarding the Pain of Others*, 24.

8 Sobchack, "Inscribing Ethical Space," 237.

9 Barthes, *Camera Lucida*, 14; Batchen, *Forget Me Not*, 17.

10 Ariès, *The Hour of Our Death*, 415, 469, 442, 411.

11 Ruby, *Secure the Shadow*, 174.

12 Faust, *This Republic of Suffering*, 61, 70.

13 E. F. Bleiler, "Introduction," in *Gardner's Photographic Sketchbook of the Civil War*.

14 Carmichael, *First World War Photographers*, 3–4; Fielding, *The American Newsreel*, 72; Mould, *American Newsfilm*, 100–131, 133–37.

15 Qtd. in Mould, *American Newsfilm*, 220.

16 Nudelman, *John Brown's Body*, 118–19; Bleiler, "Introduction."

17 Nudelman, *John Brown's Body*, 122; Schantz, *Awaiting the Heavenly Country*, 186.

18 Staging already had precedents in the short history of wartime corpse photography. In 1858, Felice Beato became the first person to photograph war corpses, after the siege of Lucknow in India. In doing so, he rearranged the bones of the slain for the camera and posed some local men behind them (Sontag, *Regarding the Pain of Others*, 54).

19 Gardner, *Gardner's Photographic Sketchbook of the Civil War*, plates 36–37; Nudelman, *John Brown's Body*, 121. Significantly, the descriptions in Gardner's book (self-published, on a small scale) may not have accompanied his pictures in other forms through which the public viewed such images: as *cartes de visite* and stereoviews, and in exhibitions at urban galleries such as Mathew Brady's (Nudelman, *John Brown's Body*, 105–6).

20 Gardner, *Gardner's Photographic Sketchbook of the Civil War*, plate 37.

21 Faust, *This Republic of Suffering*, 10–11, 17.

22 Faust, *This Republic of Suffering*, 21.

23 Raiford, "The Consumption of Lynching Images," 268. Victims of other races were also lynched, but most of those cases occurred in the frontier West, where the practice claimed to supply legitimate executions in the absence of a full judicial system. By contrast, lynchings of Blacks in the South often snatched victims from jails and purposefully denied them existing legal proceedings (Apel, *Imagery of Lynching*, 23).

24 Goldsby, *A Spectacular Secret*, 216; Leon F. Litwack, "Hellhounds," in *Without Sanctuary*, 9, 20.

25 Raiford, "The Consumption of Lynching Images," 267. The photographs were sometimes appropriated to decry racism and its violence, but their original production and distribution were generally complicit in and supportive of that violence.

26 Apel, *Imagery of Lynching*, 30; Goldsby, *A Spectacular Secret*, 273; Raiford, "The Consumption of Lynching Images," 269.

27 Litwack, "Hellhounds," 14.

28 Raiford, "The Consumption of Lynching Images," 270; Apel, *Imagery of Lynching*, 44.

29 Raiford, "The Consumption of Lynching Images," 270. Photographs were not the only available souvenir of lynchings, but not everyone could obtain pieces of cloth,

hair, teeth, bone, or even flesh torn from the corpse (Litwack, "Hellhounds," 9; Raiford, "The Consumption of Lynching Images," 270).

30 Apel, *Imagery of Lynching*, 30.

31 Goldsby, *A Spectacular Secret*, 221.

32 Hilton Als, "GWTW," in *Without Sanctuary*, 40.

33 Goldsby, *A Spectacular Secret*, 231–32. A photograph of Frank Embree (lynched on July 22, 1899, in Fayette, Missouri) standing handcuffed, naked, and visibly bleeding provides a revealing anomaly among these corpse images, underscoring Goldsby's point about their usual obstacles to identification or sympathy (*Without Sanctuary*, plate 43). His seemingly defiant look directly at the camera forces the viewer to confront his humanity and disrupts the utter powerlessness that dominates lynching photos taken after the victim's death.

34 Haggith, "Filming the Liberation of Bergen-Belsen," 39; Zelizer, *Remembering to Forget*, 88.

35 Qtd. in Zelizer, *Remembering to Forget*, 89.

36 Qtd. in Abzug, *Inside the Vicious Heart*, 30.

37 Qtd. in Zelizer, *Remembering to Forget*, 86.

38 Abzug, *Inside the Vicious Heart*, 69–73, 82, 91, 129; Gladstone, "Separate Intentions."

39 Roeder, *The Censored War*, 25. Yet there is also cause to be less suspicious of political motivations in this display of atrocities: the United States had reason to rebuild the German reputation, in the face of the developing Cold War (Roeder, *The Censored War*, 127).

40 Zelizer, *Remembering to Forget*, 39, 31, 33, 90.

41 During that time, there was a marked increase in belief, but both polls revealed that U.S. citizens still vastly underestimated the scale of the killings (Abzug, *Inside the Vicious Heart*, 10, 139).

42 Zelizer, *Remembering to Forget*, 118, 199–200, 174.

43 Rees, "*The Nazis: A Warning from History*," 147.

44 Sontag, *On Photography*, 20. She would later express second thoughts about images' anesthetizing effect in *Regarding the Pain of Others* (105).

45 Mulvey, *Death 24x a Second*, 15, 12.

46 Combs, "Final Touches," 13.

47 Banner, *The Death Penalty*, 154–56. A fascination with seeing the executions that had been shuttered from the public eye and the camera's lens registers in sensational publicity around the electrocution in 1928 of Ruth Snyder, convicted of murdering her husband. As Zelizer details, the *New York Daily News* in multiple issues published a hidden-camera photo of Snyder blindfolded and strapped to the chair. The paper's varying captions and headlines for the same photo—including "DEAD!" and "RUTH SNYDER'S DEATH PICTURED!"—shift its alleged temporality from the "moment" of death to postdeath, as the blurry and innocuous image itself cannot reveal that information (Zelizer, *About to Die*, 34–36).

48 Sobchack, "Inscribing Ethical Space," 237.

49 Further titles demonstrating the popularity of execution spectacles in this era include *Shooting the Captured Insurgents* (1898, William Heise); *Beheading the Chinese Prisoner* (1900, Siegmund Lubin); *Execution of Czolgosz with Panorama of Auburn*

State Prison (1901, Edwin S. Porter/Edison); *The Terrible Turkish Executioner* (1903, Georges Méliès); *Execution of a Spy* (1902, Mutoscope/Biograph); *Electrocuting an Elephant* (1903, Edison); and *Reading the Death Sentence* (1905, Mutoscope/Biograph) (Doane, *The Emergence of Cinematic Time*, 145; Combs, *Deathwatch*, 27–64).

50 Banner, *The Death Penalty*, 172–73.

51 Combs, *Deathwatch*, 43. Deviations from instantaneous death appear in the two electrocution films I will discuss later, but they were also reported in actual electrocutions, such as New York's first—of William Kemmler in 1890. Kemmler's body seemed to still after what should have been the fatal jolt, but then he began to moan and move shortly afterward, to the horror of onlookers (Combs, *Deathwatch*, 23–24).

52 Doane, *The Emergence of Cinematic Time*, 160.

53 Accounts of Czolgosz's actual execution also note that multiple jolts of electric current were administered to ensure death (Johns, *The Man Who Shot McKinley*, 248).

54 Combs, *Deathwatch*, 33.

55 Doane, *The Emergence of Cinematic Time*, 145; Goldsby, *A Spectacular Secret*, 225.

56 Indeed actual animal deaths, such as Topsy's, have been filmed and displayed in both documentary and fiction films far more frequently than actual human deaths—perhaps serving as a substitute spectacle. Sobchack reports that noticing this ethical discrepancy, while watching a rabbit killed on-screen in *The Rules of the Game* (1939, Jean Renoir), prompted her initial interest in writing about documentary death (245). We can watch actual animal deaths in films as geographically, temporally, and topically varied as *The Lion Hunt* (1907, Viggo Larsen, Denmark); *Blood of the Beasts* (1949, Georges Franju, France); *Pink Flamingos* (1972, John Waters, USA); *Cannibal Holocaust* (1980, Ruggero Deodato, Italy); and *The Cove* (2009, Louie Psihoyos), to name a few. Regulations now constrain U.S. filmmakers from staging animal deaths for their movies, but these do not affect unstaged documentary footage.

57 Combs, "Final Touches," 40.

58 Doane, *The Emergence of Cinematic Time*, 160.

59 Whissel, *Picturing American Modernity*, 114–15.

60 Whissel, *Picturing American Modernity*, 14, 90–91.

61 Whissel, *Picturing American Modernity*, 82, 96.

62 See the paintings *Death of Col. Edward D. Baker* (1861, Currier and Ives); *Fighting at Virginia* (1862, Currier and Ives); *Battle of Spottsylvania* [sic] (1887, Thure de Thulstrup); and *Battle of Shiloh* (1888, Thure de Thulstrup).

63 Brothers, *War and Photography*, 183; Larry Rohter, "New Doubts Raised over Famous War Photo," *New York Times*, August 18, 2009, http://www.nytimes.com /2009/08/18/arts/design/18capa.html; Kershaw, *Blood and Champagne*, 39–42, 38; "Faking Soldier: The Photographic Evidence That Capa's Camera DOES Lie . . . and That His Iconic 'Falling Soldier' Was Staged," *Daily Mail*, July 21, 2009, http://www .dailymail.co.uk/news/article-1201116.

64 Fielding, *The American Newsreel*, 67–69; Bottomore, "The Biograph in Battle," 32. Most famously, the British propaganda film *Battle of the Somme* (1916) staged an apparent on-camera death as a soldier charges "over the top" of a trench and crumples

right back down. And in the United States, the American Life Photo Film Company had been staging "German atrocities" to film in New Jersey since 1914 (Kaes, *Shell Shock Cinema*, 29–31).

65 Fielding, *The American Newsreel*, 68.

66 Kershaw, *Blood and Champagne*, 39–42.

67 Sontag, *Regarding the Pain of Others*, 55.

68 Brothers, *War and Photography*, 183.

69 Zelizer, *Covering the Body*, 18.

70 For an excellent analysis of the Zapruder film as evidence—drawing viewers in not just with the sight of death but with the tantalizing promise that documentary footage could solve this nationally shattering crime—see Bruzzi, "The Event: Archive and Imagination." Additional films shot on the other side of the road by Orville Nix and Mary Muchmore also offer evidence in this debate but have only distant, obscured views of Kennedy's death itself. The Zapruder film transfer I am working from is *Image of an Assassination: A New Look at the Zapruder Film* (1963; Oak Forest, IL: MPI Teleproductions, 1999), DVD.

71 Zapruder had to visit seven different offices and plants to get the film developed and copied—a delay during which no one even knew how much of the killing he had recorded. It took days to get (necessarily degraded) copies to all the investigators, who had to round up projectors that could slow down or freeze the film without damaging it (Wrone, *The Zapruder Film*, 19–31). Though the superpowers of digital video are often exaggerated, it remains true that such evidence today can be seen, copied, and transmitted almost instantly with little degradation.

72 Zapruder sold the film and its copyright for $150,000 plus 50 percent of future sales. Time Inc. returned its ownership in 1975 to the Zapruder family, who sold it to the U.S. government in 1999 for $16 million (Wrone, *The Zapruder Film*, 272–73).

73 Wrone, *The Zapruder Film*, 35.

74 "Split-Second Sequence as the Bullets Struck," *Life*, November 29, 1963, 24–27; "Assassination: The Trail to a Verdict," *Life*, October 2, 1964, 40–50B; "A Matter of Reasonable Doubt," *Life*, November 25, 1966, 38–48B.

75 Warren Commission, Report of the President's Commission on the Assassination of President John F. Kennedy, 108. For more on the film's underground circulation, see Wrone, *The Zapruder Film*, 59–61.

76 A bootleg copy, enhanced by Richard Groden, aired on the March 6, 1975, episode, with an audibly shocked reaction to the headshot from the studio audience. The segment appears on the *Image of an Assassination* DVD.

77 Bazin, "Death Every Afternoon," 31.

78 Instant replay was thus used to replay death actuality footage before it was used for its intended purpose of sports coverage—debuting weeks later in the 1963 Army-Navy football game (Jay, *More Than Just a Game*, 103).

79 Barnouw, *Tube of Plenty*, 334.

80 Kerekes and Slater, *Killing for Culture*, 204. Pennsylvania politician Budd Dwyer is sometimes erroneously included among famous live television deaths; his suicide during a 1987 press conference was recorded but did not air live.

81 Qtd. in Braestrup, *Big Story*, 35.

82 Pach, "And That's the Way It Was," 92. The levels of trust placed in the young medium of television were demonstrated by a series of surveys from the Roper Organization. After several years of war coverage in 1972, for example, respondents reported television as their main source of news and said they would trust television accounts over newspaper accounts in a case of conflicting information by a margin of 48 percent to 21 percent (Hallin, *The Uncensored War*, 106).

83 Implementing official censorship in a never-declared war may have been illegal, would have connoted deception and secrecy at a time when too much was already in the air, and would have taken tremendous additional spending and organization. Plus, the United States could hardly censor foreign reporters who had flocked to the action. Whether due to an ethical investment in the free press or a fear of media outcry, the United States avoided the South Vietnamese participation that would been essential for effective censorship, assuming it would be excessive (Hammond, *Reporting Vietnam*, 18, 43, 41).

84 Hammond, *Reporting Vietnam*, 53, 43; Zelizer, *About to Die*, 220.

85 Pach, "And That's the Way It Was," 95.

86 Rust, "'Passionate Detachment,'" 48.

87 Pach, "And That's the Way It Was," 95.

88 Bailey and Lichty, "Rough Justice on a Saigon Street," 223, 225; Pach, "And That's the Way It Was," 109.

89 Bailey and Lichty, "Rough Justice on a Saigon Street," 226.

90 Interview with Adams in *An Unlikely Weapon: The Eddie Adams Story* (2009), directed by Susan Morgan Cooper.

91 Sturken, *Tangled Memories*, 90; Zelizer, *Remembering to Forget*, 215; Hoskins, *Televising War*, 19–20.

92 Indeed, more 1960s viewers likely saw the widely reprinted photo than Suu's footage, which aired only a few times in the years after its debut on *The Huntley-Brinkley Report*: on *The Frank McGee Report* in March 1968 and in NBC's *From Here to the '70s* special in 1969 (Bailey and Lichty, "Rough Justice on a Saigon Street," 227). The distinction is less sharp now, when we can possess copies of the footage (on a number of DVDs featuring it or as a video file downloaded from the Internet).

93 Sturken, *Tangled Memories*, 90. Many letters from shocked or outraged readers that newspapers received upon printing Adams's photo demonstrate that as a still, too, this sight could be "extremely difficult to watch" (Zelizer, *About to Die*, 227–28).

94 Faust, *This Republic of Suffering*, 19.

95 Pach, "And That's the Way It Was," 108.

96 Sturken, *Tangled Memories*, 93. Believing Loan's assertions about mitigating circumstances in the execution, Eddie Adams regretted the damage his photograph did to Loan's reputation and its use as "perfect propaganda for North Vietnam" (Adams, "The Tet Photo," 185).

97 Zelizer, *About to Die*, 294–303.

98 "Death Jump," for example, from a canister of unused 1912 footage, appears to show the fatal descent of inventor Franz Reichelt from the Eiffel Tower as he tested a new parachute design; the clip has been viewed about 3 million times through the archive's YouTube channel as of July 2016 (YouTube video, 1:36, posted by

"britishpathe," July 27, 2011, http://www.youtube.com/watch?v=FBN3xfGrx_U).
"Prisoner Tried, Condemned and Executed in Cuba (1959)," which ends with
a clearly filmed death by firing squad, offers another instance of unused death
footage from the newsreel archives now seeing the digital light of day (YouTube
video, 0:47, posted by "WarArchives," February 1, 2012, http://www.youtube.com
/watch?v=HtfEv5kAeyE).

99 Federal Bureau of Investigation, "Malicious Software Features Usama bin Laden
Links to Ensnare Unsuspecting Computer Users," May 3, 2011, http://www.fbi.gov
/news/pressrel/press-releases/malicious-software-features-usama-bin-laden-links
-to-ensnare-unsuspecting-computer-users.

100 Zelizer, *About to Die*, 286, 290.

101 I am referencing Supreme Court justice William Brennan's well-known definition
of obscenity: that which is "utterly without redeeming social importance" (*United
States v. Roth*, 354 U.S. 476 [1957], 484).

102 Sontag, *On Photography*, 21.

Chapter 2. The Art of Dying, on Video

1 Freud, "Timely Reflections on War and Death," 185.

2 See the introduction for further discussion on the history of attitudes toward
death in Western culture, and especially Ariès, *Western Attitudes toward Death*;
Ariès, *The Hour of Our Death*; and Lundgren and Houseman, "Banishing Death."

3 Vogel, "The Ultimate Secret," 263.

4 See chapter 1, note 1.

5 Centers for Disease Control and Prevention, "Deaths, Percent of Total Deaths . . .
by Race and Sex, United States, 2009," 2012, http://www.cdc.gov/nchs/data/dvs
/LCWK10_2010.pdf, 1–3. I calculated the 7 percent figure from this data set by
adding together the percentages of deaths from all violent or possibly violent
causes that were included: accident, suicide, assault, "events of undetermined
intent," and "operations of war and their sequelae."

6 Kastenbaum, *On Our Way*, 121. Fiction films of the post–classical Hollywood
era have made some progress in rectifying these misrepresentations, but many
beloved deathbed scenes still contain them. *Love Story* (1970, Arthur Hiller), for
example, presents an emotional deathbed scene between young lovers in which
the dying cancer patient, Jennifer, appears beautiful, healthy, and strong on the
last day of her life. Amos Vogel writes that *Love Story* exemplifies "the insufferable
sentimentality and the manageable, antiseptic way in which people die in commercial films" ("The Ultimate Secret," 263).

7 Sobchack, "Inscribing Ethical Space," 236–37.

8 Combs, *Deathwatch*, 179–214.

9 Some cameras *can* penetrate the body and show us its inner workings, but (as the
next section will illuminate) death as it is currently understood cannot be localized to one visible internal event—like the heart ceasing to beat.

10 "Time of Death," Showtime, http://www.sho.com/sho/search?q=time+of+death.

11 Boyle, "A Brief History of American Documentary Video," 51–69.

12 Manovich, *The Language of New Media*, 41–42.

13   Ariès, *The Hour of Our Death*, 614.

14   It may seem that *Imitation's* anachronistic deathbed scene stems from the film's source material, Fannie Hurst's popular 1933 novel, published at a time when this kind of dying was a less-distant memory. The death scene in the novel, however, is not framed as strongly as a good death and differs significantly from the film's (Hurst, *Imitation of Life*, 265–67).

15   Ariès, *The Hour of Our Death*, 560.

16   Filene, *In the Arms of Others*, 63.

17   Anonymous, "Ars bene moriendi."

18   Kübler-Ross, *On Death and Dying*, 41–42. Kübler-Ross is herself the subject of a deathbed documentary, though one that is more interested in rehearsing her biography than in chronicling her dying process: *Facing Death: Elisabeth Kübler-Ross* (2003, Stefan Haupt).

19   Lock, *Twice Dead*, 7, 59–64, 1, 78.

20   "What and When Is Death?," 220. The question of defining this "moment" was resurfacing after its seeming resolution at the turn of the century by doctors eager to put resurgent fears of premature burial to rest. These fears had intensified with the introduction of artificial resuscitation—a procedure that cast doubt on the permanence of "death" as it was then determined. Safeguards against death's vague temporality became popular: waiting periods before burial, bell and flag alert systems to be used by those waking up in buried coffins, and even corpse mutilation (by request) to guarantee death. Consumers considering a coffin bell purchase must have been relieved when doctors in the late nineteenth century agreed that death could be declared confidently when heartbeat and respiration ceased. Alas, within decades the artificial ventilator, "brain-dead" patients, and organ transplant procedures shattered this certainty (Lock, *Twice Dead*, 66–71).

21   John Sanford, "When Are You Dead? Resurgent Form of Organ Transplantation Raises a New Question," *Stanford Medicine*, Spring 2011, http://stanmed.stanford .edu/2011spring/article5.html.

22   Lock, *Twice Dead*, 89, 79, 73–74. Lock compares the United States and Japan to demonstrate that well-educated citizens in other medically-advanced countries are less willing to accept medical assurance that "brain dead" donors are truly dead.

23   Lock, *Twice Dead*, 11. David Magnus, director of the Stanford Center for Biomedical Ethics, shares Lock's perspective, conceding in a discussion on organ donation that "there is no bright line" between a living person and a dead body, "but we need that distinction for policy reasons" (Sanford, *When Are You Dead?*).

24   So much was written that the author of a 1979 bibliography on the subject quipped, "Death is a very badly kept secret; such an unmentionable topic that there are over 650 books now in print asserting that we are ignoring the subject" (qtd. in Walter, *The Revival of Death*, 1). The late twentieth century's "badly kept secret," death, had supplanted the nineteenth century's sex as a taboo—not just simply, but in a rich, Foucauldian sense.

25   Churchill, "The Human Experience of Dying," 33. Other contributing factors in the early stages of this "revival of death" include consumer advocacy groups (which empowered patients to demand more from medical providers), popular exposés

on the funeral industry (e.g., Jessica Mitford's *The American Way of Death* and Ruth Harmer's *The High Cost of Dying*), and a widespread waning of trust in authority figures (like doctors) (Kastenbaum, *On Our Way*, 113–15).

26 Kastenbaum, *On Our Way*, 111, 110.

27 National Hospice and Palliative Care Organization, "NHPCO Facts and Figures: Hospice Care in America," November 2012, http://www.nhpco.org/sites/default /files/public/Statistics_Research/2012_Facts_Figures.pdf, 4.

28 Filene, *In the Arms of Others*, 158.

29 Kastenbaum, *On Our Way*, 132.

30 Brown, *Edgework*, 42–43.

31 Rose, "Biological Citizens."

32 Walter, *The Revival of Death*, 2; Leget, "Retrieving the Ars Moriendi Tradition," 314; Becker, *The Denial of Death*.

33 Leary, *Design for Dying*, 4. Mary Roach's popular study of the uses of human cadavers, *Stiff*, extends this principle beyond death, encouraging readers to do something unique as a corpse: "Get involved with science. Be an art exhibit. Become part of a tree. Some options for you to think about. Death. It doesn't have to be boring" (Roach, *Stiff*, 10–11).

34 In addition to Churchill, others calling for "stories over stages" include: Gavin, *Cuttin' the Body Loose*, 194; Webb, *The Good Death*, xviii; and Byock, *Dying Well*, 36.

35 Giddens, *Modernity and Self-Identity*, 52. Giddens describes the turn toward self-identity as part of "late modernity," the same period that others characterized through neoliberal ideology.

36 Centers for Disease Control and Prevention, "Deaths, Percent of Total Deaths," 4–9. Approximately 11.6 percent of annual African American male deaths are violent, compared to 7.2 percent of all annual U.S. deaths. I calculated these figure from the CDC data set by adding together the percentages of deaths from all violent or possibly violent causes that were included: accident, suicide, assault, "events of undetermined intent," and "operations of war and their sequelae."

37 Actually, Sally's was not the first segment in the original cut that aired on PBS (it was preceded by two interviews), but the only version of *Dying* in distribution during my research—a DVD from Filmakers Library [sic]—begins with Sally.

38 Michael Roemer screened and discussed *Dying* in a documentary course taught by George C. Stoney that I took at New York University in the spring of 2003 (providing my first exposure to the film and my initial interest in documentary representations of death). In his remarks, he claimed that Harriet was well aware that she would likely be perceived as "a bitch," in her words, and encouraged him to use the footage anyway. After *Dying* aired, she spent time doing invited talks on bereavement and anger.

39 See Nichols, "The Voice of Documentary." This trend is wonderfully illustrated by Albert and David Maysles's *Grey Gardens* (1975) in the year before *Dying*, in which the old "fly on the wall" pros allow eccentric subjects to bring them into arguments and to perform overtly for the camera rather than keeping up the charade of its invisibility. More radically still, others were exposing the pretensions and deceptions of the direct cinema style through parody and imitation in powerful faux docu-

mentaries such as *David Holzman's Diary* (1967, Jim McBride) and *No Lies* (1973, Mitchell Block).

40 Ariès, *The Hour of Our Death*, 592; Fleischer, "Dying to Be on Television," 30.

41 "WGBH Alumni: Susan Kubany," WGBH *Alumni*, May 22, 2007, http://wgbhalumni
    .org/profiles/k/kubany-susan/.

42 Fleischer, "Dying to Be on Television," 31.

43 Kübler-Ross, *On Death and Dying*, 8.

44 Wood, *Expressive Death*, qtd. in Walter, *The Revival of Death*, 32.

45 Jaweed Kaleem, "'Time of Death,' Showtime Documentary Series, Peers into the
    Last Days of the Dying," *Huffington Post*, November 1, 2013, http://www.huffington
    post.com/2013/11/01/time-of-death-showtime_n_4183377.html.

46 Kastenbaum recognizes that sometimes in this culture "the good death is the one
    that achieves" (*On Our Way*, 123).

47 Barnouw, *Documentary*, 254–55.

48 Michael Roemer (question and answer session, New York University, New York,
    NY, Spring 2003).

49 Combs, "Final Touches," 281.

50 Hawkins, "Constructing Death," 303–4.

51 "Show Business: Death Watch," *Time*, May 3, 1976, http://www.time.com/time
    /magazine/article/0,9171,914147,00.html.

52 Fleischer, "Dying to Be on Television," 31.

53 This section title references Laura Mulvey's book *Death 24x a Second*. "30x a sec-
    ond" reflects the change in frame rates between film and video, though these are
    not uniform across all types of video production.

54 Ross McElwee, "*Sherman's March*: Director's Statement," *Ross McElwee: Homemade
    Movies Inc.*, 2006, http://rossmcelwee.com/shermansmarch.html.

55 Kearl, *Endings*, 387.

56 Fleischer, "Dying to Be on Television," 30, 32.

57 *Near Death*, in typical Wiseman fashion, is actually about the intensive care unit
    as an institution more than it is about people dying. As one of the most generously
    funded documentarians, Wiseman—despite his notorious shooting ratios—was able
    to keep working on celluloid into the twenty-first century before making the switch.

58 Amy Souza, "Cinema Sympathy," *New England Film*, March 2003, http://www.new
    englandfilm.com/news/ archives/03march/davis.htm.

59 Kerekes and Slater, *Killing for Culture*, 261.

60 "Show Business: Death Watch."

61 Gavin, *Cuttin' the Body Loose*, 142.

62 Part of the aesthetic contrast between *Dying* and *The End* results from produc-
    tion logistics rather than types of equipment. *Dying* selected and filmed patients
    who were still mobile and well enough to spend time outdoors. *The End* found its
    subjects through a hospice organization, and therefore began documenting their
    deaths later in the process, when most were already significantly debilitated and
    unable to leave home.

63 Jason Janis, "Kirby Dick Director of *Sick* Interview," DVD *Talk*, accessed April 13,
    2011, http://www.dvdtalk.com/interviews/kirby_dick_dire.html.

64 Roemer, "Filmmaker's Report on 'Death and Dying' Film," 123.

65 Phelan, "Dying Man with a Movie Camera," 392.

66 Don McCullin, untitled contribution to "20 Years: AIDS & Photography," *Digital Journalist*, June 2001, http://digitaljournalist.org/issue0106/visions_frameset.htm, qtd. in Zelizer, *About to Die*, 154.

67 Zelizer, *About to Die*, 157.

68 Walter, *The Revival of Death*, 22.

69 For comprehensive overviews of autobiographical documentary's formation and influences, see Renov, *The Subject of Documentary*, 171–81; and Lane, "The Convergence of Autobiography and Documentary," 11–32.

70 Sobchack writes about the dying person in these rare scenarios (she mentions only *Dying* and *Silverlake Life*) as reviving a style of death ritual described by Ariès in which the dying is the organizer and the guardian of that ritual's protocols ("Inscribing Ethical Space," 253).

71 Efforts to hold onto the perishable bodies of the dead were sometimes extreme: one elaborate plan arose to vitrify the deceased's skeleton, producing a glass-like substance from which to make medallions or a portrait to commemorate that individual (Ariès, *The Hour of Our Death*, 513–16).

72 Batchen, *Forget Me Not*, 78.

73 Batchen, *Forget Me Not*, 87.

74 Renov, *The Subject of Documentary*, 186.

75 Sobchack, "Inscribing Ethical Space," 243.

76 Bazin, "The Ontology of the Photographic Image," 15.

77 This quotation comes from one of the oldest photography advertising slogans: "Secure the Shadow, Ere the Substance Fade, / Let Nature Imitate what Nature Made" (Ruby, *Secure the Shadow*, 1).

78 I am working from the samples included in Hallas, *Reframing Bodies*, 131–32.

79 Kastenbaum and Normand, "Deathbed Scenes as Imagined by the Young and Experienced by the Old," 201; Evans, Walters, and Hatch-Woodruff, "Deathbed Scene Narratives"; Tomer, "Death-Related Attitudes," 88; Bassett, McCann, and Cate, "Personification of Personal and Typical Death as Related to Death Attitudes," 163–72.

80 Sobchack, "Inscribing Ethical Space," 253.

81 Agamben, *Homo Sacer*. While I believe a loose comparison is apt, I acknowledge that the "actively dying" person does not align perfectly with Agamben's "homo sacer" (especially in that the dying party still has notable legal rights, as the cases of "brain dead" patients like Terri Schiavo demonstrate).

Chapter 3. "A Negative Pleasure"

1 A suicide into water from a bridge was also staged for the screen during this period by Vsevolod Pudovkin in the fiction film *Deserter* (1933), complete with languorous slow motion.

2 Philip Matier and Andrew Ross, "Film Captures Suicides on Golden Gate Bridge," *San Francisco Chronicle*, January 19, 2005, http://www.sfgate.com/cgi-bin/article .cgi?f=/c/a/2005/01/19/MNGENASPH31.DTL.

3 Eric Steel, "Letter to the Editor," *New York Times*, November 12, 2006, http://query .nytimes.com/gst/fullpage.html?res=9403EEDA1E3FF931A25752C1A9609C8B63& scp=3&sq=%22eric%20steel%22%20snuff&st=cse.

4 Stephen Holden, review of *The Bridge*, *New York Times*, October 27, 2006, http:// movies.nytimes.com/2006/10/27/movies/27brid.html?ref=movies; Andrew Pulver, review of *The Bridge*, *Guardian*, February 16, 2007, http://www.guardian.co.uk/film /2007/feb/16/documentary.

5 Eric Steel, "*The Bridge* Press Kit: Director's Statement," http://www.thebridge-the movie.com.

6 Matier and Ross, "Film Captures Suicides on Golden Gate Bridge."

7 Howard Feinstein, "Get Your Suicide Here, Folks," *Guardian*, June 23, 2006, http:// www.guardian.co.uk/film/2006/jun/23/3.

8 Cheryl Eddy, "Steel Will," *San Francisco Bay Guardian*, October 24, 2006, http:// www.sfbg.com/entry.php?entry_id=1942&catid=110.

9 Sobchack, "Inscribing Ethical Space," 249.

10 For more on dead time, see Doane, "Dead Time, or the Concept of the Event," in *The Emergence of Cinematic Time*, 140–71. YouTube's maximum video length is currently about twelve hours, so my assertion is that long documentary videos full of "dead time" would not succeed in YouTube's "attention economy," not that the site is technologically incapable of hosting them.

11 Camus, *The Myth of Sisyphus and Other Essays*, 4.

12 Camus, *The Myth of Sisyphus and Other Essays*, 5.

13 Plato, *The Dialogues of Plato*, 2:265–66; Tacitus, *The Annals of Imperial Rome*, 390. For a visual interpretation of Socrates's crowded bedside as he drank the hemlock, see Jacques-Louis David's painting *The Death of Socrates* (1787).

14 Friedman, *Fictional Death and the Modernist Enterprise*, 52. The fourth-century scholar Libanius records Athenian law on suicide as follows: "If your existence is hateful to you, die; if you are overwhelmed by fate, drink the hemlock. If you are bowed with grief, abandon life. Let the unhappy man recount his misfortune, let the magistrate supply him with the remedy, and his wretchedness will come to an end" (qtd. in Durkheim, *Suicide*, 330).

15 Durkheim, *Suicide*, 327–28.

16 Durkheim, *Suicide*, 183–87, 210. In contrast, France actively suppressed press coverage of suicide (291).

17 Brown, *The Art of Suicide*, 157–63, 187.

18 Brown, *The Art of Suicide*, 73–74. These seem inspired by George Cruikshank's engraving *The Drunkard's Children* (1848), plate VIII.

19 At least one of these suicides is verifiable through more reputable sources: the *Sydney Mail* of December 14, 1872, confirms that Alice Blanche Oswald did indeed jump to her death from London's Waterloo Bridge.

20 Kushner, *Self-Destruction in the Promised Land*, 30–37; Brown, *The Art of Suicide*, 109; Minois, *History of Suicide*, 191, 281, 297.

21 Maris, Berman, and Silverman, *Comprehensive Textbook of Suicidology*, 269; Kushner, *Self-Destruction in the Promised Land*, 81, 62. Modern suicidology research was sparked by Edwin Schneidman's chance discovery of a large file of suicide notes in

the L.A. County Coroner's Office in 1949, which Schneidman reflected on decades later in the most bizarre, and bizarrely earnest, quotation I have read about the study of suicide: "The golden road to the kingdom of understanding suicide was paved with suicide notes" (Maris, Berman, and Silverman, *Comprehensive Textbook of Suicidology*, 269).

22 Minois, *History of Suicide*, 321.

23 Qtd. in Kushner, *Self-Destruction in the Promised Land*, 44–45.

24 Meerloo, *Suicide and Mass Suicide*, 136. Meerloo's comment that "the suicidal tendency is infectious. It arouses the suppressed self-destructive inclinations in everybody" reveals the Freudian underpinnings of suicide contagion theory, which posit publicity on individual suicides as feeding latent impulses toward self-destruction (8). Freud's *Beyond the Pleasure Principle* controversially argued in 1920 that the life-preserving sexual instincts were in constant tension with destructive "death instincts" that could account for behaviors like suicide among individuals incapable of repressing or sublimating them effectively.

25 Phillips, "The Influence of Suicide on Suggestion."

26 Swales, *Goethe*, 58, 94, 99.

27 Duncan, *Goethe's Werther and the Critics*, 1, 23. Most scholars treat the book's alleged influence on suicide rates as unsubstantiated, though Minois lists a number of specific cases in which the corpses of suicides were found with copies of *Sorrows* (*History of Suicide*, 267). Fear, at least, of imitation was great enough to get the book banned in Leipzig, Copenhagen, and Italy (Phillips, "The Influence of Suggestion on Suicide," 340). Leipzig even made wearing the popular "Werther costume" a fineable offense (Swales, *Goethe*, 97).

28 Wasserman and Wasserman, *Oxford Textbook of Suicidology and Suicide Prevention*, 520–21.

29 American Foundation for Suicide Prevention, *Reporting on Suicide: Recommendations for the Media* (accessed November 19, 2009), http://www.afsp.org/index .cfm?page_id=0523D365-A314–431E-A925C03E13E762B1; updated version available at http://www.afsp.org/understanding-suicide/for-the-media/reporting-on -suicide.

30 Maris, Berman, and Silverman, *Comprehensive Textbook of Suicidology*, 254.

31 Maris, Berman, and Silverman, *Comprehensive Textbook of Suicidology*, 254.

32 Aaron, "Cinema and Suicide," 75. Literary representations of suicide have used similar techniques of omission to render the act romantic. Plato, for example, writes about Socrates's death as gradual and peaceful. Bringing a medical eye to this account, Robert Kastenbaum wonders "where is the agonized gulping for air, the burning sensation in the mouth, the blue tinge of the skin, the tremors, the cramps, the convulsions? Hemlock is nasty stuff. It does not make for a tranquil deathbed scene. The dying person suffers, as would any compassionate witness" (Kastenbaum, *On Our Way*, 56).

33 Centers for Disease Control and Prevention, "20 Leading Causes of Violence-Related Injury Deaths, United States" (accessed April 26, 2014), http://webappa.cdc .gov/cgi-bin/broker.exe.

34   Burke, *A Philosophical Inquiry into the Origin of Our Ideas of the Sublime and Beautiful*, 218–19.

35   Qtd. in Kant, *Critique of Judgement*, 76.

36   Ferguson, "The Nuclear Sublime," 6.

37   Ferguson, "The Nuclear Sublime," 6.

38   Habel, *On Falling*, 31.

39   Tom Junod describes his own and another reporter's quests to identify "the falling man" in "The Falling Man," *Esquire*, September 2003, http://www.esquire.com /features/ESQ0903-SEP_FALLINGMAN.

40   Qtd. in *The Falling Man* (2006, Henry Singer). This documentary, originally airing on Britain's Channel 4, does not have Region 1 DVD distribution but can be streamed on Hulu: http://www.hulu.com/watch/400148.

41   Zelizer, *About to Die*, 43–48.

42   Qtd. in *The Falling Man* (2006, Henry Singer).

43   Tom Junod, "Falling (Mad) Men," *Esquire*, January 30, 2012, http://www.esquire .com/the-side/feature/falling-mad-man-6648672.

44   Fitzpatrick, "The Movement of Vulnerability," 91.

45   Junod, "The Falling Man."

46   Marc Savlov, "The Gate Escape: Eric Steel on 'The Bridge,'" *Austin Chronicle*, January 26, 2007, http://www.austinchronicle.com/gyrobase/Issue/story?oid=oid %3A439265.

47   Nathan Rabin, review of *The Bridge*, *Onion*, October 26, 2006, http://www.avclub .com/articles/the-bridge,3733/.

48   Andrew O'Hehir, "Beyond the Multiplex: Tribeca," Salon.com, May 1, 2006, http:// www.salon.com/2006/05/01/tribeca_2_2/; Josh Rosenblatt, review of *The Bridge*, *Austin Chronicle*, January 26, 2007, http://www.austinchronicle.com/gyrobase /Calendar/Film?Film=oid%3A430985; Richard Brody, review of *The Bridge*, *New Yorker*, November 6, 2006, http://www.newyorker.com/arts/reviews/film/the _bridge_steel.

49   Kant, *Critique of Judgement*, 78–94.

50   Nye, *American Technological Sublime*, xvii.

51   Nye, *American Technological Sublime*, xx.

52   Durkheim, *Suicide*, 133, 141.

53   Aaron, "Cinema and Suicide," 75.

54   Tad Friend, "Jumpers," *New Yorker*, October 13, 2003, http://www.newyorker.com /archive/2003/10/13/031013fa_fact.

55   Sontag, *On Photography*, 20.

56   Qtd. in Nye, *American Technological Sublime*, 14.

57   Ruthe Stein, "Golden Gate Bridge Suicide Film Draws Crowd at Festival," *San Francisco Chronicle*, May 1, 2006, http://sfgate.com/cgi-bin/article.cgi?f=/c/a/2006 /05/01/BAG4AIIF6P1.DTL (my emphasis).

58   Fitzpatrick, "The Movement of Vulnerability," 102.

59   Richard Lally, "Interview: Eric Steel," *IONCinema*, October 30, 2006, http://www .ioncinema.com/news/id/1593/interview_eric_steel.

60 Whissel, *Spectacular Digital Effects*, 21–58.

61 Carolyne Zinko, "An Inside Look at Who Jumps," *San Francisco Chronicle*, July 31, 2007, http://sfgate.com/cgi-bin/article.cgi?f=/c/a/2007/07/31/BAJJR9U672.DTL.

62 Jay Slater, "Off 'The Bridge,'" *Film Threat*, December 12, 2007, http://www .filmthreat.com/index.php?section=interviews&Id=1132.

63 The study cited is Seiden, "Where Are They Now?" Seiden tracked 515 individuals who were prevented from killing themselves at the Golden Gate Bridge between 1937 and 1971 and discovered that 90 percent were still alive or had died of natural causes at the time of his data collection.

64 J. Esther, "Suicide at Sundance," *Curve* 15, no. 3 (May 2005), 67.

65 E-mail message to author, November 17, 2009.

66 In 2014, for example, the film's official website was remodeled and a new "Suicide Barrier" page appeared, featuring a short, first-person essay from Steel reviewing the history of efforts to build a barrier. In it, he overtly and causally aligns productive steps toward erecting the barrier with significant junctures in *The Bridge*'s production and release. "Notes on the Suicide Barrier at the Golden Gate Bridge," *The Bridge* official website, http://www.thebridge-themovie.com/suicide-barrier/.

67 My examination covered the 960 entries posted to the official site's message board through April 5, 2014. Later that year, the message board feature and all its archives were removed in a site remodel.

68 Sontag, *Regarding the Pain of Others*, 114–17.

69 These included the Tribeca Film Festival, the San Francisco International Film Festival, and the London Film Festival.

70 DJJOEINC, "Compelling, depressing and depressing," IMDb.com, June 7, 2007, http://www.imdb.com/title/tt0799954/usercomments?start=30.

71 Message boards are at *The Bridge*'s official site and IMDb.com. For memorial sites, see http://www.findagrave.com/cgi-bin/fg.cgi?page=gr&GRid=26753163 and http:// www.facebook.com/group.php?gid=37568059894. In the time since I first drafted this chapter, the Facebook group has been made private to Gene's friends and family.

72 Qtd. in Swales, *Goethe*, 97.

73 Lally, "Interview: Eric Steel"; Jordan E. Rosenfeld, "The Bridge," *Pacific Sun*, October 20, 2006, http://www.pacificsun.com/story_archives/bridge.html. Both of these articles have been removed, but Rosenfeld's can still be accessed at his personal site: http://jordansmuse.blogspot.com/2006/10/my-cover-story-about-controversial -new.html.

74 Carol Pogash, "Suicides Mounting, Golden Gate Looks to Add a Safety Net," *New York Times*, March 26, 2014, http://www.nytimes.com/2014/03/27/us/suicides -mounting-golden-gate-looks-to-add-a-safety-net.html?&assetType=nyt_now. Though I would not take them as proof of *The Bridge*'s imitative influence on suicide, jumper statistics at the Golden Gate do show a rise that correlates with the film's circulation. Twenty-five individuals died in 2004, as did 23 in 2005, 34 in 2006 (when *The Bridge* hit theaters), and 35 in 2007 (when the film became available on TV and DVD). *The Bridge* is only one potential factor for the increase among many (including the U.S. economy), but it has been cited as a likely contributor by Bridge District officials and local suicide prevention advocates. Analyzing the

week-by-week numbers, district spokeswoman Mary Currie notes, "The first spike in activity that we saw came on the heels of Eric Steel's film premiering in San Francisco" (Marisa Lagos, "Fatal Jumps from Bridge Rise Sharply," *San Francisco Chronicle*, January 18, 2007, http://sfgate.com/cgi-bin/article.cgi?f=/c/a/2007/01/18/MNGMMNKNN61.DTL; Carolyne Zinko, "35 Jumped to Their Deaths from Golden Gate Bridge Last Year," *San Francisco Chronicle*, January 11, 2008, http://sfgate.com/cgibin/article.cgi?f=/c/a/2008/01/11/BAG9UDDFN.DTL).

75 Bazin, "Death Every Afternoon," 31.

76 "Rise above This (The Bridge Version)," YouTube video, 4:15, posted by theVirus7, July 25, 2008, http://www.youtube.com/watch?v=O4-amEszdlo.

Chapter 4. Streaming Death

1 See chapter 1 for the full passage. Qtd. in Whissel, *Picturing American Modernity*, 63, 115.

2 Sobchack, "Inscribing Ethical Space," 237.

3 Hallin, *The Uncensored War*, 110; Hoskins, *Televising War*, 13.

4 Torchin, *Creating the Witness*, 220.

5 Henry Jenkins, "If It Doesn't Spread, It's Dead (Part One): Media Viruses and Memes," *Confessions of an Aca/Fan: The Official Weblog of Henry Jenkins*, February 11, 2009, http://www.henryjenkins.org/2009/02/if_it_doesnt_spread_its_dead_p.html.

6 Zelizer, *Remembering to Forget*, 212.

7 Dean, *Blog Theory*, 110, 125.

8 Torchin, *Creating the Witness*, 201.

9 Juhasz, *Learning from YouTube*, http://vectors.usc.edu/projects/learningfromyoutube/texteo.php?composite=14. Juhasz's innovative video-book is a necessarily online-only text, so I will cite URLs for specific pages rather than page numbers.

10 The majority of these events' recordings were made on mobile phones, but a few used stand-alone digital cameras.

11 "Community Guidelines" (accessed October 19, 2013), http://www.youtube.com/t/community_guidelines (my emphasis).

12 Perhaps in light of the site's heavy use during the Arab Spring and by Black Lives Matter activists, YouTube recently updated its guidelines to explicitly acknowledge the following: "Increasingly, YouTube is becoming an outlet for citizen journalists, documentarians and other users" whose videos may contain violent content. YouTube implores those users to contextualize such material "to help viewers understand what they are seeing" ("Community Guidelines: Violent or Graphic Content" (accessed September 29, 2015), http://www.youtube.com/yt/policyandsafety/communityguidelines.html).

13 Adrian Chen, "The Laborers Who Keep Dick Pics and Beheadings Out of Your Facebook Feed," *Wired*, October 23, 2014, http://www.wired.com/2014/10/content-moderation/; see also Roberts, "Behind the Screen."

14 Ben Quinn, "YouTube Staff Too Swamped to Filter Out All Terror-Related Content," *Guardian*, January 28, 2015, http://www.theguardian.com/technology/2015/jan/28/youtube-too-swamped-to-filter-terror-content.

15 Farhad Manjoo, "Virginia Shooting Gone Viral, in a Well-Planned Rollout on Social Media," *New York Times*, August 26, 2015. Screenshots of these defunct account pages reveal that Flanagan's tweet, "I filmed the shooting see Facebook," was retweeted more than 400 times its first twenty minutes, and the actual video post on Facebook was shared internally on the site 161 times in its first thirteen minutes. Flanagan's own recording of the murders was their second documentary record, as Flanagan made his assault while one victim was conducting an interview for live broadcast, which involuntarily aired the attack on CBS affiliate WDBJ.

16 "POV video of Bryce Williams murdering a reporter and crew on live TV in VA 8/26/15," *LiveLeak*, 0:56, posted by xone, August 26, 2015, http://www.liveleak.com /view?i=974_1440602794; "Virginia Reporter and Cameraman Killed on Live TV— Video from Shooter's Perspective," TheYNC, 0:56, posted by thadius710, August 26, 2015, http://theync.com/thadius710/virginia-reporter-and-cameraman-killed-on -live-tv-video-from-shooters-perspective.htm.

17 Zelizer, *About to Die*, 286.

18 "ISIS Militants Behead Abducted American Journalist James Foley [Real Video]," YouTube video, 1:08, posted by You Spot, August 20, 2014, https://www.youtube .com/watch?v=JvIYID5LSxk; "BARACK OBAMA 'YES WE CAN' TRUST ISIS BEHEADING US JOURNALIST JAMES FOLEY BEHEADED KIDNAPPED," YouTube video, 1:49, posted by ActingShowreel, August 22, 2014, https://www.youtube.com /watch?v=8nvNTlp13c8

19 "ISIS Burns Alive Jordanian Hostage in This BRUTAL Just Released Video from This Morning," TheYNC, 1:24, February 4, 2015, http://theync.com/shocking/isis-burns -alive-jordanian-hostage-and-just-released-video-from-this-morning.htm. In a controversial decision, FoxNews—alone among major U.S. networks—posted the full twenty-two-minute video of Al-Kaseasbeh's murder to its website.

20 Indeed, some videos on death porn sites directly blend death and sex and advertise that combination, as in TheYNC's "GORE: Dead and Mutilated Woman in Morgue (Her Tits Stay Unharmed)."

21 For a synchronization of footage from all six cameras, see "Captured by 6 Different Cameras BART Police Shoot and Kill Unarmed Oscar Grant," YouTube video, 9:39, posted by streetgangs, July 4, 2010, http://www.youtube.com/watch?v=rSN5 WF9qD3g.

22 "Iran, Tehran: Wounded Girl Dying in Front of Camera, Her Name Was Neda," YouTube video, 0:40, posted by FEELTHELIGHT, June 20, 2009, http://www.youtube .com/watch?v=bbdEf0QRsLM; "Shot by Basij [WARNING GRUESOME]," YouTube video, 0:15, posted by bowlofudon, June 20, 2009, http://www.youtube.com /watch?v=fmi-LePl894.

23 Brian Stelter and Brad Stone, "Web Pries Lid of Iranian Censorship," *New York Times*, June 22, 2009, http://www.nytimes.com/2009/06/23/world/middleeast /23censor.html?ref=neda_agha_soltan.

24 Robert Mackey, "The Lede: June 22: Updates on Iran's Disputed Election," *New York Times*, June 22, 2009, http://thelede.blogs.nytimes.com/2009/06/22/latest-updates -on-irans-disputed-election-3/?scp=1&sq=hamed,%20neda&st=cse.

25 Bazin, "Death Every Afternoon," 27–31. See the introduction for more on this essay.

26 See, for example, Scott Shane, "Spotlight Again Falls on Web Tools and Change," *New York Times*, January 29, 2011, http://www.nytimes.com/2011/01/30/weekin review/30shane.html?hp.

27 Seib, "New Media and Prospects for Democratization," 4.

28 Sobchack, "Inscribing Ethical Space," 255. For a more detailed account of Sobchack's gazes, see the introduction.

29 Quoted from a BBC interview in *Now That We Have Tasted Hope* (San Francisco: McSweeney's / Byliner, 2012), Kindle edition.

30 See, for example, the much-quoted "Don't Tase Me Bro!" video or footage of UC Davis campus police pepper-spraying Occupy protesters: "UF Police Taser Student during Kerry Forum," YouTube video, 3:33, posted by hunnybun523, September 17, 2007, http://www.youtube.com/watch?v=SaiWC S10C5s; "Occupy UC Davis—Police Pepper Spraying and Arresting Students 11–18–11," YouTube video, 8:33, posted by ieee8023, November 18, 2011, http://www.youtube.com/watch?v=0AbYHRg3qlw.

31 Zelizer, *About to Die*, 266.

32 YouTube has since discontinued providing public statistics on videos' geographic circulation, but these statistics previously accompanied the following videos and were consistent with those of other Grant and Agha-Soltan videos: "POLICE SHOOTING AT BART STATION—OSCAR GRANT," YouTube video, 3:28, from an episode of *KTVU Morning News* televised by KTVU on January 5, 2009, posted by TheDirtyNews, January 5, 2009, http://www.youtube.com/watch?v=bmJukcFzEX4; "Neda Agha Soltan, Killed 20.06.2009, Presidential Election Protest, Tehran, IRAN," YouTube video, 2:23, posted by AliJahanii, June 22, 2009, http://www.youtube.com/watch?v=76W-0GVjNEc&bpctr=1382272742.

33 Statistics on criminal charges brought against officers demonstrate how unusual Mehserle's case was. See Demian Bulwa, "Ex-BART Cop Accused of Murder in Rare Group," *San Francisco Chronicle*, February 15, 2009, http://sfgate.com/cgi-bin/article.cgi?f=/c/a/2009/02/15/MN2615QD01.DTL.

34 Comment from Sepirothkai ("Iran, Tehran: Wounded Girl").

35 PBS aired *A Death in Tehran* as part of its *Frontline* series in November 2009, and HBO's *For Neda* aired in June 2010; William Yong, "Iran Halts Production of 'Neda' Figures," *New York Times*, June 9, 2010, http://www.nytimes.com/2010/06/10/world/middleeast/10neda.html.

36 The 1968 coverage of Lém's execution provides a notable predigital precursor. For more on Hollywood's presentation of death from multiple angles, see Rust, "'Passionate Detachment,'" 22–42.

37 Taylor, *Body Horror*, 129–56.

38 Afshar, "Are We Neda?," 236–41; Shirazi, "Death, the Great Equalizer," 106–7.

39 Evelyn Azeeza Alsultany, contribution to the Roundtable "Keyword Searches: 9/11 Plus Ten" (presented at the annual meeting of the American Studies Association, Baltimore, MD, October 20–23, 2011). I am also grateful to Nazanin Shahrokni for giving me similar insights in commenting on a draft of this work.

40 Afshar, "Are We Neda?," 246; Naghibi, "Diasporic Disclosures," 61, 66.

41 Sabety, "Graphic Content," 123.

42 Sabety, "Graphic Content," 123.

43 One example showing a male protester dying from a shot to the neck has only 844 views and six comments, as of October 2015 ["Protester Shot in Neck in Iran GRAPHIC MATERIAL DISCRETION IS ADVISED PLEASE DO NOT REMOVE," You-Tube video, 0:43, posted by CensorshipIsBad, June 17, 2009, http://www.youtube .com /watch?v=eGsMfO03q_8]; another of a slain male protester covered in blood has accumulated only 1,598 views and fourteen comments ["How Many More Should Die? Tehran Demonstration 20 June 2009 (+18)," YouTube video, 1:24, posted by penguinswillfly, June 21, 2009, http://www.youtube.com/watch?v= GH8ELmefOjk].

44 Juhasz, *Learning from YouTube*, http://vectors.usc.edu/projects/learningfromyou tube/texteo.php?composite=83.

45 Jean Burgess and Joshua Green describe YouTube as a site that is "U.S.-dominated demographically to an extent; but . . . feels culturally U.S.-dominated out of all proportion" (*YouTube*, 82).

46 Juhasz, *Learning from YouTube*, http://vectors.usc.edu/projects/learningfromyou tube/texteo.php?composite=78.

47 Henry Jenkins, "From Rodney King to Burma: An Interview with Witness's Sam Gregory (Part Two)," *Confessions of an Aca-Fan: The Official Weblog of Henry Jenkins*, April 2, 2008, http://www.henryjenkins.org/2008/04/from_rodney_king_to _burma_an_i_1.html.

48 A segment from KTVU news that uses this effect is available at "Bart Police shooting in Oakland KTVU report," YouTube video, 4:17, from an episode of *KTVU News Week-end* televised by KTVU on January 4, 2009, posted by monkeyassj, January 5, 2009, http://www.youtube.com/watch?v=IKy-WSZMklc.

49 Juhasz, *Learning from YouTube*, http://vectors.usc.edu/projects/learningfromyou tube/glossary.php. Juhasz associates "bad video" mostly with talking-head vlogs but notes that "using bad form on other genres of video can limit the effectiveness of your message" (http://vectors.usc.edu/projects/learningfromyoutube/texteo .php?composite=75).

50 Comment on "Cop Shoots & Kill Unarmed Man(Oscar Grant)," YouTube video, 3:59, posted by bofoleone, January 6, 2009, http://www.youtube.com/watch?v= jFNDK8PQGNw. Comment statistics as of March 14, 2011.

51 Butler, *Precarious Life*, 37.

52 Barthes, *Camera Lucida*, 111.

53 For examples, see comments from soulstealer1995, portisalpha, and dgfmoore on "Iran, Tehran: Wounded Girl."

54 Lesley Fulbright and Steve Rubenstein, "BART Protesters in SF: 'We Are Oscar Grant!,'" *San Francisco Chronicle*, January 13, 2009, http://articles.sfgate.com/2009 −01–13/bay-area/17198450_1_police-vans-protesters-powell-street-bart.

55 Butler, *Precarious Life*, 30–31.

56 See chapter 2, note 36, for statistical details.

57 Photo count as of November 7, 2013; photos collected at http://nedaspeaks.org /gallery.

58 Dean, *Blog Theory*, 3.

59 "I Am Neda," July 17, 2009, http://iamneda.tumblr.com/.

60 The soldier writes: "i know i don't represent much of the people i serve with, and that saddens me. it's hard for me to relate to many of these people. but even in the military there are those of us that see what is happening in the world, and we are also appalled. i'm only one country away from iran, and there's still so little i can do. for what it's worth, i hope this helps, somehow," ("I Am Neda").

61 Henry Jenkins, "From Rodney King to Burma: An Interview with Witness's Sam Gregory (Part One)," *Confessions of an Aca-Fan: The Official Weblog of Henry Jenkins*, March 31, 2008, http://www.henryjenkins.org/2008/03/from_rodney_king_to _burma_an_i.html.

62 Cook, *Martyrdom in Islam*, 4, 154–55; Varzi, *Warring Souls*, 47.

63 Shirazi, "Death, the Great Equalizer," 115.

64 Qtd. in "A Death in Tehran," *Frontline*, directed by Brent E. Huffman and Katerina Monemvassitis, aired November 17, 2009.

65 Journalist Scott Peterson speculates, "Part of the strategy like that, certainly for the Islamic Republic, would be to just cast so much doubt, to really just cloud the issue so much, . . . [that] all of it would be meant to somehow undermine the power of the story of Neda's death" ("Interview: Scott Peterson," *Frontline*, September 9, 2009, http://www.pbs.org/wgbh/pages/frontline/tehranbureau/deathintehran /interviews/peterson.html).

66 These tropes are described by Cook, *Martyrdom in Islam*, 116–34.

67 Examples of Iranians reading Agha-Soltan's death through the codes of Islamic martyrdom abound in HBO's *For Neda* (2010, Anthony Thomas)—a documentary that scarcely mentions the word "martyr," let alone explains its cultural context, but includes interviewees who weave together a forceful, subtextual martyrology more accessible to viewers steeped in Islamic culture.

68 Cook, *Martyrdom in Islam*, 4.

69 "Iranian Protests, Neda, Moussavi and More—Rachel Maddow," YouTube video, 9:34, from an episode of *The Rachel Maddow Show* televised by MSNBC on June 22, 2009, posted by CheneyWatch1, June 28, 2009, http://www.youtube.com /watch?v=JRfwhYTHCcI.

70 Leslie Fulbright, "Many See Race as Central to BART Killing," *San Francisco Chronicle*, January 11, 2009, http://articles.sfgate.com/2009–01–11/news/17195723.

71 This article ran with a suggestive headline: Demian Bulwa, "Position of Mehserle's Taser Holster May Be Key," *San Francisco Chronicle*, February 14, 2010, http://www .sfgate.com/cgi-bin/article.cgi?f=/c/a/2010/02/14/MN8D1BNR8U.DTL.

72 Demian Bulwa, "Mehserle Video: Clear as Mud," *San Francisco Chronicle*, June 25, 2010, http://www.sfgate.com/cgi-bin/blogs/crime/detail?entry_id=66576.

73 Shaun King, "We'll All Remember Where We Were When We Saw Alton Sterling Killed in a Brutal Act of Police Violence," *New York Daily News*, July 6, 2016, http:// www.nydailynews.com/news/national/king-don-sense-police-killing-alton-sterling -article-1.2700578.

74 Alexander, "'Can You Be BLACK and Look at This?,'" 84, 96.

75 Bulwa, "Mehserle Video: Clear as Mud."

76 Bazin, "Death Every Afternoon," 30–31.

77 Williams, *Playing the Race Card*.

78 Although they occurred too late in this book's production schedule for me to substantively analyze them here, the recorded deaths of Alton Sterling and Philando Castile should be included in this, tragically, ever-expanding list.

79 Police and forensic experts asked to evaluate whether the corpse was properly handled largely criticized its treatment by Ferguson officers (Julie Bosman and Joseph Goldstein, "Timeline for a Body: 4 Hours in the Middle of a Ferguson Street," *New York Times*, August 23, 2014, http://www.nytimes.com/2014/08/24/us /michael-brown-a-bodys-timeline-4-hours-on-a-ferguson-street.html?_r=0).

80 To give just one example from statistics released by the U.S. government: "Young black men are killed by police in 'justified shootings' at a disproportionate rate, based on Department of Justice statistics. In 1998, there were 48 young black men killed in what were described as 'justifiable homicides,' of young white males nearly the same numbers—53. Yet, young black males made up only 1 percent of the total U.S. population and young white males made up 8 percent" (Fulbright, "Many See Race as Central to BART Killing").

81 Qtd. in Reginald James, "Vigil Held for Oscar Grant Two Years after His Death," *Oakland Local*, January 3, 2011, http://oaklandlocal.com/article/vigil-held-oscar -grant-two-years-after-death.

82 Sperb, "Reassuring Convergence," 28.

83 Demian Bulwa, "Many Police Use Cameras to Record Interactions," *San Francisco Chronicle*, July 27, 2010, http://sfgate.com/cgi-bin/article.cgi?f=/c/a/2010/07/27 /MNGI1EID8S.DTL (my emphasis).

84 Juhasz, *Learning from YouTube*, http://vectors.usc.edu/projects/learningfromyou tube/glossary.php.

85 Cook, *Martyrdom in Islam*, 11.

Conclusion

1 Bazin, "Death Every Afternoon," 30.

2 Sontag, *Regarding the Pain of Others*, 115.

3 Cherchi Usai, *The Death of Cinema*, 67, 105, 109.

4 Doane, "The Indexical and the Concept of Medium Specificity," 143.

BIBLIOGRAPHY

Aaron, Michele. "Cinema and Suicide: Necromanticism, Dead-already-ness, and the Logic of the Vanishing Point." *Cinema Journal* 53, no. 2 (2014): 71–92.

Abzug, Robert H. *Inside the Vicious Heart: Americans and the Liberation of Nazi Concentration Camps*. Oxford: Oxford University Press, 1985.

Adams, Eddie. "The Tet Photo." In *To Bear Any Burden: The Vietnam War and Its Aftermath in the Words of Americans and Southeast Asians*, edited by Al Santoli, 182–85. Bloomington: Indiana University Press, 1999.

Afshar, Sereh. "Are We Neda? The Iranian Women, the Election, and International Media." In *Media, Power, and Politics in the Digital Age: The 2009 Presidential Election Uprising in Iran*, edited by Yahya R. Kamalipour, 235–49. Lanham, MD: Rowman and Littlefield, 2010.

Agamben, Giorgio. *Homo Sacer: Sovereign Power and Bare Life*. Translated by Daniel Heller-Roazen. Stanford, CA: Stanford University Press, 1998.

Agee, James. Untitled review of the 1945 U.S. Signal Corps documentary on the liberation of the camps. In *America Views the Holocaust, 1933–1945: A Brief Documentary History*, edited by Robert H. Abzug, 202–3. Boston: Bedford/St. Martin's, 1999.

Alexander, Elizabeth. "'Can You Be BLACK and Look at This?': Reading the Rodney King Video(s)." In *The Black Public Sphere: A Public Culture Book*, edited by Black Public Sphere Collective, 81–98. Chicago: University of Chicago Press, 1995.

Anonymous. "Ars bene moriendi." 1430. In *Medieval Popular Religion, 1000–1500: A Reader*, edited and translated by John Raymond Shinners, 525–35. Peterborough, ON: Broadview Press, 1997.

Apel, Dora. *Imagery of Lynching: Black Men, White Women, and the Mob*. New Brunswick, NJ: Rutgers University Press, 2004.

Ariès, Philippe. *The Hour of Our Death*. Translated by Helen Weaver. New York: Knopf, 1991.

———. *Western Attitudes toward Death: From the Middle Ages to the Present*. Translated by Patricia M. Ranum. Baltimore: Johns Hopkins University Press, 1974.

Bailey, George A., and Lawrence W. Lichty. "Rough Justice on a Saigon Street: A Gatekeeper Study of NBC's Tet Execution Film." *Journalism Quarterly* 49 (Summer 1972): 221–29.

Barnouw, Erik. *Documentary: A History of the Non-Fiction Film*. 2nd ed. Oxford: Oxford University Press, 1993.

———. *Tube of Plenty: The Evolution of American Television*. Oxford: Oxford University Press, 1975.

Barthes, Roland. *Camera Lucida: Reflections on Photography*. Translated by Richard Howard. New York: Hill and Wang, 1981.

Bassett, Jonathan F., Polly A. McCann, and Kelly L. Cate. "Personification of Personal and Typical Death as Related to Death Attitudes." *Omega: Journal of Death and Dying* 57, no. 2 (2008): 163–72.

Batchen, Geoffrey. *Forget Me Not: Photography and Remembrance*. Princeton, NJ: Princeton Architectural Press, 2004.

Bazin, André. "Death Every Afternoon (1958)." In *Rites of Realism: Essays on Corporeal Cinema*, edited by Ivone Margulies, translated by Mark A. Cohen, 27–31. Durham, NC: Duke University Press, 2003.

———. "The Ontology of the Photographic Image." 1945. In *What Is Cinema?*, 1:9–16. Translated by Hugh Gray. Berkeley: University of California Press, 2005.

Becker, Ernest. *The Denial of Death*. 1973. Reprinted. New York: Free Press, 1997.

Berger, John. *About Looking*. 1980. Reprinted. London: Bloomsbury, 2009.

Bottomore, Stephen. "The Biograph in Battle." In *Film and the First World War*, edited by Karel Dibbets and Bert Hogenkamp, 28–35. Amsterdam: Amsterdam University Press, 1995.

Boyle, Deirdre. "A Brief History of American Documentary Video." In *Illuminating Video: An Essential Guide to Video Art*, edited by Doug Hall and Sally Jo Fifer, 51–69. New York: Aperture, 1990.

Braestrup, Peter. *Big Story: How the American Press and Television Reported and Interpreted the Crisis of Tet 1968 in Vietnam and Washington*. New Haven, CT: Yale University Press, 1983.

Bronfen, Elisabeth. *Over Her Dead Body: Death, Femininity and the Aesthetic*. Manchester: Manchester University Press, 1992.

Brothers, Caroline. *War and Photography: A Cultural History*. London: Routledge, 1997.

Brown, Ron M. *The Art of Suicide*. London: Reaktion Books, 2001.

Brown, Wendy. *Edgework: Critical Essays on Knowledge and Politics*. Princeton, NJ: Princeton University Press, 2005.

Bruzzi, Stella. "The Event: Archive and Imagination." In *New Challenges for Documentary*, edited by Alan Rosenthal, 419–31. 2nd ed. Berkeley: University of California Press, 2005.

Burgess, Jean, and Joshua Green. *YouTube: Online Video and Participatory Culture*. Cambridge: Polity Press, 2009.

Burke, Edmund. *A Philosophical Inquiry into the Origins of Our Ideas of the Sublime and the Beautiful*. 1757. Reprint. Basel: J. J. Tourneisen, 1792.

Butler, Judith. *Precarious Life: The Powers of Mourning and Violence*. London: Verso, 2004.

Byock, Ira. *Dying Well: The Prospect for Growth at the End of Life*. New York: Riverhead Books, 1997.

Camus, Albert. *The Myth of Sisyphus and Other Essays*. Translated by Justin O'Brien. New York: Knopf, 1942.

Carmichael, Jane. *First World War Photographers*. London: Routledge, 1999.

Cherchi Usai, Paolo. *The Death of Cinema: History, Cultural Memory and the Digital Dark Age*. London: British Film Institute, 2001.

Churchill, Larry. "The Human Experience of Dying: The Moral Primacy of Stories over Stages." *Soundings* 62 (Spring 1979): 24–37.

Combs, Scott. *Deathwatch: American Film, Technology, and the End of Life*. New York: Columbia University Press, 2014.

———. "Final Touches: Registering Death in American Cinema." PhD diss., University of California, Berkeley, 2006.

Connor, Stephen R. "Development of Hospice and Palliative Care in the United States." *Omega: Journal of Death and Dying* 56, no. 1 (2007–8): 89–99.

Cook, David. *Martyrdom in Islam*. Cambridge: Cambridge University Press, 2007.

Davis, Joyce M. *Martyrs: Innocence, Vengeance, and Despair in the Middle East*. New York: Palgrave Macmillan, 2004.

Dean, Jodi. *Blog Theory: Feedback and Capture in the Circuits of Drive*. Cambridge: Polity Press, 2010.

Doane, Mary Ann. *The Emergence of Cinematic Time: Modernity, Contingency, the Archive*. Cambridge, MA: Harvard University Press, 2002.

———. "The Indexical and the Concept of Medium Specificity." *differences* 18, no. 1 (2007): 128–52.

Duncan, Bruce. *Goethe's Werther and the Critics*. Rochester, NY: Camden House, 2005.

Durkheim, Émile. *Suicide: A Study in Sociology*. Edited by George Simpson, translated by John A. Spaulding and George Simpson. 1897; Reprint, New York: Free Press, 1951.

Dyer, Richard. *White*. New York: Routledge, 1997.

Evans, J. W., A. S. Walters, and M. L. Hatch-Woodruff. "Deathbed Scene Narratives: A Construct and Linguistic Analysis." *Death Studies* 23, no. 8 (1999): 715–33.

Faust, Drew Gilpin. *This Republic of Suffering: Death and the American Civil War*. New York: Vintage Books, 2008.

Ferguson, Frances. "The Nuclear Sublime." *Diacritics* 14, no. 2 (1984): 4–10.

Fielding, Raymond. *The American Newsreel, 1911–1967*. Norman: University of Oklahoma Press, 1972.

Filene, Peter. *In the Arms of Others: A Cultural History of the Right-to-Die in America*. Darby, PA: Diane Publishing, 2003.

Fitzpatrick, Andrea D. "The Movement of Vulnerability: Images of Falling and September 11." *Art Journal* 66, no. 4 (2007): 84–102.

Fleischer, Stefan. "Dying to Be on Television." *Film Quarterly* 31, no. 4 (1978): 30–36.

French, Stanley. "The Cemetery as Cultural Institution: The Establishment of Mount Auburn and the 'Rural Cemetery' Movement." In *Death in America*, edited by David E. Stannard, 69–91. Philadelphia: University of Pennsylvania Press, 1975.

Freud, Sigmund. *Beyond the Pleasure Principle*. Edited and translated by James Strachey. New York: Norton, 1920.

———. "Timely Reflections on War and Death (1915)." In *On Murder, Mourning, and Mel-*

ancholia, edited by Adam Phillips, translated by Shaun Whiteside, 183–94. London: Penguin Books, 2005.

Friedman, Alan Warren. *Fictional Death and the Modernist Enterprise*. Cambridge: Cambridge University Press, 1995.

Gardner, Alexander. *Gardner's Photographic Sketchbook of the Civil War*. 1866; Reprint, New York: Dover, 1959.

Garland, Robert. *The Greek Way of Death*. Ithaca, NY: Cornell University Press, 1985.

Gavin, William Joseph. *Cuttin' the Body Loose*. Philadelphia: Temple University Press, 1995.

Giddens, Anthony. *Modernity and Self-Identity: Self and Society in the Late Modern Age*. Stanford, CA: Stanford University Press, 1991.

Gladstone, Kay. "Separate Intentions: The Allied Screening of Concentration Camp Documentaries in Defeated Germany in 1945–46: *Death Mills* and *Memory of the Camps*." In *Holocaust and the Moving Image: Representations in Film and Television since 1933*, edited by Toby Haggith and Joanna Newman, 50–64. London: Wallflower, 2005.

Goethe, Johann Wolfgang von. *The Sorrows of Young Werther and Novella* (1774). Translated by Elizabeth Mayer and Louise Bogan. New York: Random House, 1971.

Goldsby, Jacqueline Denise. *A Spectacular Secret: Lynching in American Life and Literature*. Chicago: University of Chicago Press, 2006.

Gorer, Geoffrey. "The Pornography of Death (1955)." In *Death, Grief, and Mourning*, 192–97. New York: Arno Press, 1977.

Gunning, Tom. "Moving away from the Index: Cinema and the Impression of Reality." *differences* 18, no. 1 (2007): 29–52.

Habel, Annette. *On Falling*. London: Firebird Editions, 2009.

Haggith, Toby. "Filming the Liberation of Bergen-Belsen." In *Holocaust and the Moving Image: Representations in Film and Television since 1933*, edited by Toby Haggith and Joanna Newman, 33–49. London: Wallflower, 2005.

Hallas, Roger. *Reframing Bodies: AIDS, Bearing Witness, and the Queer Moving Image*. Durham, NC: Duke University Press, 2009.

Hallin, Daniel C. *The Uncensored War: The Media and Vietnam*. Berkeley: University of California Press, 1989.

Halverson, Jeffry R., Scott W. Ruston, and Angela Trethewey. "Mediated Martyrs of the Arab Spring: New Media, Civil Religion, and Narrative in Tunisia and Egypt." *Journal of Communication* 63 (2013): 312–32.

Hammond, William M. *Reporting Vietnam: Media and Military at War*. Lawrence: University Press of Kansas, 1998.

Hansen, Mark B. N. "Between Body and Image: On the 'Newness' of New Media." In *New Philosophy for New Media*, 20–46. Cambridge, MA: MIT Press, 2004.

Hansen, Miriam. "*Schindler's List* Is Not *Shoah*: The Second Commandment, Popular Modernism, and Public Memory." *Critical Inquiry* 22, no. 2 (1996): 292–313.

Hardwig, John. "Going to Meet Death: The Art of Dying in the Early Part of the Twenty-First Century." *Hastings Center Report* 39, no. 4 (2009): 37–45.

Hawkins, Anne Hunsaker. "Constructing Death: Three Pathographies about Dying." *Omega: Journal of Death and Dying* 22, no. 4 (1990): 301–17.

Hoskins, Andrew. *Televising War: From Vietnam to Iraq*. London: Continuum, 2004.

Hurst, Fannie. *Imitation of Life*. Edited by Daniel Itzkovitz. 1933; Reprint, Durham, NC: Duke University Press, 2004.

Jacobs, Ronald N. "Civil Society and Crisis: Culture, Discourse, and the Rodney King Beating." *American Journal of Sociology* 101 (1996): 1238–72.

Jay, Kathryn. *More Than Just a Game: Sports in American Life since 1945*. New York: Columbia University Press, 2004.

Jenkins, Henry. "What Happened before YouTube." In *YouTube: Online Video and Participatory Culture*, edited by Jean Burgess and Joshua Green, 109–25. Cambridge: Polity Press, 2009.

Jeong, Seung-Hoon, and Dudley Andrew. "Grizzly Ghost: Herzog, Bazin, and the Cinematic Animal." *Screen* 49, no. 1 (2008): 1–12.

Johns, A. Wesley. *The Man Who Shot McKinley*. South Brunswick, NJ: A. S. Barnes, 1970.

Juhasz, Alexandra. *Learning from YouTube*. Cambridge: MIT Press, 2011. http://vectors.usc.edu/projects/learningfromyoutube/texteo.php?composite=14.

Kaes, Anton. *Shell Shock Cinema: Weimar Culture and the Wounds of War*. Princeton, NJ: Princeton University Press, 2009.

Kant, Immanuel. *Critique of Judgement* (1790). Edited by Nicholas Walker, translated by James Creed Meredith. Oxford: Oxford University Press, 2007.

Kastenbaum, Robert. *On Our Way: The Final Passage through Life and Death*. Berkeley: University of California Press, 2004.

Kastenbaum, Robert, and Claude Normand. "Deathbed Scenes as Imagined by the Young and Experienced by the Old." *Death Studies* 14 (1990): 201–17.

Kearl, Michael C. *Endings: A Sociology of Death and Dying*. Oxford: Oxford University Press, 1989.

Kerekes, David, and David Slater. *Killing for Culture: An Illustrated History of Death Film from Mondo to Snuff*. London: Creation Books, 1995.

Kershaw, Alex. *Blood and Champagne: The Life and Times of Robert Capa*. New York: St. Martin's Press, 2003.

Kübler-Ross, Elisabeth. *On Death and Dying*. 1969; Reprint, New York: Scribner, 2003.

Kushner, Howard I. *Self-Destruction in the Promised Land: A Psychocultural Biology of American Suicide*. New Brunswick, NJ: Rutgers University Press, 1989.

Lane, Jim. "The Convergence of Autobiography and Documentary: Historical Connections." In *The Autobiographical Documentary in America*, 11–32. Madison: University of Wisconsin Press, 2002.

Leary, Timothy. *Design for Dying*. San Francisco: HarperEdge, 1997.

Leget, Carlo. "Retrieving the Ars Moriendi Tradition." *Medicine, Health Care and Philosophy* 10 (2007): 313–19.

Litman, Robert E. "Sigmund Freud on Suicide." In *Essays in Self-Destruction*, edited by Edwin S. Schneidman, 324–44. New York: Science House, 1967.

Lock, Margaret M. *Twice Dead: Organ Transplants and the Reinvention of Death*. Berkeley: University of California Press, 2002.

Lundgren, Burden, and Clare Houseman. "Banishing Death: The Disappearance of the Appreciation of Mortality." *Omega: Journal of Death and Dying* 106, no. 3 (2010): 223–49.

Manovich, Lev. *The Language of New Media*. Cambridge, MA: MIT Press, 2001.

Maris, Ronald W., Alan L. Berman, and Morton M. Silverman, eds. *Comprehensive Textbook of Suicidology*. New York: Guilford Press, 2000.

Meerloo, Joost A. M. *Suicide and Mass Suicide*. New York: Dutton, 1962.

Minois, George. *History of Suicide: Voluntary Death in Western Culture*. Translated by Lydia G. Cochrane. Baltimore: Johns Hopkins University Press, 1999.

Mitchell, William J. *The Reconfigured Eye: Visual Truth in the Post-photographic Era*. Cambridge, MA: MIT Press, 1992.

Mould, David. *American Newsfilm, 1914–1919: The Underexposed War*. New York: Garland, 1983.

Mulvey, Laura. *Death 24x a Second: Stillness and the Moving Image*. London: Reaktion Books, 2006.

Musser, Charles. *Before the Nickelodeon: Edwin S. Porter and the Edison Manufacturing Company*. Berkeley: University of California Press, 1991.

Naghibi, Nima. "Diasporic Disclosures: Social Networking, Neda, and the 2009 Iranian Presidential Elections." *Biography* 34, no. 1 (2011): 56–69.

Nichols, Bill. *Blurred Boundaries: Questions of Meaning in Contemporary Culture*. Bloomington: Indiana University Press, 1994.

———. "The Voice of Documentary." In *New Challenges for Documentary*, edited by Alan Rosenthal, 17–33. 2nd ed. Berkeley: University of California Press, 2005.

Nudelman, Franny. *John Brown's Body: Slavery, Violence, and the Culture of War*. Chapel Hill: University of North Carolina Press, 2004.

Nye, David E. *American Technological Sublime*. Cambridge, MA: MIT Press, 1994.

Pach, Charles J. "And That's the Way It Was: The Vietnam War on the Network Nightly News." In *The Sixties: From Memory to History*, edited by David Farber, 90–118. Chapel Hill: University of North Carolina Press, 1994.

Phelan, Peggy. "Dying Man with a Movie Camera: Silverlake Life: The View from Here." *GLQ* 2, no. 4 (1995): 379–98.

Phillips, David P. "The Influence of Suggestion on Suicide: Substantive and Theoretical Implications of the Werther Effect." *American Sociological Review* 39, no. 3 (1974): 340–54.

Plato. *The Dialogues of Plato*. Vol. 2. Translated by Benjamin Jowett. New York: Macmillan, 1892.

Post, Stephen G. *Inquiries in Bioethics*. Washington, DC: Georgetown University Press, 1993.

Raiford, Leigh. "The Consumption of Lynching Images." In *Only Skin Deep: Changing Visions of the American Self*, edited by Coco Fusco and Brian Wallis, 267–93. New York: Abrams, 2003.

Rees, Laurence. "*The Nazis: A Warning from History*." In *Holocaust and the Moving Image: Representations in Film and Television since 1933*, edited by Toby Haggith and Joanna Newman, 146–53. London: Wallflower, 2005.

Renov, Michael. *The Subject of Documentary*. Minneapolis: University of Minnesota Press, 2004.

Rilke, Rainer Maria. *The Notebooks of Malte Laurids Brigge* (1910). Translated by M. D. Herter Norton. New York: Norton, 1964.

Roach, Mary. *Stiff: The Curious Lives of Human Cadavers*. New York: Norton, 2003.

Roberts, Sarah T. "Behind the Screen: The Hidden Digital Labor of Commercial Content Moderation." PhD diss., University of Illinois at Urbana-Champaign, 2014.

Rodowick, D. N. *The Virtual Life of Film*. Cambridge, MA: Harvard University Press, 2007.

Roeder, George H. *The Censored War: American Visual Experience during World War Two*. New Haven, CT: Yale University Press, 1993.

Roemer, Michael. "Filmmaker's Report on 'Death and Dying' Film." In *Death, the Press, and the Public*, edited by David Dempsey, 122–23. New York: Arno Press, 1982.

Rose, Nikolas. "Biological Citizens." In *The Politics of Life Itself: Biomedicine, Power, and Subjectivity in the Twenty-First Century*, 131–54. Princeton, NJ: Princeton University Press, 2007.

Rosen, Philip. "Old and New: Image, Indexicality, and Historicity in the Digital Utopia." In *Change Mummified: Cinema, Historicity, Theory*, 301–49. Minneapolis: University of Minnesota Press, 2001.

Rosenberg, Charles E. *The Cholera Years: The United States in 1832, 1849, and 1866*. 1962; Reprint, Chicago: University of Chicago Press, 1987.

Ruby, Jay. *Secure the Shadow: Death and Photography in America*. Cambridge, MA: MIT Press, 1992.

Rust, Amy. "'Passionate Detachment': Technologies of Vision and Violence in American Cinema, 1967–1974." PhD diss., University of California, Berkeley, 2010.

Sabety, Setareh. "Graphic Content: The Semiotics of a YouTube Uprising." In *Media, Power, and Politics in the Digital Age: The 2009 Presidential Election Uprising in Iran*, edited by Yahya R. Kamalipour, 119–24. Lanham, MD: Rowman and Littlefield, 2010.

Schantz, Mark S. *Awaiting the Heavenly Country: The Civil War and America's Culture of Death*. Ithaca, NY: Cornell University Press, 2008.

Seib, Philip. "New Media and Prospects for Democratization." In *New Media and the New Middle East*, edited by Philip Seib, 1–18. New York: Palgrave Macmillan, 2007.

Seiden, Richard. "Where Are They Now? A Follow-Up Study of Suicide Attempters from the Golden Gate Bridge." *Suicide and Life Threatening Behavior* 8, no. 4 (1978): 203–16.

Shirazi, Faegheh. "Death, the Great Equalizer: Memorializing Martyred (*Shahid*) Women in the Islamic Republic of Iran." *Visual Anthropology* 25 (2012): 98–119.

Sobchack, Vivian. "Inscribing Ethical Space: Ten Propositions on Death, Representation, and Documentary." In *Carnal Thoughts: Embodiment and Moving Image Culture*, 226–57. Berkeley: University of California Press, 2004.

Sontag, Susan. *On Photography*. New York: Picador, 1977.

———. *Regarding the Pain of Others*. New York: Picador, 2003.

Sperb, Jason. "Reassuring Convergence: Online Fandom, Race, and Disney's Notorious *Song of the South*." *Cinema Journal* 49, no. 4 (2010): 25–45.

Stannard, David E. "Death and the Puritan Child." In *Death in America*, edited by David E. Stannard, 9–29. Philadelphia: University of Pennsylvania Press, 1975.

Sturken, Marita. *Tangled Memories: The Vietnam War, the AIDS Epidemic, and the Politics of Remembering*. Berkeley: University of California Press, 1997.

Swales, Martin. *Goethe: The Sorrows of Young Werther*. Cambridge: Cambridge University Press, 1987.

Tacitus, Cornelius. *The Annals of Imperial Rome*. Edited and translated by Michael Grant. Harmondsworth: Penguin Books, 1971.

Taylor, John. *Body Horror: Photojournalism, Catastrophe, and War*. New York: NYU Press, 1998.

Tomasulo, Frank P. "'I'll See It When I Believe It': Rodney King and the Prison-House of Video." In *The Persistence of History: Cinema, Television, and the Modern Event*, edited by Vivian Sobchack, 69–88. London: Routledge, 1996.

Tomer, Adrian. "Death-Related Attitudes: Conceptual Distinctions." In *Death Attitudes and the Older Adult: Theories, Concepts, and Applications*, edited by Adrian Tomer, 87–94. Philadelphia: Brunner-Routledge, 2000.

Torchin, Leshu. *Creating the Witness: Documenting Genocide on Film, Video, and the Internet*. Minneapolis: University of Minnesota Press, 2012.

———. "Mediation and Remediation: *La Parole Filmée* in Rithy Panh's *The Missing Picture* (*L'image manquante*)." *Film Quarterly* 68, no. 1 (2014): 32–41.

Treatment of Posttraumatic Stress Disorder: An Assessment of the Evidence. Washington, DC: The National Academies Press, 2008.

Varzi, Roxanne. *Warring Souls: Youth, Media, and Martyrdom in Post-Revolution Iran*. Durham, NC: Duke University Press, 2006.

Vogel, Amos. "The Ultimate Secret: Death." In *Film as a Subversive Art*, 263–82. New York: Random House, 1974.

Walter, Tony. *The Revival of Death*. London: Routledge, 1994.

Warren Commission. *Report of the President's Commission on the Assassination of President John F. Kennedy*. Washington, DC: U.S. Government Printing Office, 1964.

Wasserman, Danuta, and Camilla Wasserman, eds. *Oxford Textbook of Suicidology and Suicide Prevention: A Global Perspective*. Oxford: Oxford University Press, 2009.

Webb, Marilyn. *The Good Death: The New American Search to Reshape the End of Life*. New York: Bantam Books, 1997.

"What and When Is Death?" *Journal of the American Medical Association* 204 (1968): 219–20.

Whissel, Kristen. *Picturing American Modernity: Traffic, Technology, and the Silent Cinema*. Durham, NC: Duke University Press, 2008.

———. *Spectacular Digital Effects: CGI and Contemporary Cinema*. Durham, NC: Duke University Press, 2014.

Williams, Linda. "Film Bodies: Gender, Genre, and Excess." In *Film Theory and Criticism: Introductory Readings*, edited by Leo Braudy and Marshall Cohen, 701–15. 5th ed. New York: Oxford University Press, 1999.

———. *Hard Core: Power, Pleasure, and the "Frenzy of the Visible."* 1989; Reprint, Berkeley: University of California Press, 1999.

———. *Playing the Race Card: Melodramas of Black and White from Uncle Tom to O. J. Simpson*. Princeton, NJ: Princeton University Press, 2001.

Without Sanctuary: Lynching Photography in America. Edited by James Allen. Santa Fe, NM: Twin Palms, 2000.

Wrone, David R. *The Zapruder Film: Reframing JFK's Assassination*. Lawrence: University Press of Kansas, 2003.

Zelizer, Barbie. *Covering the Body: The Kennedy Assassination, the Media, and the Shaping of Collective Memory*. Chicago: University of Chicago Press, 1992.

———. *Remembering to Forget: Holocaust Memory through the Camera's Eye*. Chicago: University of Chicago Press, 1998.

———. *About to Die: How News Images Move the Public*. Oxford: Oxford University Press, 2010.

INDEX

Page numbers followed by f indicate material in figures or photographs.

concentration camps photography, 14, 39–42, 64

condolence letters describing death, 34

contagion, suicide, 122–24, 144, 150–51, 222n24

context/contextualization: and Agha-Soltan death, 189–91; and *The Falling Man,* 128; global, 188; and Grant video, 192–97; and HIV-AIDS, 95; in judging graphic material, 160–61; lack of on TheYNC, 163–64; national and historical, 8–13, 34; and Rodney King video, 193–94; through missing or superfluous detail, 193; of treatment of Black Americans, 192–93, 196; and YouTube, 22, 159–61, 180, 189–97, 225n12

controlling death through capture, 203

control through capturing death, 203

Coogler, Ryan, 185

Cook, David, 191, 199

corpse photography: becoming cliché, 157; in Civil War battlefields, 31–35; in concentration camps, 39–42; of Darfur genocide, 39–42; of lynchings, 35–39; and Michael Brown video, 196; and postmortem mourning, 29–31; rearranging, posing the dead for, 32–33; in siege of Lucknow, 211n18; sympathy and alienation in viewing, 157; as "too late," 28–29

corpses, reality and fiction: closing of eyes, 68, 98, 102; transition from lived body to, 71. *See also* moment of death

craftwork to aid mourning, 96–97

Cross, Tommy Jr., 165, 166f

Crouching Tiger, Hidden Dragon (Lee), 145–46

Crowe, Cameron, 145

Cruzan, Nancy, 76

CSI (TV show), 181–82

cultural banishment of death, 2

curiosity about death, 3; aided by digital technology, 22; death porn responding to, 15, 164, 202; evolving into apprehension, 18; feeding *Six Feet Under,* 24; natural death, 70; not inherently morbid, 203; nurtured by fiction film, 2; as only limit, 6; proper response to, 114; pushing early cinema, 43

customized death experience, 77

cystic fibrosis (CF), 90–91

Czolgosz, Leon, 45, 63, 71

Dachau concentration camp, 40

daguerreotype, 30

Darfur, Sudan, 155–56

Davis, Kate, 88

Davis, Peter, 113

Dean, Jodi, 159, 171, 189

Death 24x a Second (Mulvey), 43, 87

Death: A Love Story (LeBrun), 88, 97

deathbed documentaries, 71–72; autobiographical, 88–89; camera use in, 72–73, 82–84, 96; deemphasizing body and moment of death, 81–82, 86; demographics of, 79–80; function of, 78–79; lack of "ugly films," 88; microbudget projects, 88; providing sense of purpose, 84; as rebellion against medical "dictatorship," 75; showing death as prolonged process, 72; value of for viewers, 84–85; video and DV for, 86. *See also* documentary death footage; *Dying* (Roemer); *Sick: The Life and Death of Bob Flanagan, Supermasochist* (Dick); *Silverlake Life* (Joslin and Friedman)

deathbed scene: attendance at as privilege, 11–12; fiction of standard conventions, 68, 216n6; in *Imitation of Life* (Sirk), 67–70 (69f), 73–74, 82, 85, 184; video appearance at, 72–73, 96

death blow "embalming" time, 34–35

death culture: nineteenth-century, 11, 30, 96–97, 208n24; twentieth-century, 13, 74, 96

death-denial culture, 2, 11, 68, 76, 83

"Death Every Afternoon" (Bazin), 170

"death instincts," 222n24

"Death Jump" (Reichelt), 215–16n98

"death of one's own," 2. *See also* individualized, unique dying

Death on Request (Nederhorst), 125

death porn, 14–15; *The Bridge* and, 147–48; crossover with hard-core porn, 163; distinguishing from "redeeming social importance," 64; education versus entertainment criterion for, 112; *Faces of Death,* 15; lack of context in, 164; lynching photographs as, 35; online marketing of, 162–63; popularity and volume of, 164; and YouTube policies, 160, 162, 165

"decisive moment," 28, 48. *See also* "on time" recording; "too late"

Harriet (in *Dying*), 81, 83, 85, 218n38

Harrison, Mark, 192

Harry Potter and the Half-Blood Prince (Yates), 145

Hawkins, A. H., 85

headshots: attraction of, 52; in Kennedy assassination, 52–55 (54f); in *Saigon Execution* (Adams), 58–60 (59f), 62

"healthy dying," 70, 81

Hearts and Minds (Davis), 113

heart transplants and moment of death, 27, 75–76, 217n20

heaven, reunion in, 11–12

hejab in Agha-Soltan video, 179–80

Hejazi, Arash, 167, 171

"helpless gaze," 19, 115–16

hemlock, death by, 222n32

Herzog, Werner, 14, 144–45

Hines, Kevin, 135, 141

Hitchcock, Alfred, 144

HIV/AIDS: *The Andre Show* (Peterson), 88; in deathbed documentary, 73, 86; first-person videotaping of, 89, 94; and gay male attitudes toward death, 9, 95; and return of the body in film, 90; showing physical symptoms of, 94–95; society disassociation from, 103, 183. *See also Silverlake Life*

Holden, Stephen, 112

Holliday, George, 193–94

Holocaust, 14, 39–42, 64

"Home Burial" (Frost), 201, 203, 205

home movie cameras, 4

"homo sacer," 220n81

Hood, Miggi, 84

Hooper, Tom, 145

horror: of Holocaust, 40–41; horror genre, 14–15, 27, 65, 178; "horrors of war," 57, 150, 155–56; stylistic softening of, 145–46, 193; sublime as delightful horror, 126, 128, 144; of suicide, 130–32, 135–36, 141

hospice and palliative care, 76–77, 83, 85, 89, 94, 219n62

hospitals: aesthetic sterility of, 82, 90; Bob's death in *Sick*, 91, 92f; displacement of death to, 12, 75, 76; focus of on body, 96, 102; keeping death out of sight, 180; and machine registrants of death, 71; and neoliberalism, 79; and nostalgia for home deaths,

70; organ donation and moment of death, 27, 75–76, 217n20; prolongation of death, 13, 81, 83, 210n11; and "standard issue" death, 78; tubes as image of, 13, 74, 76, 83

How to Die in Oregon (Richardson), 125

"humane gaze"/"humane stare," 19, 174

Huntley-Brinkley Report, The, 60–61

Hussein (Shiite martyr), 190

"I am ____" declarations, 185, 188–89, 229n60

Ibrahim, Youssef, 173

Illustrated Police News (IPN), 121–22

images, ability of to wound, 65

"I Met Him on a Sunday," 102

Imitation of Life (Sirk): as anachronism, 70, 217n14; Annie's moment of death, 67–70 (69f), 73–74, 82, 85, 184; Lora in, 67–68, 71, 74, 184

immortality: in film, 115, 153, 203; and immateriality, 203–5

indexicality, loss of, 7–8

individualized, unique dying, 93, 96; failure of in *Dying*, 105; initial waning of "death of one's own," 2; neoliberalism and individual death, 73, 77–79, 85, 103; and rejection of hospital death, 74; and "revival of death," 76, 90, 217–18n25; in *Sick, Silverlake Life*, 104

Inextinguishable Fire, The (Farocki), 65

infant corpse photographs, 29–31

informed consent, 15, 19, 113, 115, 146, 202

"Inscribing Ethical Space" (Sobchack), 19–20, 71, 105, 115, 174, 210n53. *See also* Sobchack, Vivian

instantaneous death, portrayals of, 26–27. *See also* "moment of death"

instant-replay, 56, 170–71, 194, 214n78

"interventional gaze," 19, 116

interviews: with dying subjects, 82–83, 86, 105; use of in *The Bridge*, 114–16, 118, 137, 141, 146, 150

invisible made visible, 6

Islamic martyrdom, 190–91

Jackson, C. D., 53

Jackson, Peter, 145

JAMA (*Journal of the American Medical Association*), 75–76

Jarman, Derek, 14

McKinley, William, 45

Meerloo, Joost A. M., 122–23, 222n24

Mehserle, Johannes, 165, 176, 181, 185, 192–94, 196–98

melodrama soliciting tears from audience, 27

mementos of dead, 97

"memorial photographs," 31

"metallic" rites of passage, 12

"metaphysical obscenity," 3, 6, 14

microbudget projects, 88

Milford, Rebecca Leah (character), 23

Miller, Lee, 40

Minois, Georges, 122

Misérables, Les (Hooper), 145

Missing Picture, The (Panh), 9–10, 14

mobile phone cameras, 4, 158; citizen compulsion to document, 174–75; expectations of viewers, 182; outperforming security cameras, 165

modern medicine's prolongation of death, 13, 83, 210n1

"moment of death": and "about to die" moment, 210n4; as abrupt cessation of movement, 71; becoming small part of dying process, 13, 27, 75; captured in "last life-expression," 34–35; as comforting fiction, 27–28; versus duration of modern death, 81, 94; fallacy of, 7, 26–27, 46; flatline on monitor defining, 71; in *Dying at Grace*, 105, 106f; headshot as, 52; from hours of discarded footage, 117; imagining one's own, 24; legal "time of death," 72, 76; in military reenactments and fakes, 48–51 (50f); and organ donation, 27, 75–76; power of, 63; and premature burial concerns, 27, 217n20; in *Saigon Execution*, 60–61; signifiers of in war footage, 44, 48–49; in *Silverlake Life*, 98–99; in *Six Feet Under*, 24–26 (25f); technological limitations in filming, 24–26; uncertainty of in electrocution, 45–46, 213n51. *See also* deathbed documentaries; stages of death

mourning photographs, 29–31, 64, 70, 91

mourning rituals, 82, 96–97

"Moving Away from the Index" (Gunning), 8

Moving Picture World, 49

Mulvey, Laura, 43

mummifying change, 3

Mutoscope/Biograph, 44, 47

Myrick, Daniel, 178

Myth of Sisyphus, The (Camus), 120

Nabbous, Mohammed, 174

napalm, 65, 107

natural death, 5, 207n4; and African American male expectations, 80, 188, 218n36; fictions regarding, 64, 70; good and bad deaths, 84–85; and humane gaze, 19; lacking "cinematic signifier of death," 44, 71; as "last sleep," 33; medicalizing of, 12–13; as modern taboo, 13, 26, 72–73; and "moment" of death concept, 26, 70, 73; overlooked by early cinema, 44; paucity of documentary work on, 26, 70; and postmortem mourning photographs, 29–31, 64, 70, 91; as process rather than moment, 26–27; as routine, 105–7; statistic probability of, 70; versus suicide, 120; suppression of, 2; sympathizing without identifying with, 104; video as tool for recording, 73, 87–90; viewer response to, 107; YouTube favoring violence over, 5. *See also* deathbed documentaries

"natural" death of celluloid, 204

Near Death (Wiseman), 88, 219n57

"necessary mistake" of film preservation, 204

Nederhorst, Maarten, 125

"negative pleasure" of suicide, 146–47

neoliberalism and individual death, 73, 77–79, 85, 103

new media theory, 7–8, 26, 158, 171

Niagara Falls, absorbing full wonder of, 136

NicheTube, 199

Night and Fog (Resnais), 14, 17, 113

9/11. *See* World Trade Center jumpers, pictures of

nineteenth century: as age of beautiful death, 30–31, 33, 35, 74; and craftwork mementos of dead, 96–97; death seen as forecasting soul's fate, 11, 30, 34–35, 64; *Gardner's Photographic Sketchbook of the Civil War,* 32–35, 46, 49, 211n9; "memorial photographs," 31; "moment" of death pose, 48; portrayals of Black male suffering, 195; postmortem mourning photographs, 29–31, 64, 70, 91; premature burial fears, 27, 217n20; prevalence of epidemics, 11, 13, 95, 208n23;

Williams, Pat Ward, 37

Wire, The (tv show), 185

Wiseman, Frederick, 88, 219n57

WITNESS video organization, 180–81

Woodward, Richard, 6

World Trade Center jumpers, pictures of: aesthetic values in, 139; *The Falling Man* (Drew), 127–30 (129f); initial news decisions regarding, 5; later accessibility to, 5–6; spectator objection to, 1

World War I, 49

World War II, 14, 33, 39–42, 64

Yates, David, 145

YouTube, 158; attention economy of, 167, 180; "bad video" aesthetic on, 182; comments leading to video removals, 190; comments on Agha-Soltan video, 176–77, 179, 184, 191; comments on Grant video, 177, 182, 197; "Community Guidelines" of, 160–62, 225n12; cultural conventions on, 4–5; embeds in Facebook and Twitter, 162; global availability of preventing censorship, 172;

Juhasz on, 180; lack of contextualization on, 160, 189–97; maximum video length on, 221n10; "NicheTube" within, 199; not professional journalism, 174; obscurity of most death videos on, 199; as passive witnessing, 159; police body cams to counter, 198–99; racism on, 197; removal of files from, 204; "Replay" icon, 170; "Report" button and content moderation, 161; role of aesthetics in, 177–83

Zapruder film of JFK assassination: Abraham Zapruder's filming, processing of, 52–53, 99, 173, 214n71; as "accidental gaze," 173; bootleg copy of, 214n76; description of, 52; as evidence, 214n70; frame 313 headshot in, 53–55 (54f), 62; on *Good Night America*, 55; grainy quality of, 181; in *JFK* (Stone), 55; redeeming social importance of, 64; sales of, 172, 214n72

Zaritsky, John, 125

Zeindenberg, Leonard, 57

Zelizer, Barbie, 5, 41, 64, 128, 158, 210n4